Theoretical
Foundations
of
Music

**Theoretical
Foundations
of Music**

William
Duckworth
*Bucknell
University*

Edward
Brown
*Mansfield
State
College*

Wadsworth
Publishing
Company
Inc.
*Belmont,
California*

**Music
Editor**
Randy
Cade

**Production
Editor**
Catherine
Aydelott

Designer
Dare
Porter

**Editorial
Assistance**
Jeanne
Heise

Printed in the United States of America

1 2 3 4 5 6 7 8 9 10—82 81 80 79 78

Library of Congress Cataloging in Publication Data
Duckworth, William.
Theoretical foundations of music.
Includes index.
1. Music—Theory. I. Brown, Edward, date
joint author. II. Title.
MT6.D833T5   781   77-7571
ISBN 0-534-00526-8

CONTENTS iii

iv

Music excerpted: Haydn, *Symphony No. 104;* Rimsky-Korsakov, *Scheherezade,* Op. 35: I; Schubert, *Symphony No. 8:* II; Bach, "Gott sei uns gnädig und barmherzig"

V

Music excerpted: Beethoven, "Dance"; Schumann, Waltz from *Albumbläter;* Bernstein, "Candide"; Mozart, Variations on "Ah, vous dirai-je, Maman"; Schumann, "Du Ring an meinem Finger"; Clementi, *Sonatina,* Op. 36, No. 1

Music excerpted: Bach, "Du Friedensfürst, Herr Jesu Christ", Bach, "Nimm von uns, Herr, du treuer Gott"; Bach, "Jesu, meiner Seelen Wonne"; Bach, "Ermuntre dich, mein schwacher Geist"

Music excerpted: Chopin, *Mazurka,* Op. 7, No. 1; Schubert, "Du bist die Ruh"; Bach, *Brandenburg Concerto No. 3:* I; Beethoven, *Piano Sonata,* Op. 79: III; Mozart, *Sonata,* K. 284: Var. I; Bach, "Nun lob, mein Seel"; Bach, *Goldberg Variations:* Var. 18; Morley, "O sleep, fond Fancy"; Bach, "Durch Adams fall"; Mozart, *Sonata,* K. 533; Haydn, *Sonata in D major:* Finale; Mozart, *Sonata in B♭:* K. 333: III; Mancini, "Moon River"; Beethoven, *Piano Sonata,* Op. 26: Var. V; Mozart, *Sonata,* K. 283: I; Bach, "Prelude I," *WTC* I; Bach, "Christe, du Beistand deiner Kreuzgemeine"; Chopin, Op. 67, No. 2; Bach, "Nun bitten wir den heiligen Geist"; Bach, "Wenn ich in Angst und Noth"; Brahms, *Variations and Fugue on a Theme by Handel,* Op. 24

vi

viii

ix

INTRODUCTION

Music theory instruction at the college level is rapidly changing. Traditional class instruction in theory has concentrated almost entirely on a single aspect: harmony. It is becoming increasingly difficult to apply the narrow scope of seventeenth- and eighteenth-century harmonic practice to the panorama of musical styles that exists today. As musicians expand their interest into such diverse areas as 12-tone music, ethnomusicology, electronic music, and early polyphony, it becomes imperative that schools and universities teach the skills and background appropriate to these areas.

Our aim in *Theoretical Foundations of Music* is to provide a basic structure from which the student can develop an understanding of the principles of musical organization—not only tonal music, but pretonal and contemporary styles, as well. We believe that such an understanding can be best achieved through the development and application of **parametric analysis.**

We use the term *parameter* in the same way that the term *element* has often been used. The elements of music (that is, melody, harmony, rhythm and meter, timbre, texture, form, and so on) are, for us, the parameters of music. We prefer the term parameter (derived from mathematics) because it connotes a *field of possibilities.* Certain parametric controls are inherent in all music. By analyzing how a composer emphasizes, manipulates, and integrates the various parameters of music in a particular composition, the principles underlying its style can be made more apparent. Such understanding is crucial, we believe, to judging a musical composition's artistic worth and validity.

Theoretical Foundations of Music is divided into four major sections. Part A: An Introduction to Parametric Analysis introduces and explores the basic parameters of music. Within each chapter, differing musical styles are juxtaposed to illustrate how composers over the centuries have changed their methods of manipulating musical parameters. Part A concludes with parametric analyses in which the techniques discussed individually in each chapter are applied collectively to three widely different works.

Part B: The Tonal System presents much of the information traditionally offered in harmony classes, including the essentials of four-part structure, chordal writing, nonharmonic tones, altered chords, and modulation. There is also a chapter on the technical principles of figured bass. Part B concludes with parametric analyses of three compositions.

Part C: Extended Tonality completes the tonally oriented harmonic vocabulary, including chromatic harmony and expanded tonality. Important vocal and instrumental formal structures are identified and new tools for analysis, based on the work of Heinrich Schenker, are introduced. The concluding chapter of parametric analyses assumes a level of greater sophistication and complexity.

Part D: Alternatives to Tonality explores changes in music during the twentieth century. It begins with a look at the shift in relative importance of the various musical parameters in the early 1900s. It then discusses new directions in notation and explores 12-tone music, microtonality, electronic music, and indeterminate music. Part D also pursues the question of the changing relationship between composer and performer. The final chapter applies the technique of parametric analysis to three twentieth-century compositions.

Throughout *Theoretical Foundations of Music,* the relationship of parametric control to musical style is paramount. This emphasis, we feel, elucidates the basic musical controls operating in all music. In turn, this is of value in understanding compositional technique, regardless of style.

We cannot overemphasize the importance of basic musicianship. Ear training, sightsinging, and keyboard studies are essential to the development of the competent musician. In fact, consistent practice in these areas should accompany use of this text. While we suggest activities at the end of each chapter, far more basic drill is needed. In the study of scales and modes, for instance, we recommend sightsinging and taking as dictation melodies based on these pitch organizations. The parallel need not be exact, of course, but daily aural and keyboard training are indispensable to the student of music.

1

**Part A
An
Introduction
to Parametric
Analysis**

1

Musicians are continually involved in a practical application of the physical characteristics of musical sound—pitch, volume, duration, and **timbre** (tone color)—yet most musicians today pay little attention to these physical characteristics. In the Middle Ages the relationship between music and mathematics did not escape the attention of scholars. Neither is it ignored by contemporary electronic composers, who work and think in terms of wave shapes, frequency filters, and inches per second. Still, to the average musician the study of the physical properties of sound, commonly called **acoustics**, seems only distantly related to the study of music.

What we hear as musical sound is physically a pattern of oscillations of air molecules. Set in motion by a vibrating string or air column, this pattern of oscillations is the result of air molecules in the vicinity of the vibrating source being alternately crowded together and then expanding. For simplicity we have not mentioned the situation of the vibrating surface of a percussion instrument, but the process is analogous. This displacement of molecules is passed along to adjacent molecules. This is how sound is transmitted through the air. It is important to realize that it is the vibrational pattern, rather than the actual air molecules themselves, that is being transmitted, like the waves created by a stone tossed into a pond.

Frequency

Frequency is the number of times a vibrational pattern repeats itself per unit of time. Frequency, measured in oscillations or vibrations per second or Hertz (abbreviated as **Hz**), is interpreted by the ear as tone or pitch. The faster the repetition of the pattern, the higher the frequency. (When we speak of A-440—the A above middle C—

**Chapter 1
The Nature
of Sound**

we are really identifying a frequency of 440 vibrations per second [440 Hz].)

Frequency is determined, in part, by the length of the vibrating string or column of air. Basically, the greater the vibrating length, the lower the pitch. (Consider the relationship of size to pitch for an oboe and a bassoon, a trumpet and a trombone, or a violin and a viola.) Furthermore, if the vibrating length is reduced by one half, the resulting frequency will be double the original and the pitch will be an octave above the initial pitch. Further reduction of the vibrating length by one half (now one fourth of the initial length) will raise the pitch another octave. In Example 1•1 we show the vibrating frequencies for the pitch A, while Example 1•2 gives the various vibrating lengths necessary to produce a major scale. Notice in Example 1•2 that frequency is inversely proportional to length; that is, the shorter the vibrating length, the higher the frequency.

Example 1•1

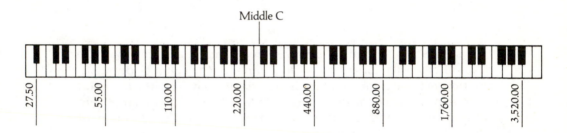

Middle C

27.50 55.00 110.00 220.00 440.00 880.00 1,760.00 3,520.00

Example 1•2

vibrating length*	1	8/9	4/5	3/4	2/3	3/5	8/15	1/2
frequency	1	9/8	5/4	4/3	3/2	5/3	15/8	2/1
frequency in Hertz	261.63	293.66	329.63	349.23	392.00	440.00	493.88	523.25

Amplitude

Amplitude is heard as volume or loudness. It is proportional to the amount of displacement of each air molecule produced by the vibrating string, surface, or air column. The greater the displacement,

---

*A scale resulting from these vibrating lengths would actually be in *just intonation.* Chapter 3 defines this and other major tuning systems in detail.

the louder the volume. For example, the more pressure a violin player exerts with the bow, the greater the distance the violin string will move when vibrating, resulting in a greater displacement of air molecules and higher amplitude. It is important to remember that amplitude can change without affecting frequency.

Harmonic Series

In addition to vibrating over its entire length, a string or column of air will vibrate simultaneously at a variety of fractional lengths, as well (one half, one third, one fourth, and so on). These secondary vibrations produce a series of pitches commonly called the **harmonic series** or overtone series (see Example 1•3). Because the overtones are not as loud as the fundamental frequency, the ear hears one composite sound. This composite is heard and notated as a single pitch. The term **partial**, often used in this context, refers to *all* of the pitches in the harmonic series, including the fundamental, while the term **overtone** refers to only those pitches generated *above* the fundamental frequency.

Example 1•3

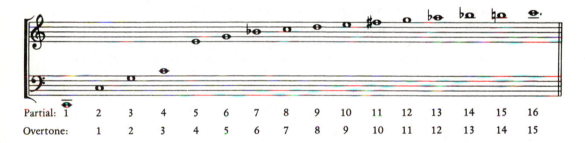

Timbre

Since pitch is determined solely by frequency, we hear a variety of vibrational patterns with the same fundamental frequency as the same pitch. The quality of musical sound by which we differentiate between musical instruments, even those at the same pitch, is timbre or tone color. Each musical instrument produces its own unique vibrational pattern, for the design of an instrument causes certain pitches in the harmonic series to be amplified and others to be suppressed. Since the vibrational pattern is different for each instrument and since the harmonic series is heard as a composite sound, each instrument, throughout its range, has its own characteristic timbre.

Suggested Activities

1. On the piano, demonstrate the existence of the harmonic series by silently depressing the second partial and sounding the fundamental. When the fundamental is released, you should be able to hear the second partial. Repeat this process with other lower partials of the harmonic series. Listen carefully to the relative strength of each partial.

2. Have someone in the class demonstrate the harmonic series on a brass instrument.

3. Have someone bring a violin or guitar to class and demonstrate the relationship of string length to pitch. This demonstration should include a discussion of harmonics and how they are employed on these instruments.

4. Write the harmonic series to the sixteenth partial from each of the following fundamentals:

5. Musicians should be able to recognize the timbre of every orchestral instrument in both solo and small ensemble settings. You can begin developing this ability by listening to recordings demonstrating each instrument individually. (Several are listed below.) The next step might be to listen to sonatas for individual instruments and piano, or to pieces for small ensembles of woodwinds, brass, or strings.

The Instruments of the Orchestra (Vanguard VRS-1017/18)
Instruments of the Orchestra (RCA Victor LE-6000)
Benjamin Britten, *Young Person's Guide to the Orchestra* (Columbia S-31808; RCA Victor LSC-2596; Phillips 6599436)

Suggested Readings

For those interested in exploring the topic of musical acoustics in more detail, we recommend the following books:

1. Backus, John. *Acoustical Foundations of Music.* New York: W. W. Norton & Co., 1969.
2. Benade, Arthur H. *Horns, Strings, and Harmony.* New York: Doubleday Anchor Books, 1960.

2

Notation serves many functions. Primarily, it is an information storage and retrieval system for composers and performers. Through notation composers store information about their musical ideas. The performer can then use this information to reproduce these musical ideas, even centuries after a composer's death. Most complex works could never be created nor survive for repeated performance without being notated. Without a notational system, performing music from the past would be limited to what can be passed on by rote, like folk music or religious chants.

For the past three hundred years, Western music has been notated through a system of signs and symbols currently referred to as **standard notation**. So much music has been written in standard notation that many musicians today consider other notational systems automatic failures. But musical concerns and interests have changed with time, and as they have, so has notation. In fact, how a composition is notated is the first clue in determining the parametric controls considered important by a particular composer or era.

While musical notation has changed and will continue to change, the basic criterion for judging the worth of a particular notational system remains the same: How accurately and clearly does it reflect the intentions of the composer? This question can and must be separated from judging the worth of the music itself, for there is nothing inherent in a notational system that makes music written in that system good or bad.

Staff

The evolution of notation has centered mainly on the increasingly precise representation of pitch and duration. The five-line staff employed in standard notation was used as early as A.D. 1200. Today, the five lines and four spaces, when used with an appropriate clef sign, identify pitch names but do not distinguish between whole-steps and half-steps. For this purpose, three accidentals are used:

♯	*sharp*	raises pitch by one half-step
♭	*flat*	lowers pitch by one half-step
♮	*natural*	cancels the previous sharp or flat

Clef

Clefs are signs placed at the beginning of a staff to provide a pitch reference. They identify the pitch that a particular line represents. Three clef signs are commonly employed:

𝄞	*G clef*	treble clef
𝄢	*F clef*	bass clef
𝄡	*C clef*	most frequently soprano, alto, and tenor clef

Normally the G clef and F clef are limited to one position on the staff, while the C clef appears in a variety of positions; all clefs may theoretically be used in any position. Example 2•1 shows an F major chord positioned on the five clefs most frequently employed. The C clef was widely employed before 1700. It still appears frequently in music written for the viola, cello, bassoon, and trombone, and musicians should learn to read it, as well as the treble and bass clefs, as quickly as possible.

Example 2•1

Gregorian Notation

Gregorian melodies for the Catholic mass have been preserved since the ninth century. Example 2•2 shows the chant "Kyrie orbis factor" as it appears in Gregorian notation in the *Liber Usualis* (the liturgical book containing the standard chants for the church year); in Example 2•3 it is rendered in standard transcription. Observe the close parallel in pitch movement between these examples. Whether there is a rhythmic correlation is not so clear.

The question of rhythmic interpretation in Gregorian chant is, in fact, still in dispute. Gregorian chant appears to place great emphasis on the words. Since words have a natural rhythmic flow, it was probably unnecessary, some scholars hold, to notate rhythm as precisely as pitch. The rhythmic details of this essentially oral tradition have unfortunately been lost.

Example 2•2 "Kyrie orbis factor"

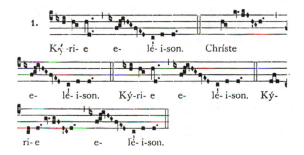

Example 2•3

Tablature

Music can be notated as a series of actions instead of as a series of pitches. Example 2•4 shows a lute **tablature** of the sixteenth century. Rather than indicating pitches directly, this notation shows where to place the fingers on the strings so as to produce the desired pitches. The six lines do not form a staff; they represent the six courses of the lute.*

Example 2•4 Dowland, *What if I never speede*

Courtesy of the British Library Board.

Example 2•5 illustrates a current use of tablature for the guitar, often found in rock and popular music.

*The lute has two strings for each pitch; each set of two strings is called a *course*.

Example 2·5

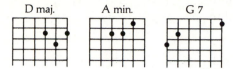

D maj.   A min.   G 7

11

Standard Notation

Example 2·6 illustrates standard notation. We can see that both pitch and rhythm are precisely represented and that phrasing and dynamics are also indicated. It is this capability for precision and dynamic control that is responsible for the steady use of standard notation over its 300-year history.

Example 2·6   Brahms, *Sonata in F♯ minor,* Op. 2: Finale, mm. 1–7

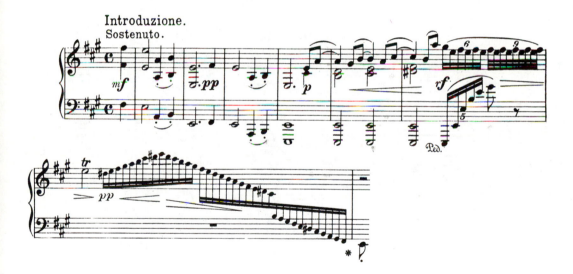

Contemporary Notation

Alternative systems of notation have appeared recently from composers interested in expressing musical ideas that are outside the realm of standard notation. For one thing, composers are demanding a more complex set of graphic controls than standard notation can offer. Example 2·7 shows the first four measures of a **microtonal** string quartet by American composer Ben Johnston. Notice the additional accidentals needed to accommodate Johnston's 53-tone scale. The lines between pitches indicate for the performers a system of tuning and pitch reference within the 53-tone system.

Example 2·7 Ben Johnston, *String Quartet No. 2:* 1, mm. 1–4

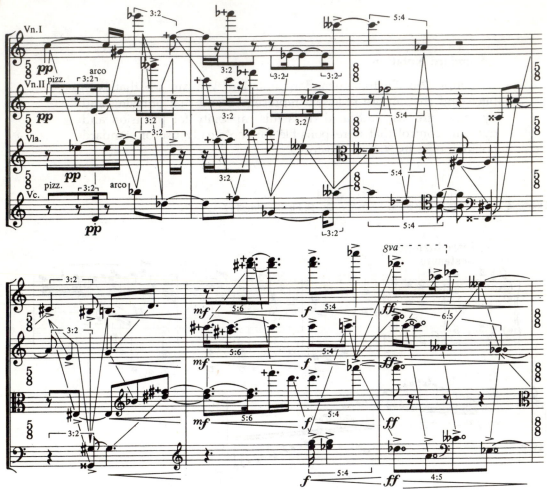

Composers are also moving toward allowing performers additional participation in the creative process, a freedom difficult to achieve with standard notation. Example 2·8 is by American composer William Karlins. Notable is the control of melodic shape rather than pitch placement, and rhythmic control in terms of clock time rather than traditional meter. However one may question Karlins' intentions in allowing this much freedom, one must conclude that he has notated his ideas clearly.

Focus

It is important to realize that not all valid musical ideas can be expressed in standard notation. As you come in contact with new systems of notation, or unfamiliar older systems, try to determine the basic intentions of the composers. Why do they notate their musical ideas as they do? Surely not to confuse. Let us assume composers choose systems of notation which store their musical ideas as clearly as possible. An understanding of these notational systems should then help elucidate the kinds of controls the composers consider important and necessary.

Example 2·8   William Karlins, *Graphic Mobile:* A

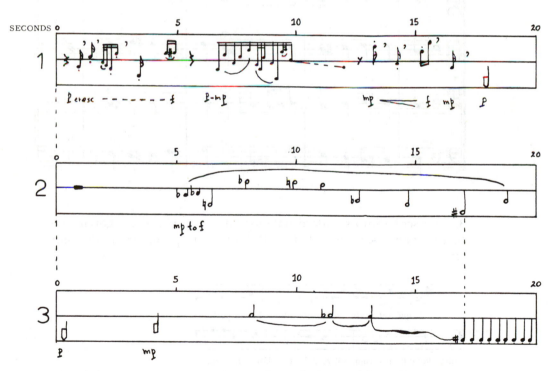

Suggested Activities

1. Rewrite the first melodic line into tenor clef, and the second line into bass clef.

Schumann, *Piano Concerto*, Op. 54, excerpt

Brahms, *Violin Concerto*, Op. 77, excerpt

2. Rewrite the following into treble and bass clefs, suitable for piano or organ.

Bach, "Herzlich tut mich verlangen"

3. Transcribe into standard notation this example of Gregorian notation. If necessary, refer to the "Rules for Interpretation" in the *Liber Usualis.*

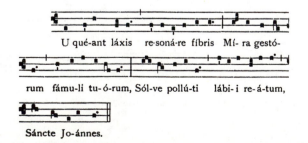

U qué-ant láxis re-soná-re fíbris Mí- ra gestó-

rum fámu-li tu-ó-rum, Sól-ve pollú-ti   lábi- i re-á-tum,

Sáncte Jo-ánnes.

4. If you cannot read treble and bass clefs simultaneously at the piano, develop this ability by practicing simple melodies in each clef individually. Useful melodies will be found in most beginning sight-singing books.

5. Determine the pitch each finger is producing in the chords of Example 2•5. (The strings indicated in guitar tablature are, from left to right [low to high pitches], E A D G B E.) Each fret raises the pitch of a string a half-step.

6. Create a short, original composition based on three nontraditional sound sources. Invent a notational system to graphically store your musical ideas. Ask members of the class to perform the piece with no other directions from you. Discuss any differences between your intentions and the actual performance.

Suggested Readings

1. Beginning music theory students often have trouble with basic musical notation. We recommend: Gardner Read's *Music Notation,* 2nd Ed. (Boston: Allyn and Bacon, 1969) as a good source of information about common notational practices.

2. A concise discussion of contemporary notational practices is "Notation" by Kurt Stone in *Dictionary of Contemporary Music,* John Vinton, ed. (New York: E. P. Dutton & Co., 1974).

3. A beautiful compendium of contemporary music manuscripts by a number of different composers is John Cage's *Notations* (New York: Something Else Press, 1969).

3

The tuning of keyboard and orchestral instruments in equal **temperament** is today so universal that little thought is given to alternate systems of tuning. However, in the development of Western music other methods of tuning profoundly influenced the way in which music was written and performed. Four major systems have been employed throughout the history of Western music: Pythagorean tuning, just intonation, meantone temperament, and equal temperament. These tuning systems continue to influence music today, and should be understood by all musicians. Each system has advantages for certain styles of music and disadvantages for other styles. A knowledge of these major tuning systems contributes to a better understanding of both the music of earlier periods and contemporary experiments in temperament.

Pythagorean Tuning

Pythagorean tuning derives its name from the Greek mathematician Pythagoras, who is credited with its invention. The basis for this system is the interval of the pure fifth (3:2). By tuning successive fifths above and below a given pitch a **diatonic** scale can be derived.

Notice that Example 3•1, when reduced to one octave, becomes C, D, E, F, G, A, B. **Chromatic** pitches may be introduced by simply extending the succession of fifths.

Example 3·1

$$\overset{\longleftarrow \quad \longrightarrow}{F - \boxed{C} - G - D - A - E - B}$$

Example 3·2

$$\overset{\longleftarrow \quad \longrightarrow}{Gb - Db - Ab - Eb - Bb - F - \boxed{C} - G - D - A - E - B - F\sharp}$$

Example 3·2 reduced to one octave becomes C, Db, D, Eb, E, F, F♯, Gb, G, Ab, A, Bb, B.

A major problem arises at this point—the more chromatic one wishes to become, the more inadequate Pythagorean tuning becomes. Unlike equal temperament, **enharmonic** tones (C♯–Db, D♯–Eb, and so on) in Pythagorean tuning are not equivalent in pitch. In Example 3·2, the F♯ will sound slightly higher in pitch than the enharmonic Gb at the other end of the tuning sequence. This discrepancy will exist between all other enharmonic tones. If, for example, a C♯ is tuned above the F♯, it will be out of tune with the low Db. The result is a tuning system perfect in one key but not in others. While key limitation is only a minor problem for singers, who can easily adjust, for fixed-pitch instruments it is insurmountable.

Another disadvantage of Pythagorean tuning concerns the interval of the third. Whereas the octave and the fifth are in tune, the third is not. The major third is too sharp and the minor third is too flat. It is significant that composers of the Middle Ages considered thirds and sixths to be **dissonances**, usable only in certain specific situations.

Just Intonation

The dissonant third derived by Pythagorean tuning became a greater problem as composers employed more thirds and sixths in their music. Just intonation was an attempt to overcome this problem by basing the tuning on both the pure fifth (3:2) and the pure major third (5:4). In this sense, it may be considered an extension of Pythagorean tuning. Note in Example 3·3 that horizontal pitches are derived from fifths, vertical pitches from thirds.

Example 3·3

```
        E  - B - F♯ - C♯
        |    |    |    |
Eb - Bb - F -⎡C⎤- G  - D  - A
             ‾
        |
        Ab
```

Although just intonation contributes concordant, as opposed to dissonant, thirds and sixths, it nonetheless retains the basic problem of Pythagorean tuning: limiting fixed-pitched instruments to a single key.

Meantone Temperament

Both Pythagorean tuning and just intonation result in acoustically correct intervals within a limited number of keys. As fixed-pitched instruments became more important, some method was needed to spread the pitch discrepancies of Pythagorean and just tunings over a wider area. The term **temperament** refers to the slight adjustments made to pure intervals in order to equalize the inherent discrepancies of pitch.

Meantone temperament, in use from the 1500s to the 1800s, was the most generally accepted system of temperament before the adoption of equal temperament. In meantone, fifths are narrowed forward and backward from C so that the major thirds resulting from four consecutive fifths are pure.

Example 3·4

```
            ┌───────────tuned either sharp or flat as desired───────────┐
Ab - Eb - Bb - F - │C│ - G - D - A - E - B - F♯ - C♯ - G♯
    └─ pure major third ─┘└pure major third┘└─pure major third─┘
          (5:4)                (5:4)                (5:4)
```

The enharmonic intervals produced by this system (Ab–G♯) result in a pitch discrepancy of almost a quarter-tone, and require that a choice be made between the Ab and the G♯.

As an alternative to previous tuning systems, meantone temperament offered distinct advantages. Since it was generally tuned from C, it made available a group of keys through three sharps and three flats, assuming both the Ab and the G♯ would be used at one time or another. This greater range of keys for fixed-pitched instruments in turn made possible greater explorations of key relationships and modulation. In addition, because in meantone temperament the pattern of just and tempered intervals is different for each key, each key possesses its own distinctive coloration.

Equal Temperament

As the interests of composers turned toward an expanded use of chromaticism, the disadvantages of meantone temperament became obvious. Equal temperament, for all practical purposes the only system in use since the 1800s, is an arbitrary division of the octave into twelve equal parts—arbitrary because it does not take into account the acoustical qualities of each interval. The only interval that *is* acoustically correct in equal temperament is the octave (2:1). But even though all other intervals are incorrect acoustically, the discrepancy is slight and the advantage of enharmonic pitches being in tune with each other is enormous.

By solving the problem of enharmonic equivalents, equal temperament allows modulation to every key, a feature which fostered the development of nineteenth-century harmonic practices. Equal temperament, however, destroys the distinctiveness of the various keys and chords inherent in meantone temperament—a major disadvantage. This will be explored in the discussion of microtonal music in chapter 26.

Suggested Activities

1. Experiment at home with tuning a guitar in equal temperament.

2. Experiment, as a class, with tuning several octaves of a harpsichord in just intonation. A tuning device may be necessary to check accuracy.

3. Diagram the tuning systems for just intonation and meantone temperament, based on the pitch G.

Suggested Readings

1. The following Musurgia recordings are difficult to locate, but they are excellent aural illustrations of the tuning systems discussed in this chapter.

  A-1   The Theory of Classical Greek Music
  A-2   Meantone Temperament in Theory and Practice
  A-3   The Theory and Practice of Just Intonation
  A-4   The History of Irregular Temperaments

2. This chapter has discussed the four most commonly employed systems of tuning. For a detailed discussion of these as well as other systems, see *Tuning and Temperament* by J. Murray Barbour (East Lansing: Michigan State College Press, 1951).

4

Rhythm and meter organize musical sounds into regular and irregular patterns of time duration. Strictly speaking, *meter* refers to a recurring pattern of strong and weak beats or pulses, while *rhythm* means the various arrangements of irregular durations of pitch within a metrical pattern. In reality, the two terms can be applied to a broader range of possibilities than the strict definitions allow.

Rhythmic Organization

Symmetrical Rhythm

Western music of the period 1600 to 1900 is characterized by **symmetrical rhythm**—that is, divided into regularly recurring patterns of strong and weak accents, clearly indicated by means of bar lines. Furthermore, each time value is proportional, being a multiple or fraction of the basic beat. The terms *metrical rhythm* and *isometric rhythm* have also been used in this way.

Within symmetrical rhythm, certain metrical patterns of strong and weak beats have been frequently employed.

Example 4·1

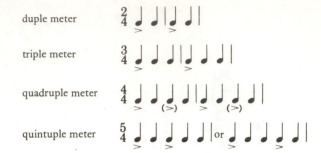

duple meter

triple meter

quadruple meter

quintuple meter

The terms *simple* and *compound* refer to the manner in which the basic beat is divided. If the basic beat has two subdivisions the meter is simple, while a basic beat with three subdivisions is a compound meter.

Example 4·2

$\frac{2}{4}$ ♩ ♩ = ♫ ♫   simple duple

$\frac{6}{8}$ ♩. ♩. = ♫♫ ♫♫   compound duple

Non-Symmetrical Rhythm

Non-symmetrical rhythm (also identified as *measured* or *multimetric rhythm*) retains the proportional time value scheme of symmetrical rhythm but avoids any recurring pattern of strong and weak accents. This is usually accomplished by continually altering the meter, as in Example 4·3.

The use of non-symmetrical rhythm has steadily increased since the early 1900s. In *Six Dances in Bulgarian Rhythm,* for instance, Bartok used such non-symmetrical rhythmic structures as $\frac{4+2+3}{8}$, $\frac{2+2+3}{8}$, and $\frac{2+2+2+3}{8}$; and jazz composers Dave Brubeck and Don Ellis have explored similar rhythmic structures. We find non-symmetrical rhythms in early music as well—for example, Gregorian chant (as currently interpreted).

Example 4·3

Free Rhythm

Since the 1950s, Western music has made wider use of **free rhythm**. In free rhythm, proportional time values and recurring accent patterns are avoided. Meter signatures are not employed in free rhythm. Instead, rhythmic structure is usually based on time lengths, as in Example 4·4, or non-proportional rhythmic symbols such as those in Example 4·5.

Example 4·4   Blatter, *A Study in Time and Space*

Example 4·5   Fulkerson, from *Patterns III*

o = long (approximately one full breath)   ♩ = circa   ♩ = 60

ȯ = less long; often a type of cadence   ● = fast

Rhythmic Systems

Rhythmic Modes

One of the earliest attempts to use rhythm in a structural way was the thirteenth-century system of rhythmic modes. This involved the constant repetition of a simple rhythmic pattern in triple meter. Example 4·6 lists the six commonly employed rhythmic modes.

Example 4·6

first rhythmic mode

second rhythmic mode

third rhythmic mode

fourth rhythmic mode

fifth rhythmic mode

sixth rhythmic mode

Certain modifications of the system were allowed. A particular rhythmic mode was not repeated indefinitely. Interruptions, usually in the form of a rest, frequently occurred at the end of phrases. Less frequently, notes on weak beats were divided or omitted.

Isorhythm

Isorhythm may be regarded as a fourteenth-century extension of the principle of rhythmic modes. In this system, a rhythmic pattern, usually of three or four measures, was repeated throughout a composition. Most frequently, the isorhythmic pattern occurred in the lowest voice (the tenor at that time), but it could occur in one of the upper voices as well. Normally, the tenor was a pre-existing melody rather than one newly composed. Known as **cantus firmus,** the tenor melody was usually based on Gregorian chant, although folk tunes were also used. The isorhythm usually disguised or obliterated the original melody. Example 4·7 presents the first phrase of the chant "Kyrie orbis factor" as it might have appeared in an isorhythmic setting. Refer to Examples 2·2 and 2·3 for comparison.

Example 4·7

Rhythmic Serialization

During the mid-1900s, the systematic rhythmic control of a composition again became important in certain styles of music. Rhythmic serialization was developed by applying the techniques of 12-tone pitch manipulation to the parameter of rhythm. By choosing a set of twelve rhythmic durations, a composer can establish and manipulate a 12-tone row of rhythms. This will be explored in chapter 25, "12-Tone Music."

**Rhythmic Controls
and Techniques**

Syncopation

Certain types of rhythmic usage have been given identifying names. Of these controls and techniques, **syncopation** is the most widely known.

Syncopation may be defined as a shifting of the normal accent structure of a composition. It is most effective in pieces written in symmetrical rhythm, since the shift is most obvious within a regularly recurring metrical scheme. Syncopation can be achieved by a variety of methods, including placing the emphasis on normally weak beats, as in Example 4•8, or holding weak beats through strong beats, as in Example 4•9. While these examples illustrate simple forms of syncopation, far more subtle and complex forms are possible.

Example 4•8

Example 4•9

Hemiola

Hemiola—a type of syncopation prevalent in the fifteenth and sixteenth centuries—is based on the relationship of 3 to 2; that is, three notes in the normal time for two, or two in the normal time for three (see Example 4•10). Example 4•11 illustrates a contemporary use of the technique.

Example 4•10

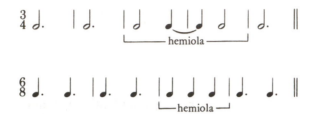

Example 4•11 Bernstein, "America": mm. 1–4

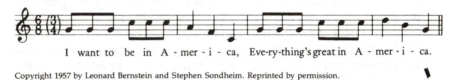

I want to be in A - mer - i - ca, Eve-ry-thing's great in A - mer - i - ca.

Polyrhythm

Polyrhythm refers to the use of contrasting rhythmic patterns within the same metric organization. These contrasting rhythmic patterns suggest the simultaneous occurrence of more than one metrical scheme. While Example 4•12 is written in 6/8 meter, the first line clearly suggests a 3/4 meter, and the second line 12/16 meter.

Example 4•12 Mozart, *Quartet in D minor* (K. 421): mm. 49–52

Polymeter

Polymeter means the simultaneous use of two or more meters (see Example 4·13.) Both polyrhythm and polymeter increase the rhythmic complexity of a composition.

Example 4·13   Mozart, *Don Giovanni:* Act One, Scene XX, mm. 455–56

Metric Modulation

Metric modulation—a relatively new technique developed by American composer Elliott Carter—is the systematic shifting of tempo or pulse within a composition. A new tempo is established and related to an original tempo by means of a cross rhythm within the original. In Example 4·14, the quarter-notes of the second measure are at the tempo of the quarter-note triplet of the first measure. Metric modulation not only provides increased control of tempo, but also allows a new means of structural development, since the rhythmic relationship between sections is precisely controllable.

Example 4·14

Suggested Activities

1. Musicians should be able to aurally identify different symmetrical meters, and to distinguish between symmetrical rhythm and non-symmetrical or free rhythm. We recommend the following recordings for class identification and discussion:

Tielman Susato, Basse Danse "Bergeret sans roch" (Angel S-36851)
Haydn, *Symphony No. 31:* I
Tchaikovsky, *Symphony No. 6:* II
Paul Desmond, "Take Five" (Columbia CS-8192)
John Dowland, *Frog Galliard* (Decca DL-79434)
Ravel, *Bolero*
Ben Johnston, "Passing Days" from *Carmilla* (Vanguard VSD 79322)
Terry Riley, *In C* (Columbia MS-7178)
Machaut, *Douce dame jolie* (Vanguard 71179)
David Crosby, *Deja Vu* (Atlantic Records SD 7200)
Dave Brubeck, "Unsquare Dance" (Columbia CS 8490)
Dave Brubeck, "Blue Rondo à la Turk" (Columbia CS 8192)
Rimsky-Korsakov, *Capriccio Espagnol*
Don Ellis, *Live in 3 2/3 /4 Time* (Pacific Jazz 20123)

2. Write a short composition in free rhythm for solo instrument, and arrange for a performance in class. Discuss the advantages and disadvantages of free rhythm compared with non-symmetrical rhythm. Is free rhythm less musical than non-symmetrical rhythm?

3. Basic drill in hearing, writing, and performing simple and compound symmetrical meters and rhythms is essential at this point. You might begin with simple rhythmic dictation by both you and the teacher, or play rhythmic exercises written by other class members. As the text adds new concepts, they can be included in the drill.

4. Clap out the metric modulation in Example 4·14.

5. Write an example of metric modulation with an original tempo of mm. 60 and a new tempo of mm. 90.

6. Use a currently popular song or a well-known folksong as a cantus firmus in an isorhythmic setting with an additional voice. Arrange for a performance in class.

7. Write a short composition in non-symmetrical rhythm for three to five performers. Limit your sound sources to non-pitched sounds ordinarily available in the classroom.

8. As a class, select a first movement, or section of the movement, from a Haydn string quartet, a Beethoven quartet, and an Ives quartet. Perform the three selections rhythmically by dividing into groups and clapping the four parts. Discuss the similarities and differences.

5

Octave Identification

To facilitate discussion of pitches, scales, and melodies, we will use the system of octave identification shown in Example 5·1, with all notes of the octave referred to C.

Example 5·1

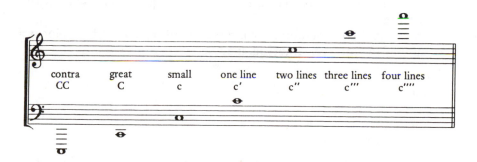

Example 5·2

Intervals

Interval Classification

An interval is the distance between two pitches. It may be **harmonic** (sounding simultaneously), or **melodic** (sounding successively).

Example 5·3

In calculating an interval we first consider the arithmetical distance. In Example 5·4, g′ to a′ is described as a second; g′ to b′ as a third; g′ to c′′ as a fourth.

Example 5·4

Observe that we consider the total number of letter names between and including the two pitches. Note also that the staff itself is of great help in interval recognition—seconds always appear on adjacent lines and spaces, thirds on consecutive lines or spaces, and so on with other intervals.*

The second consideration for interval identification is the color or quality of the interval. Intervals may be

perfect   P
major   M
minor   m
augmented   A or +
diminished   d or °

Perfect intervals include unisons (primes), fourths, fifths, and octaves. If a perfect interval is increased by a half-step, it becomes augmented. If it is decreased by a half-step, it becomes diminished.

---

*The layout of the piano keyboard is also an aid to interval measurement. We recommend using printed keyboards to physically count the notes within intervals, especially for the student who has difficulty visualizing the keyboard in his mind.

Example 5·5

**Chapter 5
Melody:
Pitch
Resources**

31

Note that Example 5·5b remains a fourth and Example 5·5d a fifth, even though both contain six half-steps. This is because the arithmetical distance of each is different.

Seconds, thirds, sixths, and sevenths can be major, minor, diminished, or augmented in quality. If a major interval is increased by a half-step, it becomes augmented; if decreased by a half-step, it becomes minor. When a minor interval is decreased by a half-step, it becomes diminished.

Example 5·6

Through this system, the identification of intervals can now be very precise as to size and quality.

The importance of the arithmetical distance in calculating intervals cannot be overemphasized. Without such careful calculation, intervals such as those in Example 5·7 could easily create analytical problems.

Example 5·7

Purely aural analysis would undoubtedly result in these intervals being identified as a minor second and a major second. By taking into account the arithmetical distance involved, however, the theoretical description would become "augmented prime" and "diminished third."

Intervals larger than an octave are described as *compound*. Example 5·8 illustrates a major ninth (compound second) and a minor tenth (compound third).

Example 5·8

Inversion of Intervals

Any interval may be inverted by reversing the pitches from top to bottom. When intervals are inverted, the arithmetical distance always changes; the quality, on the other hand, remains the same in some cases and changes in others. This type of inversion is known as *harmonic inversion*. (Melodic inversion is discussed in chapter 6.)

Perfect intervals, when inverted, remain perfect in quality.

Example 5·9

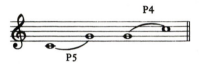

When inverted, major intervals become minor and minor intervals major in quality.

Example 5·10

Inverted augmented intervals become diminished and inverted diminished intervals become augmented.

Example 5·11

Note that in every case the sum of the interval plus its inversion totals nine. Thus, a seventh inverts to a second, a sixth to a third, and so on. Remember that this identifies the arithmetical distance only and not the quality of the interval.

Scales and Modes

Chromatic Scale

The basic pitch resources for most scales and modes are contained within the twelve notes of the chromatic scale. The chromatic scale consists entirely of half-steps, the smallest interval in equal temperament.

Example 5·12

By selecting different pitches from the chromatic scale it is possible to construct many different scales, each with its own unique arrangement of notes. Traditionally, however, composers have used only certain arrangements of pitches, systematized into consistent patterns.

Major–Minor Scales

An examination of music written between 1600 and 1900 reveals a practice based predominantly on the major–minor scale system. Major and minor scales utilize seven pitches in a particular arrangement of five whole-steps and two half-steps. In the major scale, half-steps appear between the third and fourth degrees, and the seventh and eighth degrees. All other degrees of the scale are separated by whole-steps.

Example 5·13

This pattern of whole-steps and half-steps, which gives the major scale its characteristic quality, may be started on any other pitch; as long as the pattern is kept intact, the result is a major scale.

Example 5·14

Example 5·14 illustrates that in transposing the major scale pattern, additional accidentals are needed to keep the pattern of whole-steps and half-steps intact. This predictable order of pitch alterations is the basis for a system of key signatures.

Example 5·15   Major Key Signatures

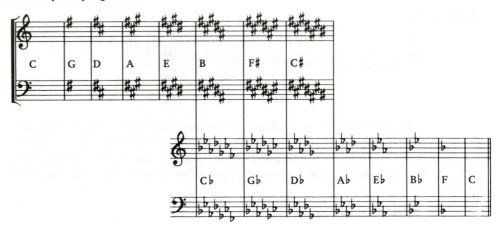

Like the major scale, the *natural minor scale* (Example 5·16) contains five whole-steps and two half-steps, but the half-steps occur between degrees two and three, and five and six.

Example 5·16

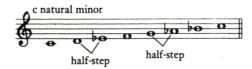

In addition to the natural minor, two other minor scales are commonly used. The *harmonic minor scale* is constructed by raising the seventh degree of the natural minor scale by a half-step, and thus contains three whole-steps, three half-steps, and one augmented second (see Example 5·17).

Example 5·17

Chapter 5
Melody:
Pitch
Resources

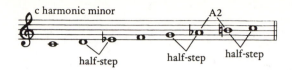

In the *melodic minor scale* (Example 5•18), the sixth and seventh degrees are raised when ascending and lowered when descending, thus avoiding the interval of the augmented second inherent in the harmonic minor scale. Notice that the descending version of the melodic minor scale is the same as the natural minor scale.

Example 5·18

Minor scales use the same set of key signatures as major scales, and one key signature identifies all three forms of the minor scale. Compare Examples 5•15, 5•19, and 5•20 and you will see that major and minor scales sharing the same key signature are related by a minor third.

Example 5·19   Minor Key Signatures

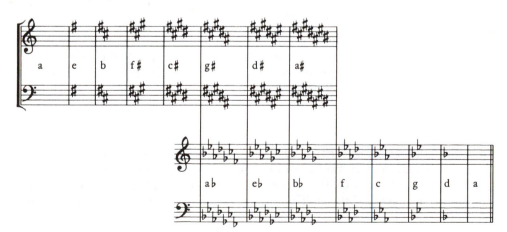

Example 5·20 The Circle of Fifths

Major keys

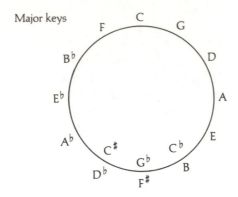

Minor keys

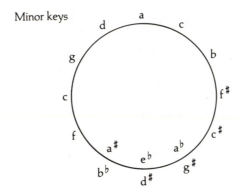

The terms *relative major* and *relative minor* identify the major and minor scales sharing the same key signature, while the terms *parallel major* and *parallel minor* refer to the major and minor scales beginning on the same pitch.

Modes

Most music written before 1600 is based on pitch sets called *modes*. These church modes (unlike the modes of ancient Greece) are based on a pattern of five whole-steps and two half-steps; the changing placement of the half-steps gives each mode its own unique sound.

Example 5·21*

Chapter 5
Melody:
Pitch
Resources

37

Dorian

Phrygian

Lydian

Mixolydian

Aeolian

Locrian

Ionian

Fluency in recognizing and using modes is essential for understanding not only early music, but also music written since the time of Chopin and Debussy. Since major and minor scales are already familiar to the majority of students, it should be helpful to relate the modes to them. Such a comparison is presented in Example 5·22.

*The Locrian mode is primarily a theoretical mode and is seldom found in actual practice. The Ionian mode corresponds to the major scale, and the Aeolian mode to the natural minor scale.

Example 5·22

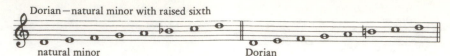

Dorian — natural minor with raised sixth

natural minor   Dorian

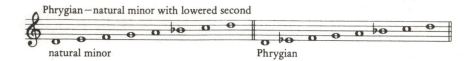

Phrygian — natural minor with lowered second

natural minor   Phrygian

Lydian — major with raised fourth

major   Lydian

Mixolydian — major with lowered seventh

major   Mixolydian

Pentatonic Scales

Many varieties of pentatonic (five-note) scales are in use throughout the world. Although some contain half-steps, the variety known as *anhemitonic* does not. This variety is found primarily in Chinese music, as well as in primitive and folk music. Because it contains only five notes and no half-steps, this variety suggests no strong tonic. In Example 5•23, any of the pitches in either of the two forms can function as the tonic.

Example 5·23

Pentatonic (anhemitonic variety)

Pentatonic scales are normally associated with Eastern music, but they have been used in Western music as well (see Example 5•24). They also form the pitch basis for most of the folk music of the world.

Example 5·24a Rossini, *William Tell*: Overture, mm. 176–180

b "Tom Dooley" (Southern ballad): mm. 1–8

Whole-Tone Scale

The whole-tone scale—made up entirely of whole-steps—has only two possible forms, shown in Example 5·25.

Example 5·25

It is associated primarily with the musical style known as *Impressionism*. The whole-tone scale lacks the perfect fifth, perfect fourth, and major seventh of the major–minor scale system, resulting in an ambiguous tonal center.

12-Tone

Arnold Schoenberg is credited with the development in the early 1900s of the compositional system known as 12-tone technique. In 12-tone music, the basic pitch resource is the chromatic scale, which is arbitrarily arranged into a **tone row**. This ordering becomes the structural basis for the entire composition. Example 5·26 is a tone row developed by Schoenberg; Example 5·27 gives it in a melodic and rhythmic framework.

Example 5·26

Example 5·27 Schoenberg, *Fourth String Quartet*, mm. 1–6

Examples 5·26 and 5·27 copyright 1939 by G. Schirmer, Inc. Reprinted by permission.

Microtonal Scales

Scales which utilize intervals smaller than a half-step are referred to as *microtonal*. Microtonal scales vary from those which divide the octave into quarter-steps to those which divide the octave into as many as ninety-six divisions. Some of the composers who have worked with microtonal pitches are Julián Carrillo, Harry Partch, Krzysztof Penderecki, and Alois Hába (who has written an opera in quarter-tones).

When dealing with intervals smaller than a half-step, performance and notational problems are major. Example 5·28 gives the 53-note microtonal scale employed in much of the music of American composer Ben Johnston. (Refer to Example 2·7 to see how Johnston has used this scale.)

Example 5·28

Copyright © 1977 by Ben Johnston. All rights reserved. Used by permission.

Suggested Activities

1. Locate the following pitches on the staff and at the keyboard:

Treble clef:	a′	c♭	GG	d′′′	f
Bass clef:	b	d′	e′′	A	b♯′
Tenor clef:	g♯	G	b′	d♯′′	a

2. Write, sing, play at the keyboard, and identify by ear the following intervals:

Above the pitch e′:   M3, P5, m2, M7, A4, M6, m3
Below the pitch d′:   P4, m3, M2, P5, M3, m6, M7
Above the pitch f: m3, m6, A4, P5, m2, P4, M3
Below the pitch a♭:   M7, M6, M3, m7, M2, P5, P4

A great amount of drill work, both in class and individually, is essential to become proficient with intervals. Teacher and student should take these exercises as suggestions and should devise their own drills for further practice.

3. Write the following scales and modes from the indicated pitch. Use accidentals rather than key signatures, and a clef appropriate to the beginning pitch. Develop the abilities to sing them and to play them at the keyboard.

Harmonic minor from B♭
Lydian mode from f♯′
Dorian mode from e♭
Whole-tone scale from g♭
Phrygian mode from a′
Major scale from g♭′
Melodic minor scale from c
Mixolydian mode from a

4. Select a well-known melody written in a major key. Rewrite it in harmonic minor, Dorian mode, Lydian mode, and whole-tone. Play the different versions in class and discuss the changing character of each version.

5. Construct a 12-tone pitch row and set it, plus two repetitions, as a melody for solo instrument.

6

Melody is so complex and subtle a combination of elements that it practically defies definition. Throughout the history of music, melody has been the parameter which allowed the most personal and individually creative expression. While in each stylistic period composers have usually shown much in common in their use of the parameters of rhythm, form, and harmony—that is, been able to work within commonly established harmonies and forms—they have consistently expressed their individuality through their approaches to melody.

Some of the factors that determine the success of a melody are the choice of pitch materials, motion, placement of arrival points, contour, and harmonic considerations. The interaction of these elements can produce an infinite number of melodic possibilities covering the entire emotional and expressive spectrum. A closer look at specific elements within the melodic parameter will provide insight into how a composer controls and manipulates his melodic material.

Melodic Elements

The elements within the melodic parameter are: melody, tune, theme, subject, motive, phrase, and period. **Tune** usually denotes an easily recognized, easily remembered melody, such as a folk song or a popular song. **Theme** refers to the pitch material used for sonatas, symphonies, theme and variations, and other generally homophonic compositions. **Subject** describes the pitch material of contrapuntal compositions such as inventions and fugues. A **motive** is a short arrangement of pitches identifiable as a melodic unit. It usually lends itself well to further transformation or development. The **phrase** is the basic unit of melodic construction. It gives a feeling of completeness, although the degree of completeness may vary with the setting in which the phrase is used. Historically, phrases have tended to be symmetrical in length, that is, two, four, or eight measures in length. A **period** is the combination of two or more phrases. If a period consists of two phrases, the first generally ends with a feeling of incompleteness that the second phrase acts to complete.

Melodic Contour

An important consideration in melodic analysis is the contour shaped by the arrangement of pitch materials. Related factors include vocal or instrumental range, tempo, expressive mood, and texture. Example 6•1 shows a melodic contour of almost continuous ascent. The pitches span a range of two octaves, beginning with c' and rising to c' ' '.

Example 6•1   Beethoven, *Sonata in F minor*, Op. 2, No. 1: mm. 1–8

An important aspect of the contour of a melody is the placement of high and low points. Example 6•1 reveals a careful placement of these points for maximum tension and interest within the eight-measure structure. The first arrival point within the contour is the ab' ' in measure 2. The upward motion is used again in measure 3, rising this time to bb' '. The material in measures 5 and 6 fragments and reinforces the material of the earlier arrival points, thus creating even more expectancy for the c' ' ' in measure 7. The melody also shows a balance of conjunct motion (motion by step) and disjunct motion (motion by leap). Although basically disjunct, it contains descending conjunct motion to balance each upward thrust.

Example 6•2 illustrates a melodic line with predominately descending motion and thrust. This is accomplished through the initial dramatic upward leap.

Example 6·2 Richard Strauss, *Also sprach Zarathustra:* mm. 131–134

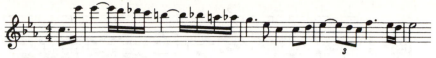

A more typical contour—one found in thousands of melodies—has a gradual rise in pitch from the beginning of the melody through a climax approximately two-thirds or three-fourths from the end. Example 6·3 shows two such melodic contours.

Example 6·3 Bach, *B minor Mass:* Sanctus, mm. 1–7;
Sea chantey

Melodic Motion

The impact of motion is primary in the shaping and manipulation of pitch, as a re-examination of Example 6·1 will reveal. The drive to the longer note value in measure 2 draws even greater attention to the placement of the pitch. This rhythmic pattern continues for each successive arrival point. The pattern (𝅘𝅥𝅭 𝅘𝅥𝅯𝅘𝅥𝅯𝅘𝅥𝅯 𝅘𝅥), stated four times, sets up an air of stability that is destroyed in measure 7 by the unexpected 𝅗𝅥 𝅘𝅥𝅘𝅥𝅘𝅥𝅘𝅥 , drawing even greater attention to the climax.

Example 6·4 is an illustration of the control of pitch and motion through the careful placement of **rhythmic cells**. The fugal subject is based on three such cells. By juxtaposing the three, a melody coherent in pitch and rhythm is achieved.

Example 6·4 Bach, *Fugue No. 21*, mm. 1–4

$1 = $

$2 = $

$3 = $

Melodic Manipulation

In addition to contour and motion, there are other elements the composer must consider when dealing with the melodic parameter. These include such manipulative devices as sequence, repetition, inversion, retrograde, retrograde inversion, augmentation, diminution, and variation.

Sequence is the repetition of a melodic pattern at a new pitch level.

Example 6·5 Sequence

Melodic inversion is the changing of direction of each interval of a melody (an ascending fourth becomes a descending fourth, and so on.) The term *mirror* is often used to mean the same thing. In melodic inversion the interval remains the same and the pitches change; in harmonic inversion (discussed in chapter 5) the pitches remain the same and the interval changes.

Example 6·6 Melodic Inversion

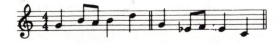

Retrograde motion begins with the last note and ends with the first. This device, used as early as the thirteenth century, is a basic technique of 12-tone composition.

Example 6·7   Retrograde*

Retrograde inversion is the combination of inversion and retrograde.

Example 6·8   Retrograde Inversion*

Augmentation refers to increasing (usually doubling) the time values of the original melodic motive.

Example 6·9   Augmentation

Diminution is decreasing (usually by one half) the time values of the melodic motive.

Example 6·10   Diminution

Variation includes less formal procedures, such as rhythmic alteration, contour expansion or contraction, transposition, or embellishment.

*In these examples, only the pitches have been written in retrograde, although it would also be possible to write the rhythm in retrograde.

We can now return to Example 6•1 to give an overall analysis that will illustrate the subtle interaction of elements within the melodic parameter.

Pitch basis: F minor

Contour: Basically ascending, predominantly disjunct, reaching a high point in measure 7.

Motion: Recurring rhythmic motives give unity of motion. Longer note values emphasize important pitch arrival points.

Manipulation: Chordal outlines and important resting tones support the F minor tonality. Motive and sequence are extensively used.

We can apply this same technique to widely different melodies. Sing and analyze Example 6•11 before reading our analysis.

Example 6•11   American folksong

Pitch basis: Mixolydian mode on D.

Contour: Basically conjunct, with a balance of ascending and descending motion. High point is reached with the d′′ in measure 9. In preparation for this, the melody rises to c′′ in measures 2 and 6. The gradual descent is strengthened by the a′ in measure 13.

Motion: Regular, predictable, straightforward. Note, however, the longest note value coincides with the high point in measure 9.

Manipulation: The modal framework is strongly established by careful placement and repeated use of the C natural (lowered seventh degree). Repetition is of prime structural importance.

Example 6•12 is a melody created on a 12-tone row to which we have applied the same analytical techniques. Perform and analyze the melody before reading our analysis.

Example 6•12

Pitch basis: Chromatic

Contour: Basically disjunct. Preliminary high points reached in the first two measures on pitches 2 (ab') and 9 (d' '). Major high point in measure 3, pitch 10 (eb' '). Low point begins and ends the melody.

Motion: Unpredictable. Constant juxtaposition of ascending and descending motion. Constant rhythmic activity with no major point of rest.

Manipulation: The chromatic scale manipulated by 12-tone technique. Measures 3 and 4 are a pitch and rhythmic retrograde of measures 1 and 2.

Focus

To many listeners, melody is the crucial factor in any composition. If they approve of the melody, the piece is excellent; if they do not, it is terrible. To such listeners, the absence of a melody indicates a non-musical sound event. Historically, melody has varied in importance. In monophonic compositions, certainly, melody is paramount. With styles such as Impressionism, however, melody is sometimes secondary to such parameters as timbre and harmony. Today's compositions for percussion ensemble or electronic tape vividly demonstrate that melody is only one of many musical parameters. Melody can be of little or no importance when material of sufficient worth and interest makes use of other musical parameters.

Suggested Activities

1. Write down or discuss in class the characteristics that unify and shape the melodies given below. Consider, when appropriate, such factors as pitch resources, contour, motion, and manipulation.

Bach, *Passacaglia in C minor*, opening measures

Medieval English carol

Haydn, *Symphony No. 104*

Anon., *L'Homme armé*

L'hom - me, l'hom - me, l'homme ar - mé,

Smetana, "The Moldau" from *My Country*

Chopin, *Prelude,* Op. 28, No. 7

Mozart, *Eine kleine Nachtmusik*

Gregorian chant, "Dies irae"

I- es írae, di- es ílla, Sólvet saéclum in favílla :

Téste Dávid cum Sibýlla. Quántus trémor est futúrus,

Quando jú-dex est ventúrus, Cúncta stricte discussúrus!

Berlioz, *Symphonie Fantastique*

Bach, *Brandenburg Concerto No. 5*

Dvorak, *Symphony in E minor*

Susato, *Ronde*

Beethoven, *Symphony No. 9*

Rachmaninoff, *Piano Concerto No. 2*

Suggested Readings

As indicated at the beginning of this chapter, *melody* is an elusive term to define. Compare the definitions in *Harvard Dictionary of Music,* 2nd Ed., and *Oxford Companion to Music,* 10th Ed.

7

Our discussion of pitch resources and manipulation has concentrated on the horizontal or linear aspect of music. In examining the harmonic parameter, we will consider both vertical and horizontal elements.

The term **chord** means the vertical structure created when three or more notes are sounded simultaneously. **Harmony** refers to a horizontal progression of chords. Harmony is generated directly from basic pitch materials. For example, if the Mixolydian mode is the basis for a melody, then the harmony as well will probably be constructed from Mixolydian pitch resources. Or if a composer works with microtones, the harmony, too, will consist of microtonal elements.

Triads

The **triad** is the primary component of the major–minor harmonic system. It is a three-note chord constructed by the superposition of thirds. The four species of triads are:

Major triad: a major third and a perfect fifth (Example 7•1a)
Minor triad: a minor third and a perfect fifth (Example 7•1b)
Augmented triad: a major third and an augmented fifth (Example 7•1c)
Diminished triad: a minor third and a diminished fifth (Example 7•d)

Example 7•1

Triads can be constructed on each degree of a major or minor scale.

Example 7·2

Notice in Example 7·2 how the Roman numeral designation (upper–lower case) agrees with the quality of the triad (major–minor). The symbol ° beside a lower-case Roman numeral indicates a diminished triad, while the sign + beside an upper-case Roman numeral indicates an augmented triad. Additional nomenclature used interchangeably with Roman numerals includes:

I   tonic
ii   supertonic
iii   mediant
IV   subdominant
V   dominant
vi   submediant
vii°   leading tone (subtonic when positioned a whole-step
                   below the tonic)

The significance of the scale degree names is shown in Example 7·3.

Example 7·3

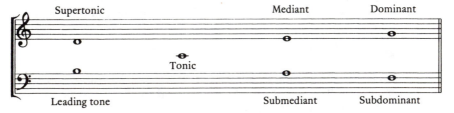

Notice in particular that the dominant is a perfect fifth above the tonic and the subdominant a perfect fifth below, while the mediant and submediant are located halfway between. The primary scale degrees (tonic, subdominant, and dominant) effectively establish a tonality.
Every major scale will generate the same pattern of triads:

3 major triads   I, IV, V
3 minor triads   ii, iii, vi
1 diminished triad   vii°

The harmonic minor scale will produce the following triads:

2 major triads   V, VI
2 minor triads   i, iv
2 diminished triads   ii°, vii°
1 augmented triad   III⁺

Inversions

Triads made up of superimposed thirds are said to be in root position. In addition, any triad may be inverted or rearranged into the two other positions. Remember that rearranging a triad into one of the other positions does not change the quality of the triad.

Example 7·4

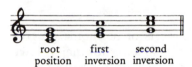

root   first   second
position   inversion   inversion

The lowest-sounding pitch determines the label of an inversion. Arabic numerals are used in conjunction with the Roman numerals, as in Example 7·5, to label the inversion positions more precisely. The Arabic numbers refer to the intervals from the bass note. It is important to remember the distinction between the lowest sounding pitch, or bass note, and the root of the chord. The two are the same only when a chord is in root position.

Example 7·5

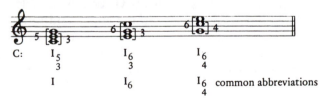

Of course, the spacing of the notes of a triad vary with the compositional context. Composers often spread out the pitches of a chord to achieve a particular effect. When determining the inverted position of a chord, however, octave displacement is never considered (see Example 7•6).

Example 7•6

In labeling chordal structures for an analysis of harmonic progression, key is indicated at the beginning: capital letter for major, lower case for minor. Example 7•7 shows such a labeling procedure.

Example 7•7

Occasionally an extra pitch, located a seventh above the root, is added to a triad. The additional note adds tension to the chord and to the harmonic progression. Such four-note chords, known as **seventh chords**, should not be confused with triads built on the seventh degree of the scale. Example 7•8 demonstrates the procedure for labeling seventh chords.

Example 7•8

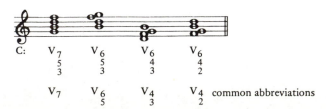

Seventh chords are identified according to the quality of both the triad and the interval of the seventh. Thus, Example 7•8, consisting of a major triad plus the interval of a minor seventh, is labeled a *major minor-seventh* chord (Mm7). (This terminology, based on the chord in root position, also applies to any inversion.) Usually, however, a major minor-seventh is referred to as a *dominant seventh* chord, a major major-seventh is called a *major seventh* chord, and minor minor-seventh is abbreviated as *minor seventh* chord. In jazz and popular music, the figure *E7* indicates a *major major-* (*dominant*) *seventh*, *A♭ maj. 7* refers to a *major major-seventh,* and *Bm7* indicates a *minor minor-seventh.* Example 7•9 gives the three different seventh chords. (There is further discussion of seventh chords in Part B.)

Example 7•9

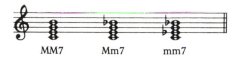

Harmonic Rhythm

The character and momentum of a composition are determined in part by the **harmonic rhythm**, or rate of chord change. This does not necessarily coincide with the tempo indication. A fast tempo combined with a slow rate of chord change can produce a static feeling; a slow tempo and fast rate of chord change can result in great tension and momentum. In Example 7•7, there is a chord change with each beat, thus producing a fast harmonic rhythm. Example 7•10 has a much slower harmonic rhythm.

Example 7•10 Fr. Kuhlau, *Sonatina*, Op. 20, No. 1: mm. 1–8

Cadences

The term **cadence** is used to describe a temporary or permanent point of rest. It applies to both melody and harmony, and can occur at the end of a phrase, period, or section. Within the major–minor system, certain harmonic cadential formulas have become standard.

Authentic cadence: V to I in major, V to i in minor.

Example 7·11

Plagal cadence: IV to I in major, iv to i in minor.

Example 7·12

Half cadence or *semi-cadence:* ending on V.

Example 7·13

Deceptive cadence: V to vi in major, V to VI in minor.

Example 7·14

Phrygian cadence: iv₆ to V in minor.

Example 7·15

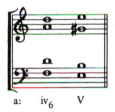

Modal cadence has a tonic chord preceded by a subtonic chord (a major chord built on the lowered seventh degree of the scale). A cadence which occurs normally in Mixolydian mode, it is used frequently in rock music.

Example 7·16

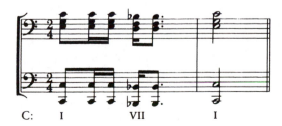

Jazz Neopolitan cadence has a tonic chord preceded by a major chord built on the lowered second degree.

Example 7·17

All cadences sound stronger when the final chord contains the root of the chord in both the bass and soprano voices. This is called a *perfect cadence*. The term *imperfect cadence* is used when the third or fifth of the chord is in the soprano voice of the final chord. Since the authentic cadence is the strongest of the cadential formulas, it tends to be identified as perfect or imperfect more frequently than other cadences. In certain places in a composition, composers want a cadence less final than it is capable of sounding. To accomplish this, they often make the cadence imperfect. In addition, they may further weaken the cadence by inverting one or both of the chords.

Cadences generally denote important structural points within a composition. Examples: a half cadence usually divides a period; an authentic cadence completes a period; a deceptive cadence indicates an extension of musical material.

An Introduction to Modulation

Modulation is the moving of pitch materials from one key to another. The changing of keys adds harmonic variety to a composition, and contributes to its shape and structure. Modulations do not have to involve a change of key signature, for they can be accomplished with the use of accidentals. In fact, most modulations occur without a key signature change. A change from a major key to its parallel minor, or the reverse, is generally called *change of mode* rather than modulation.*

Harmony in Non-Tonal Music

Typically, triads function harmonically when a composer is dealing with major–minor pitch materials. Other tonal systems, however, have been used as the basis for harmony. Example 2·7 was an illustration of microtonal harmony. Example 7·18 shows how a 12-tone row

*The harmonic understanding of specific types of modulations and developing fluency in writing these modulations is fully explored in chapters 15 and 16. At this point we wish merely to introduce the concept for use in our upcoming discussion of the parameter of form.

was used to generate the harmonic materials of a 12-tone composition. (See Example 5•26 for the basic tone row of this quartet.)

Example 7•18   Schoenberg, *Fourth String Quartet*, Op. 37: I, mm. 1–3

Suggested Activities

1. Practice spelling, singing, and playing at the keyboard major, minor, augmented, and diminished triads, in both root position and inversions, beginning on any pitch.

2. Write the following triads in the bass clef:

F major, root position
Gb minor, first inversion
E augmented, second inversion
Db major, first inversion

3. For each of the following, determine the key and write out the chord.

IV   III$_6^+$ VI$_6$ ii$_2^4$ iv   vi$_5^6$ III$_6^+$ ii$_6^o$

4. Analyze the following pieces in terms of cadences. Discuss the relative strengths of the cadences.

Bach, *Invention No. 4 in D minor*
Beethoven, *Sonata in F minor*, Op. 2, No. 1: II

5. Continue in the third measure the 12-tone numbering of pitches of Example 7•18.

6. Write the bass line for the following progressions in the indicated keys:

Ab major ⎫
D major ⎬   I   vi   ii$_6$ V   vi   ii$_5^6$ I$_4^6$ V$_7$ I

G minor ⎫
E minor ⎬   i   V$_4^6$ i$_6$ ii$_5^o$ V   i   VI   iv   V   V$_5^6$ i

8

Types of Texture

Texture is a multi-faceted parameter capable of many interpretations and manipulations. In Western music, three primary types of texture have been historically important. **Monophonic texture** is one melodic line without accompaniment. **Homophonic texture** is one predominant melody with accompaniment. Often the accompaniment is chordal or it outlines chords. **Polyphonic texture** is two or more equally important melodic lines occurring simultaneously. The term is synonymous with **contrapuntal texture**. Polyphony may be imitative or non-imitative. Imitative polyphony uses the same melodic material in more than one voice, as in a round, canon, or fugue. When more than one type of texture occurs in a single composition, such juxtaposition of textures often contributes to the structural design.

The term *texture* applies to more than the various kinds of melodic settings. Through judicious use of texture, a composer can control such elements as density, contrast, and dynamic intensity. The excerpts of Example 8•1 show how density (thickness or thinness) can be easily discerned in both visual and aural analyses.

Example 8·1 Chopin, *Nocturne*, Op. 15, No. 1: **a** mm. 1–2; **b** mm. 25–26

This Nocturne by Chopin also shows how a composer's choice of texture creates both unity and contrast. The opening section (Example 8·1a) is structured around a lyrical, single-note melodic line, with a simple, chordal accompaniment. We might describe this texture as both homophonic and thin. Example 8·1b, from later in the work, is in striking contrast, for it has a much thicker, dense texture. The additional changes of range and tempo, plus the change to the parallel minor add to the contrast.

Dynamic intensity as well as density can be achieved by a gradual buildup of texture. Both the well-known *Passacaglia in C minor* by Bach and the *Passacaglia* by Aaron Copland exemplify this technique. The opening statement of each is monophonic, and the variations that follow, employing both polyphonic and homophonic textures, build in density and dynamic intensity as lines are added.

Layers of Sound

Composers have periodically explored the device of layering sound to achieve specific textural aims. Example 8·2 is a passage from the Bach *Passacaglia in C minor;* four distinct layers of sound can be seen. (An ornamented version of the subject is stated in the lowest voice.) Today's rock musicians imply depth and layers when they speak about listening into and fully experiencing the multiple levels of the rock sound.

Another composition which graphically illustrates the layering of sound is the organ composition *Volumina* by Transylvanian composer György Ligeti. Still another, the choral composition *Epitaph for Moonlight* by Canadian composer R. Murray Schafer, is given in Example 8·3.

Example 8·3 R. Murray Schafer, *Epitaph for Moonlight*

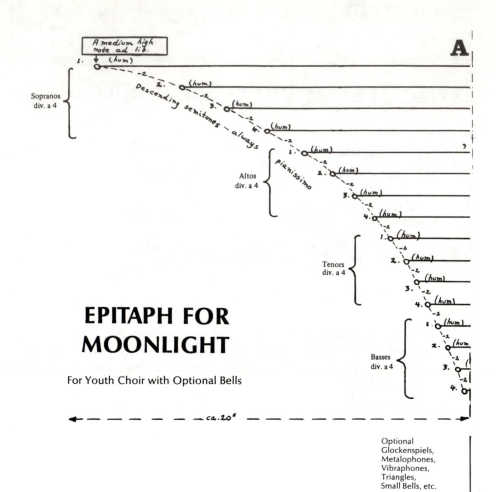

EPITAPH FOR
MOONLIGHT

For Youth Choir with Optional Bells

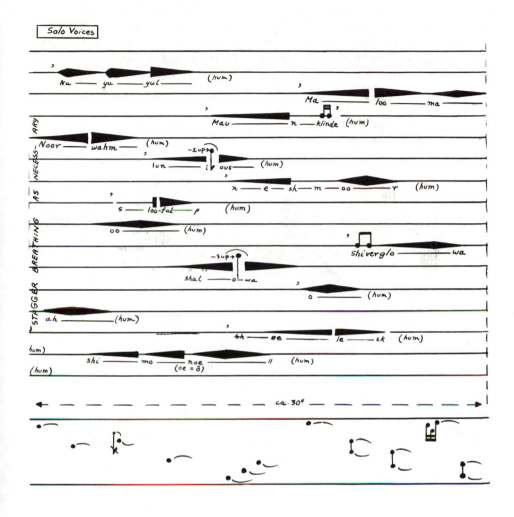

Space As a Textural Element

The concept of spatial placement has interested composers for hundreds of years. Gabrieli often employed a polychoral style of writing which involved placing choirs in various parts of the performance area. Hundreds of years later, Berlioz experimented with placing instrumentalists offstage. More recently, the compositions of Henry Brant have made the placing of performers an essential part of performance. Example 8•4 is a piece in which spatial placement is a basic premise of the composition.

Example 8•4   Pauline Oliveros, *Meditation on the Points of the Compass*

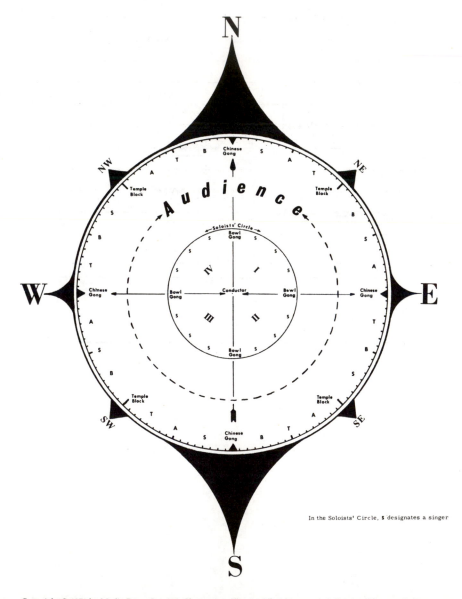

In the Soloists' Circle, **s** designates a singer

Suggested Activities

1. Perform in class a composition for small instrumental or vocal ensemble with the performers positioned as for a traditional concert. Then, perform it again, this time positioning the performers around or within the class. Compare the textural qualities of the two performances.

2. If possible, experiment in class with the spatial/textural qualities of monophonic, stereophonic, and quadrophonic recordings of tonal music, as well as two-channel and four-channel electronic compositions.

3. Analyze the following pieces for texture. (Do not expect each piece to maintain the same type of texture throughout.) How does each composer utilize texture in a structural way?

Bartok, "Melody in Tenths" from *Mikrokosmos,* Vol. II, No. 56
Bach, "Fuga V" in D major from *WTC,* Book 1
Riley, *In C*
Schumann, "Traümerie" from *Carneval,* Op. 9
Chopin, *Prelude in C minor, No. 20*
Ligeti, *Volumina*
Penderecki, *Threnody for the Victims of Hiroshima*
Gabrieli, *Fuga on the VIIIth Tone*
Bach, Menuet and Trio from *French Suite No. 3*
Cage, *Variations I* (discuss in terms of spatial texture)
Ravel, Menuet from *Le Tombeau de Couperin*
Schoenberg, *Five Pieces for Orchestra*

Suggested Readings

1. Henry Brant was one of the first composers in recent times to rediscover the musical importance of spatial placement. See his "Space As an Essential Aspect of Music Composition" in Elliott Schwartz and Barney Childs, eds., *Contemporary Composers on Contemporary Music* (New York: Holt, Rinehart and Winston, 1967).

2. Compare the discussions of "texture" in *Harvard Dictionary of Music,* 2nd Ed., and *Dictionary of Contemporary Music.* Explain the difference in emphasis and relative importance.

9

As every musician knows, each musical instrument has its own distinctive quality of sound. This quality, or timbre, is the result of the structural design of each instrument, which amplifies certain pitches in the overtone series and suppresses others.

Composers have always realized the importance of timbre as a compositional element. At times they have centered their interest around combining homogeneous sounds, while at other times they have emphasized differences in tone color. In compositions for the symphony orchestra we see the manipulation of tone colors at its most intense.

Orchestral Instruments

Instrumental Families

Instruments of the orchestra are usually grouped into four families, reflecting the manner in which their sound is produced:

Strings (violin, viola, cello, string bass): a vibrating string set in motion by a bow.

Woodwinds (flute, piccolo,* oboe, English horn,* clarinet, bass clarinet,* bassoon, contra bassoon*): a vibrating air column set in motion by a single cane reed (clarinet), a double cane reed (oboe, bassoon), or blowing across an air hole (flute).

Brass (trumpet, French horn, trombone, tuba): a vibrating column

*Auxiliary instrument, the tone of which is produced in the same manner as the preceding instrument.

of air set in motion by means of a cup-shaped mouthpiece through which the performer buzzes his lips.

Percussion (timpani, snare drum, xylophone, cymbals, piano, and others): instruments, both pitched and non-pitched, that are sounded by striking.

Transposition

Certain instruments of the orchestra sound at a pitch other than the written pitch. This practice developed at a time when certain instruments could not play in all keys equally well, and families of instruments were developed that played in particular keys. Music for these instruments was written transposed so the performer had to learn only one set of fingerings. With the technical improvements of the past century, today's orchestral instruments are chromatic, but the custom of transposition persists. Example 9·1 lists the commonly employed instruments of the orchestra, their transposition if any, and their range.

Example 9·1*

	Instrument	Transposition	Written Range
Strings	Violin	sounds as written	
	Viola	sounds as written	
	Cello	sounds as written	
	String Bass	sounds 8va lower	

*For many instruments—woodwinds and brass in particular—the *possible* range is not always the *practical* range. The pitches at the extremes tend to be hard to control and are often out of tune. For this reason we have sometimes indicated a practical range (darkened note) within the possible range. In writing for these instruments, you should take into account these problematic extremes. Use them only when it seems important.

	Instrument	Transposition	Written Range
Woodwinds	Piccolo	sounds 8va higher	
	Flute	sounds as written	
	Oboe	sounds as written	
	English Horn	sounds P5 lower	
	B♭ Clarinet	sounds M2 lower	
	A Clarinet	sounds m3 lower	
	Bass Clarinet	sounds M9 lower	
	Bassoon	sounds as written	
	Contra bassoon	sounds 8va lower	
Brass	B♭ Trumpet	sounds M2 lower	
	F French Horn	sounds P5 lower	
	Trombone	sounds as written	
	Tuba	sounds as written	

Example 9·2 gives one melody (the violin at original pitch) transposed for two other instruments. (In both cases the actual pitch *sounds* lower than the written pitch.)

Example 9·2 Haydn, *Symphony No. 104*

The Orchestral Score

Because of the many instruments involved, the orchestral score is sometimes hard for inexperienced musicians to read. In order to facilitate score reading, certain common practices have evolved over the years. The score is arranged by instrumental family: woodwinds, brass, percussion, and strings. Within each family, the order extends from the highest in pitch to the lowest. The exception to this order is the French horn—written above the trumpet—since it plays with both woodwinds and brass.

Suggested Activities

1. Practice score reading by following these recorded works with their scores.

Bach, *Brandenburg Concerto No. 2 in F major*
Mozart, *Symphony No. 40 in G minor*
Beethoven, *Symphony No. 5 in C minor*

2. Make a piano reduction of the following:

Schubert, *Symphony No. 8:* II, mm. 32–40

3. Transcribe the following for four instruments available for class performance (as many as possible should be transposing instruments). Perform the work in class. Discuss how the instrumental timbres affect the character of the work.

Bach, "Gott sei uns gnädig und barmherzig"

77

Suggested Readings

The following texts in orchestration contain useful information on scoring for instruments, both individually and in groups:

1. Kennan, Kent. *The Technique of Orchestration,* 2nd Ed. Englewood Cliffs, N.J.: Prentice-Hall, 1952, 1970.
2. McKay, George F. *Creative Orchestration,* 2nd Ed. Boston: Allyn and Bacon, 1969.
3. Piston, Walter. *Orchestration.* New York: W. W. Norton & Co., 1955.

10

79

A piece of music is shaped and controlled by the interaction of parameters, including the parameter of **form**. Yet the study of form in music is often grouped with advanced theory courses and is approached only after completion of the basic music theory sequence. For a truly complete understanding of parametric interaction, however, the study of the formal structure of music cannot be postponed. This chapter, then, discusses the parameter of form.

Without exception, every musical composition has a discernible organizing principle, or structure, resulting from the relationship of its parts. Traditionally, certain forms and procedures have become so established during a particular era that they have acted almost as molds for shaping the creativity of composers. This does not mean that all compositions of the same form are structurally alike (even two sonatas by the same composer are never exactly alike in structure), for within a particular form, composers have always manipulated the structural materials over a wide range of possibilities. Very few pieces of music exactly match in form the textbook models. Each piece must be analyzed for its own unique structuring of materials.

A major principle of formal organization is *repetition and contrast*. A composition may be structured around either or both of these elements. For example, binary (two-part) form is based on contrast, while ternary (three-part) form is based on contrast *and* repetition. Many other traditional forms, such as strophic, theme and variations, rondo, and sonata form, consist of a complex interplay of these elements of contrast and repetition.

Binary Form

The **binary form** (principle of contrast; two-part form) has two parts that contrast with each other. Example 10•1 is a relatively short com-

Chapter 10
Form

position of sixteen measures subdivided into two symmetrical sections of eight measures each. (Although the binary procedure typically involves a change of key, we have chosen an example that remains in D major throughout in order to substantiate the point that musical forms are not inviolable molds or blueprints.)

Harmonic interest and contrast are achieved in Example 10•1 by varying the chord progression and harmonic rhythm. Section A is oriented around the tonic-dominant, while section B is tonic-subdominant oriented. The faster harmonic rhythm in the B section further delineates the sections, as does the introduction of chromatic pitches in the B section.

Example 10•1 Beethoven, "Dance"

The **rounded binary form** is a two-part structure in which a portion of the A material is repeated at the end of the B material. Sometimes this repeat only hints at the A material, while at other times a considerable amount is repeated. Although similar to ternary form, the rounded binary retains its two-part structure with the use of repeat signs in the middle and at the end.

Ternary Form

The **ternary form** (principle of contrast and repetition; three-part form) is a three-part structure: statement, departure, and return. The structure of the Schumann "Waltz" in Example 10·2 is typical of many short instrumental and vocal works. This piece subdivides into three distinct sections: A—measures 1 to 16, B—measures 17 to 28, and the repeat of A—measures 29 to 44.

The most important element of contrast is the change of key in the B section. Both A sections are in the key of A minor, while the B section moves to F major. While composers often use melodic elaboration and ornamentation in the repeat of the A section, the final A section of Example 10·2 is an *exact* repetition of the opening material. Other elements that give contrast to the B section include the introduction of a new rhythmic pattern, the introduction of melodic and harmonic sequence, and a change from phrases of irregular length to four-bar phrases.

Example 10·2 Schumann, Waltz from *Albumbläter*

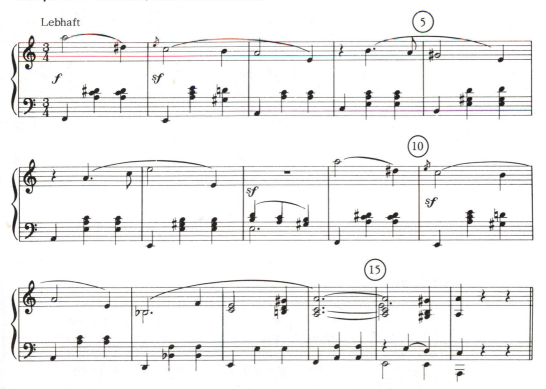

Strophic Form

The term **strophic** (principle of repetition) describes a vocal composition in which the same musical material is repeated for every
stanza of the text. Example 10•3 illustrates the effectiveness, as well
as some of the possibilities of the strophic procedure. The repetition
of the music achieves a feeling of unity and predictability, and helps

focus attention on the changing text. Since the repetition is exact, repeat signs are used. In some compositions, however, slight melodic variations necessitate writing out each stanza of music.

Example 10·3   Bernstein, "Candide"

Theme and Variations

In the theme and variations procedure (principle of repetition and contrast), one element usually remains constant (melodic material, harmonic progression, or the like). Surrounding this constant element are elements of contrast (change of rhythmic setting, change of mode, and so on). The following examples from "Ah, vous dirai-je, Maman" by Mozart illustrate the theme and variations technique.

Example 10·4   Mozart, Variations on "Ah, vous dirai-je, Maman": Theme, mm. 1–8

In Variation V (Example 10·5), the melodic pattern remains constant while the rhythmic pattern is altered.

Example 10·5   Mozart, "Ah, vous dirai-je, Maman": Var. V, mm. 121–128

A change of texture and rhythmic pattern gives additional contrast to Variation VI (Example 10·6). The increased rhythmic activity in the lower part heightens the sense of momentum and rhythmic thrust.

Example 10·6   Mozart, "Ah, vous dirai-je, Maman": Var. VI, mm. 145–152

Variation III (Example 10•7) retains the harmonic progression as the constant element, and disperses the theme through arpeggiated figurations.

Example 10•7 Mozart, "Ah, vous dirai-je, Maman": Var. III, mm. 73–80

Contrast is achieved in Variation VIII (Example 10•8) by a change of mode from C major to C minor.

Example 10•8 Mozart, "Ah, vous dirai-je, Maman": Var. VIII, mm. 169–176

Rondo

The **rondo** procedure (principle of repetition and contrast) involves a statement and restatement of A material, interspersed with contrasting digressions, or episodes. Contrast is achieved by change of key, change of melodic material, change of texture, or the like. Although rondo form is more frequently found in instrumental works, Example 10•9 ("Du Ring an meinem Finger" by Schumann) is a vocal piece. The form (ABACA) appears to follow the structure of the poem. Of the five stanzas, the first and fifth are alike, while the third only has the same first line.

The song is symmetrically balanced in shape, each section containing eight measures. The strongest element of contrast is found in the use of new melodic material for sections B and C. Although the key level remains Eb major throughout, harmonic tension is created by the introduction of chromatically altered chords in the C section, by a change of texture in the accompaniment, as well as by a change of rhythmic intensity. The interaction of these elements gives not only contrast, but also a feeling of climax for the entire composition.

Example 10·9   Schumann, "Du Ring an meinem Finger"

Sonata Form

The term *sonata* (principle of repetition and contrast) usually describes an instrumental work in three or four movements, while the term **sonata form** applies specifically to the structure of a single movement. (Sonata form has been used so frequently in the first movement [allegro] of multi-movement works, that the term *sonata-allegro form* is used interchangeably with sonata form.) Sonata-form has three distinct sections: exposition, development, and recapitulation. An important structural element is the use of contrasting key levels.

The following chart summarizes the procedure:

Exposition: Statement of thematic material.
  Group I   Group II
    I (tonic)   V (most often modulates
                      to dominant key)

(If Group I is in minor, then Group II will generally
  move to relative major.)

Development: Fragmentation and development of thematic materials. Exploration of new key areas. Unstable tonality. New material sometimes introduced.

Recapitulation: Restatement of thematic materials. Return to tonic for both themes.

Example 10•10, a concise use of the sonata form procedure, is outlined as follows:

	Exposition		Development	Recapitulation	
Theme	*A*	*B*	*A*	*A*	*B*
Measures	*1–8*	*9–15*	*16–23*	*24–31*	*32–38*
Key	*CM*	*GM*	*cm*	*C major*	
Harmonic function	*I*	*V*	*i*	*I*	

Example 10•10   Clementi, *Sonatina*, Op. 36, No. 1

Focus

The discussion of structural procedures in this chapter is meant merely to introduce the parameter of form. More information and greater sophistication in analysis will lead to greater insight. Most important, even at this preliminary stage, is making concrete observations about the form or structure of a composition. Doing so will aid both listening and performing.

Once again we emphasize that it is unnecessary to make all compositions fit the molds and labels discussed in this chapter. In many instances this will produce nothing but frustration and disillusionment with the analytic process. Try to understand the structuring of musical ideas, however they may exist. If a composition appears to subdivide into sections, then make note of this, and look for other factors of unity and repetition—recurring rhythmic motives, recurring melodic motives, changes of texture, changes of key, or the like—that give coherence to the musical structure.

Suggested Activities

1. The following works are grouped by principles of formal organization. Analyze several from each group. (Begin by following their recordings with a score.)

Binary
    Bach, "Prelude in E minor," *WTC*, Book 1 (2-Col. M2-32500)
    Handel, Bouree from *Water Music* (Col. M-33436)
    Chopin, *Prelude in E minor*, Op. 28, No. 4 (Phi. 6500622)
    Gershwin, "Summertime" from *Porgy and Bess* (RCA LSC-2679)

Ternary
Bach, Gavotte from *Suite No. 3 in D major* (DG-139007)
Beethoven, *Sonata in E♭ major,* Op. 27, No. 1: II (Van. C-10055)
Desmond, *Take Five* (Col. CS-8192)

Theme and variations
Beethoven, *Variations in C on Mozart's "La Ci Darem"* (3-Vox SVBX-580)
Brahms, *Variations on a Theme of Haydn* (DG-138926)
Rachmaninoff, *Rhapsody on a Theme of Paganini* (Col. MS-6634)
Copland, *Piano Variations* (Odys. 32160040)

Rondo
Mozart, *Sonata in C* (K. 545): III (Lyr. 781)
Chopin, *Mazurka in B♭,* Op. 7, No. 1 (3-RCA LSC 6177)
Schumann, *Arabesque,* Op. 18 (Col. KS-6371)

Sonata form
Haydn, *Symphony in G major,* No. 100: I (Ang. S-36364)
Mozart, *Symphony in G minor,* No. 40, K. 550: I, (Ang. S-36183)
Mozart, *Sonata in C major,* K. 279: II (Col. MS-7097)
Brahms, *Rhapsody,* Op. 79, No. 2 (RCA LSC-3240)

2. Using only non-pitched sounds, write short exercises that illustrate the formal principles of rondo and theme and variations.

11

Previous chapters have focused on individual parameters of music in an effort to define the various means of control to which each may be subjected. We will now examine the various parameters of a composition simultaneously to determine the primary methods by which a composer controls his musical material. We will focus on how the parameters interact with one another, as well as the manner in which parametric independence is asserted. In looking at music in this way, we will try to determine which parameters the composer is most interested in controlling, how he controls them, and how they contribute to the success of the composition.

The following three examples exhibit strikingly different forms of parametric control. You may wish to attempt your own analyses before reading ours.

Clementi, *Sonatina*, **Op. 36, No. 2: I**

Example 11·1

Form

Since a sonatina is usually like a small sonata, the first movement can be expected to be in sonata form. As we have seen, sonata form exerts a strong influence over other parameters, in effect dictating much of what happens in thematic and harmonic development. The form of this sonatina may be outlined as follows:

	Exposition		Development		Recapitulation	
Theme	*A*	*B*	*A expanded*		*A*	*B*
Measures	*1–8*	*9–22*	*23–36*		*37–44*	*45–59*
Keys	*GM*	*DM*	*am, GM, dominant preparation*		*GM*	
Harmonic function	*I*	*V*	*ii*	*I*	*I*	

Melody

Although the choice of sonata form establishes certain demands in regard to the melodic parameter, it does not determine the character and individuality of a melody. For Clementi, melodic balance and proportion seem to have been of utmost concern. Notice how the predominantly disjunct motion of the A theme is balanced by the predominantly conjunct motion of the B theme, and how the upward movement of the A theme is balanced by the descending sweep of the B theme.

In the development section, the A theme, with slight modification, predominates. By its strong presence, the A theme provides a degree of unity that offsets the transitory key cells being explored at this point in the harmony.

Harmony

The manipulation of key centers is an essential characteristic of sonata form. By placing the B theme in the key of the dominant and the recapitulation in the tonic, functional harmony actually contributes to the development of the form. Notice, too, that the movement away from the tonic is emphasized in the development section, first by moving to A minor, then to G major with a long dominant preparation. This contributes harmonically to the feeling of return in the recapitulation.

Another important harmonic feature can be found in the broken chord figurations, or **Alberti bass**, given to the left hand. Employed in this manner, the left hand not only outlines the harmonic structure but also provides an element of motion. This device draws attention as much to the horizontal harmonic movement as to the vertical chord structure. Finally, observe how the Alberti bass gives way to a more independent bass line in the development section.

Rhythm and Meter

It is evident that regularity and stability of rhythm and meter are major concerns. Within the simple duple meter the rhythm proceeds mainly in eighth-notes and sixteenth-notes, and the regularity is seldom broken. Little that can be called unique or unusual is allowed to happen. Basically, the rhythmic parameter is subservient to the parameters of melody and harmony.

Texture

The texture is homophonic. The left hand does not have a melodically equal, independent voice and cannot stand alone. Instead, it provides a harmonic outline supporting the melody.

Thirteenth-Century Conductus Motet

Example 11·2 "Deo confitemini—Domino"

Reprinted by permission of the publishers from *Historical Anthology of Music* by Archibald T. Davison and Willi Apel, Cambridge, Mass.: Harvard University Press; copyright © 1946, 1949 by the President and Fellows of Harvard College; © renewed 1974 by Alice D. Humez and Willi Apel.

Melody

Of major interest in Example 11•2 is the distinction between the voices. The tenor has a cantus firmus text separate from the text of the upper two voices. This text and the tenor melody itself are taken directly from a much older Gregorian chant. The upper two voices—the **triplum** and the **duplum**—are composed of original material. There is even a difference in style of melodic writing between the tenor and the upper voices; each syllable of the tenor text is set to several different pitches (**melismatic style**), while each syllable of the upper text has a separate note **(syllabic style).**

Some overall integration of the voices is achieved, since all voices are in the Dorian mode. Also, each voice has a limited range, reducing the possibility that one voice will stand out. Finally, the continual crossing of voices further destroys the independent character of each line.

Rhythm

Perhaps the parameter contributing most to musical unity is rhythm. The tenor is written in isorhythm. This superimposing of the cantus firmus melody (the color) on a repetitive rhythmic pattern (the talea) unifies, contributes coherence of form, and creates a concealed structure—all of which delighted composers of that time. In this example the color repeats twice and the talea (𝅗𝅥. | 𝅗𝅥 𝄾 | 𝅗𝅥 ♩ 𝅗𝅥 𝄾 |) repeats five times for each color.

The two upper voices are primarily in the first rhythmic mode (𝅗𝅥 ♩ 𝅗𝅥 ♩ |), although some departure from this pattern can be observed. The use of a rhythmic mode superimposed on a tenor in isorhythm gives the piece a basic, unchanging motion.

Harmony

This composition is modal rather than tonal. And while composers of that time paid little attention to the harmonic dimension of music, certain vertical considerations are being made which demand our attention. With but three exceptions (mm. 4, 29, 33), each phrase cadences to a unison. Observe also the places where the triplum and duplum are consonant with each other and the duplum and tenor are consonant with each other, but the three voices together produce a striking dissonance (mm. 11, 19, 38).

Texture

The texture of this piece might at first glance be incorrectly identified as homophonic, but the use of two separate texts and the melodic independence of each voice undeniably represent non-imitative polyphony.

Greg Bright, *The Balkan Sobranie*
Smoking Mixture

Example 11·3

Six players, seated as shown in the audience:

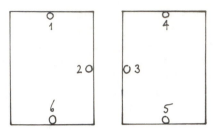

The tempo is indicated by a conductor who signals the start. At his signal, all 6 players tap. Player 1 soon begins the chanting. When the chanting is completed, the conductor allows the final 'schh' to continue until he sees fit to stop it. The start and end should be crisp, all players together.

Tapping:

All players should tap at about the same volume.
Each player's tapping should have completely different sound quality.
The total volume of the tapping should be less than that of the chanting.

Player 1:

2:

3:

4:

5:

6: (Shakes or rattles continually)

Chanting:

A	LONG	COOL	SMOKE
TO CALM	A	TROUBLED	WORLD
AN	AROMA	TO	ANSWER
ALL	LIFE'S	WORRIES	WORRIES WORRIES
WITH	THE	ADDITION	OF
RAREST	YENIDJE	LEAF	AS
THE	AUTHENTIC	SOBRANIE	TOUCH . . .

The words should be spoken on the first beat of the bar (ie. when player 1 taps). They should be said in a normal voice, clearly; do not shout. The text is spoken as a round. Player 1 speaks 'A', and as he speaks 'LONG', player 2 speaks ('A', and so on. After player 1 has said 'WORRIES WORRIES' (to be spoken as one word) he waits for the other players to reach this point and fall silent in their turn. After player 6 has said 'WORRIES WORRIES' there is a pause of one bar (tapping continues), then the rest of the text is spoken in the same manner.
As each player reaches 'TOUCH' he continues the final 'schh' sound, pausing only to take breaths. When all 6 players are making this sound, the conductor can end the piece. The 'schh' should not be too short, neither should it be disproportionate to the rest of the piece.

Notation

The most striking feature of "The Balkan Sobranie Smoking Mixture" is its notation. Unlike the previous examples in this chapter, it is written in tablature, or operational notation. The performers are given instructions for a sequence of actions, rather than an accurate diagram of melodic and rhythmic shape, as with standard notation.

In chapter 2 we said that the criterion for judging the validity and worth of such notational experiments is whether or not the composer has presented, in a lucid manner, the sounds and sequences he wishes to achieve. In this case, we will examine the performance instructions to determine the parameters being controlled and the manner of controlling them.

Melody

Melody, in its usual sense, is absent from this composition. The notation provides no means for controlling pitch contour. However, the chanting of the performers is a type of uncontrolled melody.

Rhythm

The rhythmic parameter is tightly controlled, the appearance of the notation notwithstanding. Within the simple quadruple meter, a six-part rhythmic **ostinato** (repeated rhythmic pattern) is employed in the percussion.

Texture

The texture presents a multi-layered sound composite of a polyphonic sentence chanted over the rhythmic ostinato. This repetition of the same sentence or melody beginning at different times is known as **canon**. Another textural consideration is the use of the performance space. The symmetrical positioning of the performers in the audience creates a sense of depth that allows the various sounds and words to be perceived individually, while at the same time contributing to the overall fabric of the work.

Form

Form functions on two levels. The combination of the rhythmic ostinato and the vocal word-canon are one level. These are subjected to another level of control—because of the vocal silence in the middle—which results in an overall form of A A'.

Timbre

The timbre of the percussion instruments will vary from performance to performance. The composer is not interested in limiting the choice of instruments, but in ensuring that the sounds chosen will have completely different qualities. Superimposed on the various percussive timbres is the composite timbre of the chanting voices.

Focus

It should be clear by now that a composer's choice of important parameters and their means of control greatly affects the stylistic characteristics of a composition. It should be equally clear that understanding a composition, whether for performance or historical–analytical purposes, depends on the appreciation of the parameters the composer considered important, as well as a thorough understanding of the nature and means of their control. One has only to imagine a performance of the Clementi *Sonatina* without an understanding of sonata form, the thirteenth-century motet without a knowledge of rhythmic modes and isorhythm, or *The Balkan Sobranie Smoking Mixture* without an appreciation of the structure of the canon or of the notation, to see why it is necessary for musicians to understand the essential controlling features inherent in all styles of music.

Part B
The
Tonal
System

12

With a four-voice texture, either vocal or instrumental, we consider both the vertical and horizontal aspects of the sound. The vertical aspects of the block chord involve deciding which pitch to double and how to space pitches; the horizontal, or linear considerations involve the connection and succession of chords.

Traditionally, the voices of four-part texture are designated as in choral music, that is, soprano, alto, tenor, and bass. Their normal ranges are shown in Example 12•1.

Example 12•1

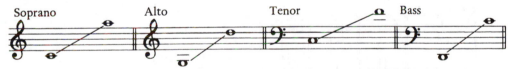

In notating this kind of texture, the soprano and alto voices are usually in the treble clef and the tenor and bass voices in the bass clef, as in Example 12•2. Alternating the direction of the stems allows for easier identification of individual voices.

Example 12•2

Occasionally, piano style of notation is used, as in Example 12•3.

Example 12•3

D: I   V   I

Writing chords in the choral style of Example 12•1 has the advantage of making individual voices easier to distinguish. In playing such examples on a keyboard instrument, however, soprano, alto, and tenor voices should be taken with the right hand and bass voice with the left.

Vertical Considerations

Doubling

Since the pitch resources for four-part structure are based on the three-note triad, one pitch is always doubled.

Example 12•4

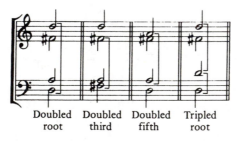

Doubled   Doubled   Doubled   Tripled
root   third   fifth   root

Doubling practices vary by composer as well as by stylistic period, and many factors are involved in choosing which pitch to double (for example, a particular "special effect," such as omitting the third or fifth of the chord, or tripling the root). In general, however, it is possible to say for major and minor chords that (1) in root position the root is doubled, (2) in first inversion the soprano is doubled, and (3) in second inversion the bass is doubled. Diminished chords most often appear in first inversion with the third doubled. Augmented chords are usually in root position with the root or third doubled.

Example 12·5

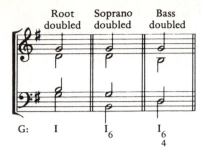

Root doubled   Soprano doubled   Bass doubled

G: I   I₆   I⁶₄

Spacing

The vertical spacing or positioning of the pitches of a particular chord is of great importance in arriving at a desired sonority. Perform the Example 12·6 to compare the differences in sound possible with various spacings of the same triad.

Example 12·6

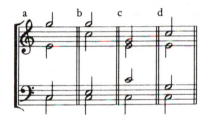

a   b   c   d

Examples 12·6c and 12·6d are in better balance. Intervals smaller than an octave are usually found between the soprano and alto voices, and alto and tenor voices, while intervals larger than an octave are often found between the tenor and bass.

Examples 12·6c and 12·6d illustrate the types of spacing called, respectively, *close* and *open position*. To write in close position, it is necessary to use each member of the chord, without omitting tones, from the soprano down through the tenor. If every other chord tone is omitted, the resulting sonority is called open position. These two techniques are illustrated in Example 12·7.

Example 12·7

Close   Open

Horizontal Considerations

When working with the horizontal aspect of four-part structure, it is important to keep in mind the contour of the melodic line, the voice leading, and the motion between voices (contrary, parallel, or oblique), as well as the basic chord progression. Perform Example 12•8 and compare the overall effects.

Example 12•8

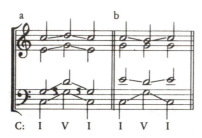

The parallel motion of voices in Example 12•8a destroys the independence of the melodic lines. Compare the effect of the contrary motion of voices in Example 12•8b.

The smoothest chord progression can be obtained by observing the following basic techniques of four-part chordal writing:

1. Retain the common chord tone (or tones) between chords with roots a fifth or a third apart.

2. Move the other voices to the nearest chord tone, using contrary or oblique motion whenever possible.

3. Avoid parallel fifths and parallel octaves, since they destroy melodic independence.

4. Avoid doubling the leading tone, any non-harmonic tone, any altered tone, or the seventh of a seventh chord.

5. Avoid the melodic interval of an augmented second.

These suggestions for part writing will, if carefully followed, ensure a smooth chord progression, although chords always connected in this manner can sound too predictable. If valid musical reasons suggest alternatives, use them.

Dominant Seventh Chords

The dominant seventh chord is practically indispensable in the harmonization and part writing of four-part structure. The additional note a minor seventh above the root adds harmonic color and tension. Because it uses four different pitches, special attention is needed.

In root position, the fifth can be omitted, and the root tripled. In an inversion, however, all four voices are usually present. Remember that the dominant seventh is always a major minor-seventh chord in quality.

A significant part of the effect of the dominant seventh chord has to do with how it resolves to the following chord. Since the third of the dominant seventh chord is the leading tone of the key, and the seventh is the fourth degree of the key, the most satisfying resolution occurs when the leading tone ascends to the tonic, and the seventh descends to the mediant.

Example 12·9

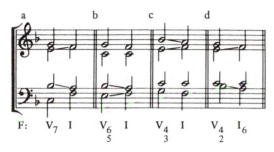

Observe that the resolution in Example 12·9a produces an incomplete tonic chord of three roots and one third. If the sonority of a complete tonic chord is preferred, the leading tone, when placed in an inner voice (tenor or alto), may descend to the dominant, as in Example 12·10.

Example 12·10

Resolution of the dominant seventh chord demands additional attention because it also contains the interval of a *tri-tone* (three whole-tones wide). Depending upon position and spacing, the tri-tone will appear sometimes as a diminished fifth, and sometimes as an augmented fourth. The augmented fourth will expand, while the diminished fifth will contract in resolving to the next chord.

**Part B
The
Tonal
System**

Example 12·11

106

Example 12·11 shows that our earlier suggestions of resolving the third of the chord upward and the seventh of the chord downward produce the same result.

Root Bass–Melodic Bass

If only root position chords are used, it is practically impossible to shape a bass line into a conjunct, melodic contour. Observe the progression of Example 12·12 as it appears in root position.

Example 12·12

Using inversion with the same chord progression, it is possible to produce a very different bass line.

Example 12·13

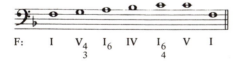

Compare the root bass progression (Example 12·12) with the melodic bass (Example 12·13). The melodic qualities of the bass voice are important and should be considered when determining which chord or inversion to use in a particular harmonic setting.

Inversions

First inversion chords may be used as frequently as desired. In fact we recommend the inversion of diminished triads because these triads in root position often sound too dissonant in relation to the rest of the harmony.

Even though second inversion chords are possible with every diatonic triad, they should be used with restraint. Composers have traditionally limited the use of second inversion chords to the following four situations:

Cadential $^6_4$: Occurs at cadence points on a strong beat. Two of the voices move down by steps (Example 12•14a).

Passing $^6_4$: Often occurs between the root position and first inversion of a chord. Usually found in a rhythmically weak position (Example 12•14b).

Pedal $^6_4$: Occurs over the same or repeated bass note, while two upper parts move stepwise (Example 12•14c).

Arpeggiated $^6_4$: Occurs from the melodic outline of a chord. Usually found on a weak beat (Example 12•14d).

Example 12•14

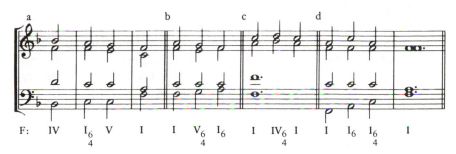

Harmonizing a Melody

We are now ready to apply our knowledge of chords and harmonic movement to harmonizing a melody. Certain basic steps, if carefully followed, will help ensure success. First, determine the form of the melody.—Does it divide into phrases? Do the phrases form periods?—Then decide where cadences should occur and what kind each should be. Establishing cadences before you consider the harmonic progression of each phrase means that each phrase has a harmonic goal and does not simply wander from chord to chord.

The next step in harmonization is to determine the chord progression for each phrase. Keep in mind that root movement by fourths or fifths is stronger than root movement by seconds or thirds. Once you have settled the basic progression, construct the bass line. First write down the root of each chord. Then consider inversions to strengthen the melodic qualities of this root bass. (Caution: too many root-position chords create a melodically weak bass line; too many inversions weaken the feeling of root movement.) Once you have established the bass line, fill in the inner voices. Here you should consider such factors as doubling practices, avoiding parallel fifths and octaves, voice leading, and so on.

Focus

Careful attention must be given to both the vertical and horizontal aspects of four-part writing. Without such dual consideration, the vertical characteristics of each chord can become over-important, and the melodic quality of the lines seriously weakened. In addition to serving a proper function within each chord, all four voices should be as melodically interesting as possible. Observe in Example 12•15 the careful attention given by Bach to voice leading, contrary motion between voices, and the composite rhythm produced by the four voices.

Example 12•15   Bach, "Du Friedensfürst, Herr Jesu Christ"

If you have noticed that some of the pitches that contribute to the horizontal motion and harmonic color of Example 12•15 are not part of the chord with which they occur, you are correct. These pitches, identified collectively as *non-harmonic tones*, are discussed in the next chapter.

Suggested Activities

1. Sing or play the following chorale* excerpt in class, remembering to make instrumental transpositions when necessary. Then answer the questions.

Bach, "Nimm von uns, Herr, du treuer Gott"

Indicate the motion between the soprano and bass voices.
Indicate the motion between the alto and tenor voices.
Identify the intervals between the soprano and bass voices.

*It should be noted that although the chord before the first fermata appears to be a $^6_4$ chord, it will actually sound in root position when performed on the organ, as was common in performances of Bach chorales.

Identify the intervals between the alto and tenor voices.
Identify the root and quality of each chord.
Indicate the harmonic progression.
Identify and label the cadences.

2. Write out the following as four-part, root-position chords, with the root doubled.

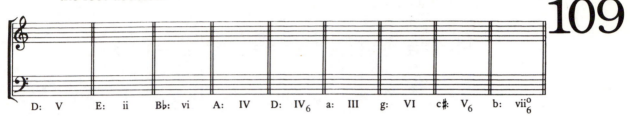

D: V   E: ii   B♭: vi   A: IV   D: IV₆   a: III   g: VI   c♯: V₆   b: vii°₆

3. Write out and resolve the following dominant seventh chords.

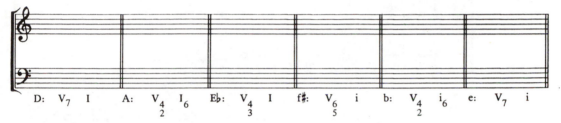

D: V₇ I   A: V₄₂ I₆   E♭: V₄₃ I   f♯: V₆₅ i   b: V₄₂ i₆   e: V₇ i

4. Write the bass line for the following progression. Using inversions, rewrite the progression to create a melodic bass line with a conjunct, melodic contour. Using close position, add the soprano, alto, and tenor voices.

G minor: i   V   i   ii°   i   V₇   i

5. Using either close or open position, write the following chord progressions in four voices.

F major: I   IV   V   I
D major: I   vi   IV   V   I
G minor: i   VI   iv   V   i
C minor: i   vii°₆   i₆   iv   V   i
G major: I   V   vi   ii₆   V   I
B♭ major: I   iii   vi   ii   V   I
A major: I   IV   I₆₄   V₇   vi   ii   V₇   I
E minor: i   iv   V   VI   ii°₆₅   V₇   I

6. Harmonize the following melodic excerpts from Bach chorales. (Include a Roman numeral analysis.) Compare your harmonization with the original chorales.

Bach, "Jesu, meiner Seelen Wonne"

Bach, "Ermuntre dich, mein schwacher Geist"

7. Fill in alto and tenor voices in the following: (Add key name and
   Roman numeral analysis.)

110

13

The preceding chapter focused primarily on chord structure and harmonic movement. Few compositions, however, are based entirely on chords or on melodies made up exclusively of chord tones. Most tonal compositions incorporate a variety of pitches that do not belong to the chord structure, although they may sound simultaneously with it. These non-chord pitches are called *non-harmonic tones*. In this chapter we discuss the various kinds of non-harmonic tones: passing tones, neighboring tones, changing tones, anticipation, suspension, retardation, appoggiatura, escape tones, and pedal point.

First, some general observations. Since non-harmonic tones are not part of the chords with which they occur, they are, to varying degrees, dissonant. This dissonance (1) calls attention to the voice in which the non-harmonic tone occurs, (2) adds movement to the phrase, and (3) creates ambiguous tonality at that point in the harmonic framework.

Because of their dissonance, non-harmonic tones have traditionally been used cautiously. While conventions have varied from style period to style period (strict during the Baroque, less so during the Classical and Romantic), we can identify certain underlying precautions in the use of non-harmonic tones:

1. They are generally approached stepwise or by direct preparation, in which case the non-harmonic tone appears in the preceding chord as a chord tone;

2. they usually resolve stepwise;

3. they are seldom doubled;

4. the pitch to which the non-harmonic tone resolves seldom occurs in another voice simultaneous with the non-harmonic tone (so as to retain the dissonant quality of the non-harmonic tone);

5. several non-harmonic tones can occur simultaneously.

Passing Tones

Non-harmonic tones which fill in or pass melodically between two chord tones are called *passing tones*. Most commonly, the interval filled is a third. Composers have occasionally filled in other intervals, the most frequent being a fourth (filled in with two consecutive passing tones) or a second (with a chromatic passing tone).

Some theorists make a distinction between accented and unaccented passing tones. They reason that unaccented passing tones (those falling on weak parts of the beat or measure) contribute more to melodic movement than to dissonance, while accented passing tones (those falling on strong parts of the beat or measure) contribute equally to melodic movement and dissonance. In Examples 13•1 and 13•2, a passing tone, accented or unaccented, is marked *PT*.

Example 13•1   Chopin, *Mazurka*, Op. 7, No. 1: mm. 1–4

Example 13•2   Schubert, "Du bist die Ruh": mm. 24–25

Neighboring Tones

Neighboring tones (also called *auxiliary tones* or *embellishing tones*) are used by composers to embellish a repeated chord tone. They occur a step or half-step above or below, and between the repeated chord tones. Like passing tones, neighboring tones can be accented or unaccented, and can occur in several voices simultaneously. In Examples 13•3 and 13•4, the neighboring tones are indicated by the letter *N*.

Example 13•3   Bach, *Brandenburg Concerto No. 3:* I, mm. 1–2

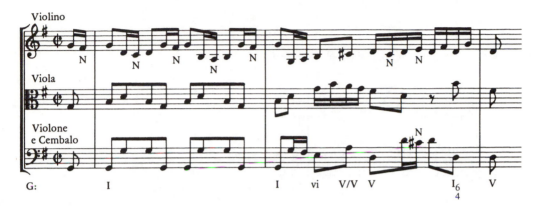

Example 13•4   Beethoven, *Piano Sonata*, Op. 79: III, mm. 1–4

Changing Tones

Changing tones may be thought of as the combined use of upper and lower neighboring tones. In the changing tone figure, the chord tone is followed by two dissonances a step or half-step above and below (or reversed). The chord tone is then repeated, with an optional change of harmony. In Example 13•5, changing tones are indicated by the letters *CT*.

Example 13•5   Mozart, *Sonata*, K. 284: Var. I

Anticipation

An anticipation results when a chord tone appears before the chord to which it belongs. At the moment it is introduced, the anticipation is dissonant to the surrounding pitches. Ordinarily, the anticipation is unaccented, rhythmically weak, and of shorter duration than the chord tone itself. The anticipations in Example 13•6 are indicated by the letter *A*.

Example 13•6 Bach, "Nun lob, mein Seel": mm. 7–8

Suspension

In contrast to the anticipation, the suspension results from *prolonging* a chord tone into the next chord. Traditionally, great care has been taken with the treatment of suspensions, partly to ensure against too abrupt a dissonance.

The suspension figure contains three main elements:

1. Preparation: The tone to be suspended occurs as a chord tone on a weak beat.

2. Suspension: The tone is held over and becomes dissonant to the succeeding chord.

3. Resolution: The suspended tone resolves downward one scale step to become a member of the new chord.

Although a less frequent occurrence, suspensions may resolve upward. This is referred to as a *retardation*.

In Examples 13•7 through 13•11, suspensions are labeled *S;* the numbers in the bass refer to the intervals produced between the suspension or retardation figure and the bass note (not to be confused with the root of the chord which in an inversion may appear in another voice). Suspensions occur as 9-8, 7-6, 4-3, or 2-1. The most common retardation is 7-8. While the interval 6-5 may have the appearance of a suspension, it is not dissonant and thus is not a true suspension.

Example 13·7 Bach, *Goldberg Variations:* Var. 18, mm. 1–2

P = preparation
S = suspension
R = resolution

Example 13·8 Morley, "O sleep, fond Fancy": mm. 19–20

Example 13·9 Bach, "Durch Adams fall": m. 2

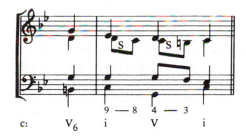

Example 13·10 Mozart, *Sonata,* K. 533: mm. 1–3

Example 13·11   Haydn, *Sonata in D major:* Finale, mm. 1–6

A common device in popular music is to suspend an entire chord. In Example 13·12, the fifth and seventh of the Gm7 chord function as 9-8 and 4-3 suspensions, resolving to the C chord. The procedure continues sequentially with the suspension of the Fm maj. 7 chord over the Bb chord.

Example 13·12

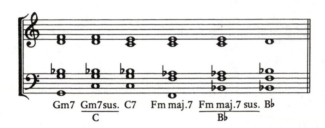

Appoggiatura

The appoggiatura is a non-harmonic tone whose definition has given theorists trouble for years. Some argue that it is an accented non-harmonic tone approached by skip and resolved stepwise up or down. Others feel that when a dissonance occurs on the strong part of the beat and resolves on the weak part it should be called an appoggiatura. This second view, however, is ambiguous, since it can refer to an accented passing tone, an accented neighboring tone, or a suspension in which the suspended tone is rearticulated rather than tied as an appoggiatura.

To clarify the issue, let us examine the linguistic derivation of *appoggiatura*. The word comes from the Italian verb *appoggiare,* meaning "to lean." Thus, an appoggiatura is a non-harmonic tone which "leans" on and toward the tone to which it resolves. Although both of the earlier definitions are valid, we prefer the first; that is, an appoggiatura is a dissonance approached by leap and left by step. Either way, it is important to remember that rhythmically strong dissonances, unlike rhythmically weak dissonances, contribute equally to melodic movement and dissonance. In Examples 13·13 and 13·14, the appoggiatura is indicated by *app.*

Example 13·13   Mozart, *Sonata in B♭*, K. 333: III, mm. 1–4

B♭:   I   vi   ii   V₇   I₆ V₆ I ii₆   I⁶₄   I

Example 13·14   Mancini, "Moon River": mm. 1–4

C major   a minor   F major   C major

Copyright ©1961 by Famous Music Corporation. Reprinted by permission.

Notice that the definition we prefer allows us to call the unaccented dissonances in Example 13·15 appoggiaturas. This infrequent unaccented form of the appoggiatura is known as a *passing appoggiatura*.

Example 13·15   Beethoven, *Piano Sonata*, Op. 26: Var. V, mm. 1–2

Escape Tones

The escape tone is a rhythmically weak dissonance approached by step and resolved by leap. In addition, the escape tone either moves opposite to the basic direction of the melodic line and must leap back, or it skips in the same direction. The resolving leap is usually the interval of a third, although larger intervals occur. In Example 13·16, escape tones (also known as the *échappée*) are marked *ET*.

Example 13·16   Mozart, *Sonata*, K. 283: I, mm. 26–28

D: V   I₆   V⁴₃   I   V₆   vi⁷   V

Pedal Point

The pedal point is a sustained tone over which the other voices move. As the harmony changes around it, the pedal point may become dissonant; it is therefore classified as non-harmonic. Although most common in the bass, the pedal point may be found in any voice. A typical use of pedal point is in dominant preparation, particularly in establishing a new key center. In Example 13•17 the pedal point is lettered *P*.

Example 13•17 Bach, "Prelude I," *WTC* I: mm. 24–32

Focus

Used well, non-harmonic tones focus the listener's attention on the interaction of melody and harmony through the subtle shift in emphasis between the consonant–dissonant qualities of the harmony and the accented–unaccented movement of the melody. This quality of subtle melodic and harmonic ambiguity is demonstrated in Examples 13•18 through 13•20.

Example 13•18 presents a chord progression void of non-harmonic pitches. Notice how attention is drawn to the harmonic movement and the vertical qualities of the chords.

Example 13·18

Chapter 13
Non-Harmonic
Tones

119

Example 13·19 is the same chord progression indiscriminately loaded with non-harmonic tones. Does this draw too much attention to the melody?

Example 13·19

Finally, Example 13·20 gives the same chord progression with carefully chosen non-harmonic tones, as it was originally written by Bach. Compare the quality and effect with the earlier versions.

Example 13·20 Bach, "Christe, du Beistand deiner Kreuzgemeine": mm. 1–4

Suggested Activities

1. Identify the circled non-harmonic tones in the following. Play the example in class, first omitting all non-harmonic tones, then including them. Discuss the differences between the two versions.

Chopin, Op. 67, No. 2: mm. 6–9

120

2. The following phrases are taken from Bach chorales. Make a Roman numeral analysis of the harmonization. Then, carefully supply non-harmonic tones, and compare your versions with the originals. (See Mainous and Ottman, *The 371 Chorales of Johann Sebastian Bach.* New York: Holt, Rinehart and Winston, 1966.)

Bach, "Nun bitten wir den heiligen Geist"

Bach, "Wenn ich in Angst und Noth"

3. Analyze the harmonic structure and non-harmonic tones in the following, accounting for every note as part of the harmony or as a type of non-harmonic tone.

4. For the following works, analyze the harmonic structure and locate and identify the non-harmonic tones

    Bach, "March" from *Notebook for Anna Magdalena Bach*, mm. 1–5
    Bach, "Two-Part Invention No. 4," mm. 1–18
    Chopin, *Etude*, Op. 10, No. 3, mm. 1–8
    Couperin, "La Bandoline" from *Pieces de Clavecin*, Book 5, mm. 1–8
    Schubert, *Valse Sentimentale*, Op. 50, No. 10
    Schumann, "Traumerei" from *Kinderscenen*, Op. 15, No. 7, mm. 1–7
    Jimmy Webb, "Up, Up and Away"

Suggested Readings

    A major controversy in the identification of non-harmonic tones centers around the question of whether accented non-harmonic tones are sufficiently different from unaccented ones to warrant a labeling system different from the one we recommend. For a good discussion of an alternate system, see chapters V and VII of Roger Sessions' *Harmonic Practice* (New York: Harcourt, Brace & World, 1951).

14

Our attention to this point has centered primarily on diatonic chords, that is, chords built within the framework of a single key or tonality. Any diatonic chord, however, can be altered by the addition of one or more accidentals. Altered chords can heighten the harmonic color and tension of a composition. This chapter discusses three types of altered chords: secondary dominant chords, secondary leading tone chords, and bimodal chords.

Secondary Dominant Chords

The strongest chordal relationship in tonal music is that of dominant to tonic. Composers have consistently carried this V-I relationship to other diatonic triads. This means that any major or minor diatonic triad in a given key may be preceded by a chord which functions as its own dominant. While this would appear to weaken a tonality, in reality it serves to strengthen it.

Perform Example 14•1 as written; then play it again, changing the penultimate chord to G minor.

Example 14·1 Chopin, *Mazurka*, Op. 68, No. 3: mm. 1–8

The G major chord, of course, resolves more strongly to the following C major chord. In the key of F major, this chord would be a major supertonic. Further observation, however, will show that the relationship of the G major chord to the C major chord is temporarily that of dominant to tonic. Since the phrase does not modulate to the key of C major, the functional analysis of the G major chord is "dominant of the dominant" or secondary dominant. A secondary dominant is indicated in Roman numeral analysis as V/V.

Much of the thrust from the secondary dominant to the following chord stems from the altered tone temporarily assuming the sound of leading tone to tonic. In Example 14·1, observe the relationship of the B natural to the C. This type of relationship is true of all secondary function chords. In Example 14·2, notice the relationship of the altered tone to the root of the following chord (m.7).

Example 14·2 Haydn, *Sonata in D major:* Finale, mm. 1–8

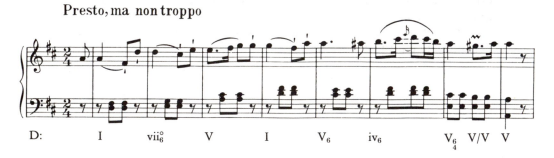

A secondary dominant relationship can be established for any diatonic chord. Just as the altered supertonic chord becomes V/V, the altered mediant chord becomes V/vi, the altered submediant becomes

V/ii, and the altered leading-tone chord becomes V/iii (Example 14•3). In a similar manner, the tonic chord can, on certain occasions, become V/IV. If the I chord is heard as a triad, it normally maintains its identity as tonic. However, if a minor seventh is added to the triad, its sonority is altered and it assumes the function of V_7/IV. Remember that all secondary dominant chords must be major in quality, and all secondary dominant seventh chords must be major–minor in quality to function as secondary dominants. Example 14•4 illustrates a popular usage of this chord.

Example 14•3   Mozart, *Piano Trio No. IV*, K. 548: I, mm. 38–45

Example 14•4   Joseph Lamb, "Reindeer": mm. 1–4

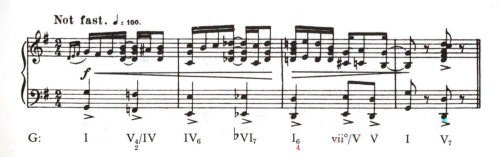

Secondary Leading
Tone Chords

Each major or minor diatonic triad can also be preceded by its own leading-tone triad. The function of a secondary leading-tone chord is similar to that of a secondary dominant.

Example 14·5

C: vii°/ii   ii   vii°/iii   iii   vii°/IV   IV   vii°/V   V   vii°/vi   vi

Notice that the altered tonic chord becomes vii°/ii, the altered supertonic becomes vii°/iii, the altered mediant becomes vii°/IV, and so forth. Because of this relationship, the secondary leading-tone triad is often used between two chords which progress up by seconds. For example, the progression V–vi often becomes V–vii$^o_7$/vi–vi (Example 14·6).

Example 14·6

G: V   vi   V   vii$^o_7$/vi   vi

Example 14·7 illustrates a sequential use of secondary dominants and secondary leading-tone triads.

Example 14·7 Schumann, *Nachtstucke*, Op. 23, No. 2: mm. 3–4

F: vii$^o_7$/V   V   vii$^o_7$/iii   iii   vii$^o_7$ I   vii$^o_7$/vi   vi   V$^4_2$/ii   ii$_6$ V$^6_4$/ii   ii   V   I

Bimodal Chords

To vary the harmonic color of a composition, composers often substitute diatonic chords from the parallel major or minor key. For example, a work in C major will normally have an F major subdominant chord. For a different sonority, however, an F minor chord can be substituted without destroying the basic key center of C major. Chords normally found in one key but used in a parallel key are classified as borrowed or **bimodal chords**.

Example 14·8 Chopin, *Nocturne*, Op. 9, No. 2: mm. 28–30

E♭ I   iv   I   iv   I

Focus

Altered chords allow a composer to introduce new elements of harmonic color and tension into a composition without shifting the tonality of the work. In fact, secondary dominant chords and secondary leading-tone chords strengthen the basic key center at the same time as they create momentary diversions to new key areas. The technique of altering diatonic chords can, however, also obscure the key center, temporarily or permanently. The process of modulating to a new key area by means of altered chords will be explored in chapter 19. A less complicated method of modulation is available diatonically, and will be discussed in the next chapter.

Suggested Activities

1. Write out and resolve the following secondary function chords:

G major:	V/V–V	V_4^3/V–V	vii°/V–V
D minor:	V/V–V	vii_7°/VI–VI	$vii_6^\circ{}_5$/iv–iv
B♭ major:	vii°/ii–ii	V_7/IV–IV	V_4^2/V–V_6
C minor:	$vii_6^\circ{}_5$/V–V	V_4^2/V–V_6	V_4^3/V–V

2. Write two examples of each of the following chord progressions, using contrasting textures and harmonic rhythms.

D major: I IV vii°/V V V_7 I
F major: I IV V/V V vii°/vi vi ii_6 I_6^4 V_7 I

G minor: i VI iv vii°/V V V_7 i
E♭ major: I V/vi vi V_4^3/IV IV V vi

3. At the keyboard, play and resolve in a variety of keys, the secondary function chords written for the first activity. Play each of the chord progressions written for the second activity, also in a variety of keys.

4. Analyze the harmonic structure of the following three works. (Be alert for secondary function chords.)

Schubert, "Daphne am Bach"

**Part B
The
Tonal
System**

Schubert, "An die Geliebte"

130

5. Select a chord progression from one of the songs analyzed in activity 4. Change the key and set the progression as a solo for piano.

6. Analyze the following works for secondary dominant and secondary leading-tone chords:

Beethoven, *Sonata,* Op. 13: II, mm. 1–8
Brahms, *Waltz,* Op. 39, No. 15: mm. 1–15
Chopin, *Mazurka,* Op. 41, No. 2: mm. 1–8
Mendelssohn, *Song Without Words,* Op. 62, No. 4: mm. 1–12
Mozart, *Fantasia in D minor,* K. 397: mm. 1–8
Schumann, *Arabesque,* Op. 18: mm. 1–12

15

Modulation is a change of key or tonality within a composition and involves either a change of key signature or, more often, the use of accidentals. Almost every long piece of music contains some change of key or shift of tonality, and in all but the shortest compositions this is necessary for tonal interest and contrast. In large compositions, the contrast of key levels helps delineate the formal sections. Modulations are classified as *diatonic, chromatic,* or *enharmonic,* depending on how the modulation is brought about. This chapter concentrates on the technique of diatonic modulation.

Diatonic modulation is a modulation to a closely related key through the use of a common or pivot chord. The transition from the old key center to the new can be smooth, and the new key can go practically unnoticed until it is already firmly established.

Closely related keys are those with the same key signature, or with one accidental more or less than the original key. To illustrate, the keys closely related to D major and E♭ major are shown in the following chart.

One sharp	G major	e minor
Two sharps	*D major*	b minor
Three sharps	A major	f♯ minor
Two flats	B♭ major	g minor
Three flats	*E♭ major*	c minor
Four flats	A♭ major	f minor

Another method of determining the keys that are closely related to a given key is to extract the diatonic triads of that key. Each triad, omitting any diminished chords, can become the tonic of a related key (see Example 15•1).

Example 15·1

For a minor key, use the triads resulting from the natural form of the minor. Remember that diminished chords are always omitted (see Example 15·2).

Example 15·2

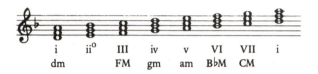

Diatonic Modulation

Diatonic modulation, also called *common chord* or *pivot chord modulation,* uses a chord common to both the new and the old key. Remember that, depending upon the key orientation, a chord can have many identities. For example, the C major triad can have the following diatonic identities:

I in C major
IV in G major
V in F major
VI in e minor
VII in d minor

This ambiguity can be used to establish the relationship between two keys. The pivot chord is the chord common to both keys. Example 15·3 illustrates the relationship between the triads in C major and A natural minor.

Example 15·3

Notice that each chord can function in both keys. Some triads, however, tend to produce a stronger feeling of progression and modulation than others. Consequently, it is preferable to avoid using the dominant of the new key as a pivot chord. The basic procedure for common-chord modulation is as follows:

1. The old key is firmly established through a dominant–tonic relationship.

2. The pivot chord, common to both keys, is introduced.

3. The new key is firmly established through a dominant–tonic relationship.

In a common-chord modulation, the ear will not detect the move to the new key until after the pivot chord has been introduced. If you perform Example 15•4, you will observe that the A minor chord still sounds as if it were in C major. In fact, the D minor iv could even sound as ii in C major. With the introduction of the G♯ in the V chord, however, the new tonality of A minor is clearly established.

Example 15•4

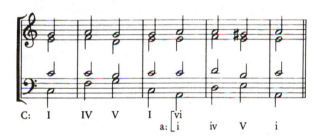

Example 15•4 shows a pivot-chord modulation in a block chord, four-voice texture. Example 15•5 shows the use of a pivot chord for modulation in an instrumental work.

Example 15•5   Haydn, *Piano Sonata in E minor:* I, mm. 9–14

Change of Mode

Another method for achieving tonal contrast is to employ a change of mode from major to parallel minor, or the reverse. This is not, however, a modulation, for the same tonic note remains as the key center. This technique, effective in many compositions, is especially common in theme and variations (see Example 10•8), as well as in sonata movements. A favorite device in developing the thematic material of sonatas written in minor mode is restating the material in the development section in the parallel major.

Example 15•6 Haydn, *Piano Sonata in E minor*: I, mm. 46–50

Transient Key Cells

Composers often move to new tonal levels for a few measures, only to move away without firmly establishing the new tonality. We prefer to call this type of tonal shift a **transient key cell**, and reserve the term *modulation* for a more stable change of key, in which the new key is firmly established and maintained for a longer time. For example, a piece in the key of E♭ major could move to the mediant for a transient key cell on G minor or G major. It could then move back to E♭ major, or to the submediant for another key cell on C major or C minor.

Example 15•7 is clearly in G minor. However, the second phrase has a strong feeling of B♭ major, even though the phrase ends in G minor. We have analyzed this as a transient key cell on III, with the harmonic progression inside the cell reflecting the key of B♭ major.

Example 15•7 Bach, "Wer weiss, wie nahe mir mein Ende": mm. 1–5

Example 15•8 gives us an ingenious use of a transient key cell combined with an unexpected cadence. The piano has a trill on the dominant for four beats. But rather than resolving to the tonic, as expected, it resolves to a bimodal submediant chord (♭VI). The expected deceptive cadence in the key of G major is, of course, D major to E minor

(V–vi). The move to an E♭ major chord adds dramatic intensity, which is maintained while the material is extended through the use of a transient key cell on the E♭. The progression then moves back to G major and comes to rest on the expected tonic six-four chord which introduces the cadenza.

Example 15·8 Mozart, *Concerto in G major*, K. 453: I, mm. 316–27

Focus

The musical importance of modulation cannot be overestimated. The mechanical process of changing keys within a composition, particularly by means of a common or pivot chord, is relatively simple, yet the structural implications of this simple technique are significant.

Contrasting key levels as a component of the parameter of form can be seen in most of the music written from 1600 to the 1900s. Our distinction between modulation (a key change from one firmly established key to another) and transient key cell (a brief excursion into an area of new tonality) is important in this context. Modulations within the harmonic framework of a large composition contribute not only to the formal structure but to the establishment of the basic tonality of the whole work. Consider sonata form and the relationship of key levels to its formal structure. In sonata form, the exposition normally moves from the area of the tonic to the area of the dominant, if in major, or to the area of the mediant if in minor. The development section becomes tonally unstable, and a variety of key levels are explored simultaneous with the transformations of the melodic material that normally occur. Finally, the recapitulation restates the original thematic material in the tonic key. Similarly, the rondo principle usually involves a change of key in the digressions from the A material, and the minuet and trio often involve a change of key in the trio.

The transient key cell, on the other hand, provides momentary new color and tension within the framework of a single key. In normal use a transient key cell seldom has significant effect on the formal structure of a work; continued use—as in repeated chains of transient key cells—can actually obliterate, momentarily or permanently, the basic key center of a work.

Suggested Activities

1. Write and play at the keyboard the following modulatory passages, in four-voice texture:

D major: I   vi   ⎡ii
              e: ⎣i   iv i_6^4 V_7 i

G major: I   vi   IV   ⎡vii_6^o
                    e: ⎣ii_6^o V   VI i_6^4 V_7 i

B♭ minor: i   iv   V   i ⎡i_6
                    A♭: ⎣ii_6 I_6^4 V_7 I

F♯ minor: i   V   i ⎡iv
                    G: ⎣iii ii_6 V_7 I

2. Identify all common chords (possible pivot chords) for the following pairs of keys.

Eb major – Ab major
F major – A minor
Bb major – F major
A major – B minor
Eb major – F minor
C minor – Ab major
Db major – Bb minor

3. Using pivot chords, write and play at the keyboard short passages that modulate between the following keys.

A minor – F major
Ab major – Db major
Bb major – G minor

4. Analyze the pivot-chord modulation in the following example.

Mozart, *Sonata in D major*, K. 284: Theme

5. The following sonatina exhibits transient key cells in the transition between the first and second thematic groups. The piece begins in G major and modulates to D major for the second thematic group at measure 43. Locate the transient key cells and analyze the work harmonically.

Fr. Kuhlau, *Sonatina*, Op. 20, No. 2

140

6. The following example utilizes sequential transient key cells as a transition to the second thematic group. Locate and analyze these key cells.

Beethoven, *Sonata,* Op. 10, No. 1: I, mm. 21–44

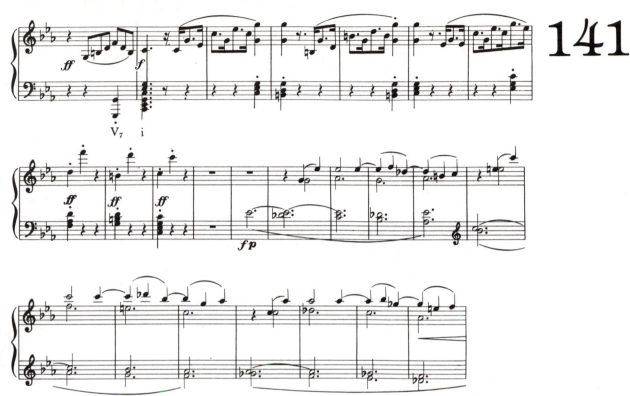

141

7. Analyze the following example for a transient key cell on B♭.

Bach, "Wachet auf, ruft uns die Stimme"

16

As in the 1600s and early 1700s, keyboard players in contemporary jazz ensembles are expected to be skilled improvisors. Within a given harmonic progression, for example, the jazz pianist is free to determine the spacing and voicing of the chords, as well as their melodic and rhythmic framework. With only the basic chord progression indicated, he is both guided and restricted by the style in which he plays. A good jazz pianist must be able to do more than change chords at the right time. He also must be able to imitate musical material in other parts, improvise melody, and provide a suitable rhythmic framework, to name only a few skills required. The competent jazz musician, therefore, not only reads chord symbols, but also generates from this harmonic scaffolding a sensitive accompaniment to the melodic material.

Like the jazz pianists of today, keyboard players of the seventeenth and eighteenth centuries were expected to have superior improvisatory skills. Ensemble music of that period used the **continuo**, which actually consisted of two instruments. One instrument, such as viola da gamba or bassoon, played the bass line, while the other, usually harpsichord or organ, played the harmonies suggested by the bass line. Keyboard players were expected not only to recognize the harmony implied by the bass line, but like the jazz pianist, to provide a suitable musical framework.

Technical Principles of Figured Bass

Figured bass, also called *basso continuo* or *thoroughbass*, assumes the triad as the norm. A bass pitch without a number or sign under it is automatically considered to be the root of a triad. The quality of that triad is determined by the function of the bass pitch in the key. (For example, an A in G major will be the supertonic and the resulting chord will be minor in quality, while the same A in D major will require a major chord because of its dominant function.) Inversions or chord alterations are indicated by one or more figures below the bass pitch. Such additional figures are used for identifying the inversion of a chord, indicating an altered chord tone, or indicating the use of non-harmonic tones (most frequently a suspension).

Inversions

In figured bass, the notation for the inversion of triads and seventh chords resembles the system used in this book for the harmonic analysis of those same chords, except that Arabic numerals appear without Roman numeral identification. The performer must, however, understand the harmonic function of each chord to correctly interpret its quality.

Two points from previous discussions should be restated. First, the figured bass numerals always refer to intervals above the bass note, *not* to intervals above the root of the chord. Second, figured bass never indicates the voicing or spacing of a chord. While we have written the chords of Examples 16•1 and 16•2 in close position, they would be equally correct in other voicings.

Example 16•1   Triads

Root position — Figures omitted unless chord otherwise unclear.

First inversion — Generally abbreviated to 6.

Second inversion — Generally written as 6̥4.

Example 16•2   Seventh Chords

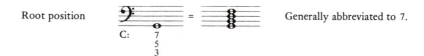

Root position — Generally abbreviated to 7.

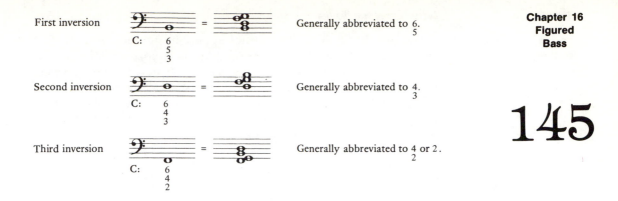

First inversion   =   Generally abbreviated to 6.
5

C: 6
5
3

Second inversion   =   Generally abbreviated to 4.
3

C: 6
4
3

Third inversion   =   Generally abbreviated to 4 or 2.
2

C: 6
4
2

Altered Chords

The quality of a chord is always determined by the relationship between the root of the chord and the key, whether or not the root is the bass note. Hence, in a major key the chord built on the supertonic is minor, the chord built on the subdominant is major, and the chord built on the leading tone is diminished. In figured bass, adjusting the quality of a chord to conform to the key is the normal practice and requires no indication of pitch alteration. An alteration *is* indicated in the figures, however, if the quality of the chord is altered from the norm. Figured bass alterations are also indicated for several chords in minor keys and for modulation.

Example 16·3

Note, as shown in Example 16·3, that a flat, sharp, or natural sign, when used alone, always refers to the third above the bass pitch.

Any pitch of a chord may be similarly altered. A raised pitch is indicated by a sharp beside the numeral, by an oblique line through the numeral, or in fewer instances, by a plus sign beside it (see Example 16·4).

Example 16·4

Non-Harmonic Tones

Some non-harmonic tones do not appear in figured bass. Passing tones and neighboring tones, for example, are almost never indicated, even when they occur in the bass voice. Other non-harmonic tones, such as suspensions and anticipations, appear as adjacent numerals. In realizing (performing) a continuo part, the keyboard player must supply all indicated non-harmonic tones, and may add others if appropriate to the style of the work.

Example 16·5

Example 16·6

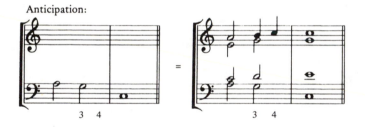

Figured Bass Realization

Constructing a musical accompaniment from a bass line and a set of figures implying the harmony has always been a subtle skill demanding both technical proficiency and stylistic understanding. Today the task of writing out such accompaniment is complicated by the knowledge that the literature on figured bass realization encompasses several diverse styles, ranging from an Italian style of the 1600s to mature French and German styles of the 1750s, and may demand anything from homophonic chords to a richness of texture satisfied only by arpeggios and ornamentation.

The degree of personal expression possible in writing out figured bass can be seen in the following examples. Example 16·7 is an excerpt from Handel's *Sonata in F major,* Op. 1, No. 11, for recorder and continuo, realized by Waldemar Woehl.

Compare Woehl's realization with a realization of the same excerpt by Joscelyn Godwin of Colgate University.

Example 16·8   Handel, *Sonata in F major:* I, mm. 1–9

Finally, notice the graceful interrelationship of lines in the realization written out by Bach for his own *B minor Flute Sonata* (BWV 1030).

Example 16·9 Bach, *Sonata in B minor* (BWV 1030)

Focus

A sufficient understanding of figured bass requires a technical knowledge of the system, as well as a broad familiarity with performance practices. In this chapter we have introduced the basic techniques of figured bass realization. Most musicians today can easily learn enough of the technical essentials to complete basic part-writing exercises or block-chord keyboard realizations. Few, however, will grasp the delicate nuances of stylistic improvisation needed to properly perform a full-fledged figured bass realization. Remember, there is a vast difference between playing block chords and realizing a figured bass. Still, abilities at figured bass realization will improve with practice and careful listening, and some degree of proficiency in this area will add to an understanding of the music written in this style.

Suggested Activities

1. Write out the chords indicated by the figured bass symbols, and identify the harmonic function of each chord.

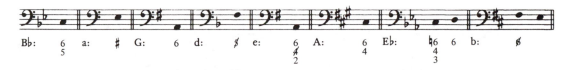

2. The following figured bass progressions are from Bach chorales. Realize each of the progressions on paper and at the keyboard. (Use

non-harmonic tones when appropriate.) Give an harmonic analysis
of each progression.

3. Realize the following melodies with figured bass on paper and at
the keyboard. (Use non-harmonic tones when appropriate.)

Bach, "Auf, auf, die rechte Zeit ist hier"

Bach, "Brunnquell aller güter"

4. For the following, prepare a realization of the continuo that complements the flute melody. Arrange for class performances of the realizations.

Handel, *Sonata for Flute and Continuo in A minor*

151

5. Ask someone to bring a typical jazz chart to class. Transcribe the chart into figured bass with a bass line and Arabic numerals. Discuss the differences between the jazz chart and the figured bass transcription. How would these differences affect a performance of the work?

6. Write a melody and figured bass for a solo instrument and keyboard. Ask several members of the class to prepare a realization. Discuss the results.

Suggested Readings

The following works will be useful in preparing the realization of the Handel Sonata, as well as for general knowledge of figured bass realization.

1. Williams, Peter. *Figured Bass Accompaniment* (Edinburgh: Edinburgh University Press, 1970) includes hints on accompanying and styles of accompaniment.

2. Keller, Herman. *Thoroughbass Method,* trans. Carl Parrish (New York: W. W. Norton & Company, 1965) includes an historical perspective on changes in stylistic practices during the seventeenth and eighteenth centuries.

3. Arnold, F. T. *The Art of Accompaniment from a Thorough-Bass,* Vols. 1, 2 (New York: Dover Publications, 1965), first published in 1931, is the most comprehensive study available on the technique of figured bass realization.

17

Part B has given us the increased understanding and additional analytical tools we need to explore in more systematic detail the parametric interaction and independence within a composition. As we did in chapter 11, we will investigate the ways particular composers have controlled and shaped their musical materials by examining simultaneously the various parameters and types of parametric control in these compositions. We again recommend that you attempt your own parametric analyses before reading ours.

Chopin, *Mazurka in F major,*
Op. 68, No. 3

Where to begin the parametric analysis of a complex musical work is always a question. Usually, one or two details stand out that suggest starting places. Here, it is quickly apparent that the piece changes key centers and has definite sections. We will therefore begin with the harmonic parameter, since this should give us the necessary clues from which to determine the formal structure.

Harmony

Our chord-by-chord analysis of the harmonic motion on the Example 17•1 score reveals that the first sixteen measures function solidly in the key of F major, with a half cadence (V/V – V) between measures 7 and 8, and a perfect authentic cadence (V – I) in measure 16. With

Example 17·1

154

155

the single exception of the major supertonic chord functioning as a secondary dominant, the chromatic pitches are not an alteration of chord structure, for they function more as non-harmonic tones that add color to the basic chord progressions.

Beginning in measure 17, there is a direct shift of key, from a center on F to a center on A. In this section—measures 17–24—the harmonic motion is less stable, the result of ambiguity about whether the section is in A major or A minor. The use of F rather than F♯ creates a minor subdominant chord and suggests the key of A minor, but the C♯ in the tonic chord strongly suggests A major. The question is further complicated because each measure can be seen as alternating between A minor and A major. That is, measures 17, 19, 21, and 23 suggest A minor while measures 18, 20, 22, and 24 suggest A major. But we believe that the section centers on A major and explain the D minor chord as a bimodal subdominant. Measures 25–32 return, again by a direct shift of key, to F major, and firmly re-establish this key in a manner identical to measures 9–16.

Measures 33–44 present another unusual problem in harmonic analysis. The key signature changes to two flats, suggesting B♭ major or G minor. The accompaniment has a B♭–F pedal figure, further suggesting the key of B♭ major. The melody, however, continually uses E natural. If the key center of these measures is B♭, then this section is in Lydian mode on B♭. However, the longer note values associated with the pitch F in the melody, and the half-step relationship created by the E natural, suggesting leading tone to tonic, make the melody center more on F than on B♭. Although it would be possible to harmonically analyze these measures in B♭ major and explain the E natural as a variety of non-harmonic tones, our analysis identifies the key center as B♭ Lydian with the accompaniment functioning as a drone. That the section stays in F major and functions harmonically at the level of the subdominant is, we think, a less plausible solution. How, for instance, can the change of key signature be explained?

Rhythm

A two-measure rhythmic motive ($\frac{3}{4}$ ♫. ♩ ♩ | ♫. ♩ |) dominates the composition. In fact, it is only in measures 33–44 that this rhythmic motive does not appear. Measures 33–44 thus function as an important rhythmic contrast to the rest of the composition.

Melody

The melodic parameter supports and extends the rhythmic parameter. The melody functions within the dominant rhythmic motive and is made up of an ascending perfect fourth on the second and third beats of the first measure, filled in by diatonic, conjunct motion in the second measure of the motive. (See Example 17•2.)

Example 17·2

Chapter 17
Parametric
Analysis 2

157

This pattern occurs twenty times within measures 1–16, 25–32, and 45–60. Within measures 1–16 and 45–60, the melody is symmetrically structured into phrases of eight measures, with the first phrase ending on a half-cadence, the second phrase ending on a perfect authentic cadence. In each case, these two phrases combine to form one period. Measures 25–32 make up only one phrase, but it has a feeling of completeness because it ends with a perfect authentic cadence.

Between measures 17 and 24, the rhythmic motive remains the same but the melodic material changes to a descending figure based on thirds. This section consists of one eight-measure period of two four-measure phrases. Measures 33–45 offer an even stronger contrast. Here, the melodic material is based on Lydian mode and the rhythmic motive is replaced by a static quarter-note drone over which the melody moves, predominately in eighth-notes. Structurally, this section consists of a four-measure introduction and two four-measure phrases.

Form

Both the harmonic and melodic parameters suggest a five-part formal structure, with the same melodic and harmonic materials in the first, third, and fifth sections. This example of rondo form may be diagrammed as follows:

measures	1–16	17–24	25–32	33–44	45–60
sections	A	B	A	C	A

Notice that the A section, which by its recurrence lends unity to the structure, is the most stable section harmonically and the most dramatic melodically. The A sections are firmly in the key of F major. The phrases cadence on either a half-cadence or a perfect authentic cadence, and chromatic alterations are explainable as non-harmonic tones.

The B section and the C section, however, are far less stable harmonically. The omission of the third of the tonic chord every other measure and the bimodal subdominant chord in the B section, plus the use of Lydian mode in the C section, contribute to a state of harmonic ambiguity. Since the B and C sections are presented at two contrasting key levels from the A sections, their harmonic instability makes each return to the home-key A sections seem even stronger and more secure. The chart of Example 17·3 makes the complex interaction of the parameters in this mazurka more apparent.

Example 17·3

Measures

	1————16	17———24	25———32	33————44	45————————60
Form	A	B	A	C	A
Keys	F major	A major	F major	B♭ Lydian	F major
Dynamics	*f* ∣ *p*	*ff* ∣ *p*	*p*	*p*	*f* ∣ *p*
Cadences	V/V-V ∣ V-I	iii-V ∣ iv₆-I	V-I		V/V-V ∣ V-I
Rhythm	¾ 𝅘𝅥𝅮♩♩∣𝅘𝅥𝅮♩♪	same	same	¾ ♩♩♩	same as A

Historical Considerations

Pieces of music are not isolated from the time in which they are written nor from the materials on which they are based. Historical information can affect both our performance of a piece and our understanding of compositional ambiguities in a score. With regard to the piece under consideration, then, two points along these lines are worth making. First, the mazurka began as a folk dance and only later became a source for art music. Knowledge about the manner in which the mazurka was danced should certainly affect performance of this piece. Second, the C section is less confusing melodically and harmonically when we learn that early mazurkas were accompanied by a bagpipe, an instrument capable of producing a tonic-dominant drone below the melody.

Telemann, Gigue from
Little Clavier Book for Wilhelm Friedemann Bach

Example 17·4

A: I   V   I   V₇   I₆   vii°₆   vi₆   V₆   IV₆   V₆   I   V₆   I

Melody

The Telemann Gigue is a monothematic work based on a two-measure melodic motive. This motive is characterized by a descending interval of a perfect fourth in measure 1, suggesting the tonic harmony, and a descending triadic outline of the dominant chord in measure 2. The motive, even when heard alone, suggests a two-voice texture moving in contrary motion. The descending character of the motive is contradicted by the ascending a' to b'.

A *gigue* was one of a number of popular dance forms Baroque composers often used in larger compositions. Telemann chose to treat this melodic motive contrapuntally even though the gigue, as a dance, was not contrapuntal. Throughout most of the composition, there is an obvious relationship between the contrapuntal treatment of the melodic motive and the motive as it is presented in the first two measures. Several instances, however, deserve particular attention.

Notice, first, the entrance of the second voice in measure 3. While this voice is repeating the motive, the first voice continues the ascending line suggested in the motive of measures 1 and 2. Contrary motion of this type appears throughout much of the composition. The material in measures 5–8 suggests an inversion of the motive. It is not, however, an exact inversion, due mainly to harmonic and voice leading considerations. Finally, notice measures 21–36. Measures 21–28 seem related to the first measure, while measures 29–36 suggest an extended inversion of measure 2. This can be observed again in measures 71–86.

Rhythm

The rhythm of this piece is characteristic of the gigue. Written in compound duple meter, the rhythmic parameter supports the work primarily as a unifying element. The work uses only two basic rhythmic patterns, $\frac{6}{8}$ ♩♪♩♪ or $\frac{6}{8}$ ♫♩♫♩ . This is quite characteristic of the gigue, and Telemann's alternation between the two patterns is never monotonous. Notice, in particular, the special rhythmic effect achieved between measures 21 and 36. Measures 21–28 extend the first pattern for eight measures while measures 29–36 extend the second pattern. This makes the measures immediately following measure 36 sound rhythmically fresh and interesting. The same rhythmic manipulation closes the work.

Harmony

Within the linear, contrapuntal character of the gigue, Telemann ignores neither the vertical relationships nor the horizontal progression of harmonies. He has, in fact, carefully constructed the chord-to-chord motion and the overall harmonic scheme around the individual lines. The gigue begins in the key of A major. With the entrance of the third voice in measure 9 it is still firmly in A major but moves quickly, through a tonally ambiguous section, to a cadence in

E major in measure 17. This change of key is accomplished through a use of secondary dominant chords in measures 12–16. We could have indicated a common-chord modulation to the dominant a few measures earlier, but the statement of the melodic motive in measure 17 draws attention to the key of E major there. The gigue remains in E major through the perfect authentic cadence in measure 36.

Two additional harmonic devices in the first thirty-six measures deserve mention. First, measures 5–7 contain a sequence of chords in first inversion. This sequence of first-inversion, parallel sixth chords, sometimes referred to as **fauxbourdon**, occurs primarily because of voice leading considerations. Second, measures 21–26 represent a key cell on B major, the dominant of E major. This key cell and a similar one on E major in measures 71–77 strengthen the harmonic tension inherent in the dominant sound.

While measure 37 begins in E major, the key of D major is quickly established. Between measures 52 and 53, a strong authentic cadence occurs in D major, although the D chord in measure 53 assumes the function of V_7/IV with the addition of the C natural in the upper voice. This chord, however, does not resolve to a subdominant chord, and the chord progression ascends chromatically from this point to an F♯ major chord in measure 57. The F♯ chord becomes the dominant for the key of B minor, the relative minor of D major. Finally, the original key of A major returns in measure 65.

Form

This gigue is in monothematic, rounded binary form. Within this structure, however, several unusual events occur. As would be expected, the A section modulates to a cadence on the dominant. The B section begins in E major, again as expected, but quickly moves to the unexpected key of D major. This section is further confused by chromatic movement to the key of B minor, and the non-symmetrical grouping of sections into measures of eight, eight, four, and ten. Measure 67 marks the return of the key of A major. Measures 67–86 are similar in content to measures 17–36 from section A. Example 17•5 diagrams the structure of this gigue.

Example 17•5

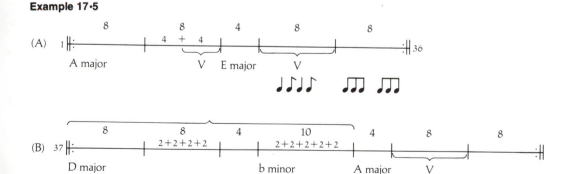

One additional point. In some ways, measures 37–66 foreshadow the classical concept of development—new keys are explored, measures are grouped irregularly, and chromaticism becomes increasingly important. All of this prepares for the return of the A material in measure 67. This is also the point at which Telemann extends the range of the voices and strongly announces the melodic motive in the bass voice.

Bach, Chorale from
Cantata No. 18

Melody

A chorale is a hymn tune of the German Protestant Church. Many chorale melodies date from the fifteenth and sixteenth centuries. German composers, particularly during the seventeenth and early eighteenth centuries, used these tunes as the basis for extended compositions such as cantatas, fugues, preludes, and fantasias. Perhaps the best-known chorales are Bach's four-part harmonizations of these hymn tunes. For the most part, they are found within his larger choral works.

Example 17·6 Bach, Chorale from *Cantata No. 18*

We recommend beginning the analysis of this chorale by singing the hymn tune (soprano line). You should immediately notice that the melody divides into eight two-measure phrases, primarily in conjunct motion. These phrases complement each other but do not form periods and double periods, as is common in instrumental dance forms. Please note that the fermata in a Bach chorale indicates phrasing and is not to be interpreted as a held note. The Reformation in Germany encouraged participation in the religious service through congregational singing. The symmetrical phrases and conjunct motion made such participation easier, as did the steady, symmetrical rhythm (predominately quarter-notes and eighth-notes).

According to one authority,* this melody existed as early as 1529, approximately 185 years before the chorale was written. Although the melodic shape was probably altered during the interim, it is still possible to detect some modal characteristics. If G is considered as the tonal center of the first four phrases (first four measures repeated), the pitch basis is natural minor or Aeolian mode because of the F natural (lowered seventh). (Play or sing the first two phrases while sustaining the pitch G.) Our harmonic analysis, however, has the first phrase beginning in the key of C minor. (Now play or sing the two phrases while sustaining the pitch C.) If we consider C as the tonal center, then the pitch basis becomes Dorian mode. This can explain why Bach begins the chorale in C minor even though the key signature has two flats (two flats is the key signature for transposed Dorian on C.) The abbreviated key signature was common in Baroque music; used in this particular work, it shows the influence of modal thinking more than 100 years after the beginning of tonal music. These modal implications are not as evident in the fifth and sixth phrases of the melody (measures 5–8) and are even less apparent in Bach's harmonization.

Harmony

As is true for most chorales, the harmonic rhythm of this chorale is both fast and even; chords change almost every beat. In the few instances where the same chord occurs on two consecutive beats, the strong beat, never the weak beat, is always first. Harmonic motion is strengthened by a change of chord on a strong beat, particularly if it is the first beat of a measure. Notice the number of times chord changes occurring across a bar line are from dominant to tonic or tonic to dominant.

In analyzing the shifting tonal centers of a chorale, let your ear be the final judge. Often, a modulatory progression that looks ambiguous will sound firmly in one key or the other. It is possible to analyze the first two phrases of this chorale in C minor, explaining the B♭ in measure 3 as a modal influence and the F♯ in measure 4 as a secondary dominant. This analysis is further supported by the final chord of the

*Charles Sanford Terry, ed. *The Four-Part Chorales of J. S. Bach* (London: Oxford University Press, 1929), p. 77.

second phrase being a G major rather than a G minor chord, functioning as a dominant to C minor when the four measures are repeated. Nevertheless, we hear the second phrase as a modulation to G minor and have analyzed it accordingly. A strong case can be made for either approach; you base your choice on what *you* hear. The fifth phrase (measures 5–6) definitely moves to the area of Eb major, only to return to C minor in the sixth phrase. The seventh phrase begins in C minor, but briefly explores the area of F major. The final phrase is firmly in G minor.

Pieces in which the harmonic rhythm moves at such a fast pace will, unless skillfully constructed, draw too much attention to the vertical aspects at the expense of the horizontal motion. Observe how successfully Bach has avoided this problem. First, his use of non-harmonic tones brings out the linear qualities of each line. Second, through skillful inversion, he has created a melodic bass line that has a linear quality second only to that of the hymn tune itself.

Rhythm

The rhythmic parameter is more subtly structured than is at first apparent. The composite rhythm created by the four voices is indicated below each line of the score. Together the voices generate an almost steady stream of eighth-notes, broken only by a few quarter-notes, usually at cadences. The individual lines show wide variety, and each moves in a rhythmically satisfying manner that belies the steady stream of eighth-notes.

Timbre

In addition to soprano, alto, tenor, and bass voices, the chorale is scored for 2 flutes, 4 violas, bassoon, and continuo, the instruments that accompany the other sections of the cantata from which this is drawn. The absence of violins is unusual. If, as mentioned earlier, the chorale melody was already familiar to the congregation for whom it was written, the instrumental accompaniment would have added support to the congregational singing.

**Part C
Extended
Tonality**

18

Composers of tonal music have shown a consistent interest in exploring new harmonic sonorities. At times this has merely added harmonic color; at other times it has significantly altered the concept of harmonic function. Few compositions exist which use only the diatonic pitches associated with the basic key center. But as long as chromaticism is limited to modulation or to secondary dominant or to secondary dominant or secondary leading-tone function, the harmonic character of a work remains diatonic and feels harmonically secure and stable. As chromaticism assumes an increasingly important role in a piece, feelings of harmonic ambiguity and uncertainty are created.

To understand how chromaticism extends the concepts of tonality, the next two chapters explore two basic components of chromatic harmony: expanding chordal possibilities and expanding tonal centers. This chapter considers the harmonic implications of diminished seventh chords, augmented sixth chords, and Neapolitan sixth chords, as well as ninth, eleventh, and thirteenth chords. Chapter 19 explores chromatic and enharmonic modulation, and re-examines transient key cells.

Diminished Seventh Chords

The diminished seventh chord is one of the most ambiguous and fascinating sonorities in the harmonic vocabulary. It consists of a diminished triad plus a diminished seventh, producing a chord built entirely on minor thirds. Various names are used to identify this chord, such as *fully diminished, diminished-diminished,* and *doubly diminished.* We prefer the term *fully diminished seventh* to identify a diminished triad with a diminished seventh, and the term *half diminished seventh* to identify a diminished triad with a minor seventh.

A diminished seventh chord can be spelled with any of its four notes as the root of the chord. This makes possible four different, non-deceptive resolutions from the same chord. Only three basic spellings of the fully diminished seventh chord are possible, however, one each on C, C♯,and D. Beyond this, enharmonic equivalents occur.

170

Example 18·1

Observe that Example 18·1d is enharmonically the same as Example 18·1a. Because of its enharmonic character, the diminished seventh chord is especially useful for modulation to remote keys. Furthermore, it can resolve to either a major or minor triad.

Example 18·2

In example 18·2, the same diminished seventh chord can resolve to C major, C minor, E♭ major, E♭ minor, F♯ major, F♯ minor, A major, or A minor. In each case, the normal resolution of the seventh of the chord is downward.

The diminished seventh chord was a favorite sonority with composers of the Romantic era. A series or sequence of diminished seventh chords can lessen the sense of tonal stability and, as a result, was often used in opera to create a mood of mystery, anticipation, or suspense. Use of the chord has not been limited, however, to any one period of music. Example 18·3 presents a striking effect in the Gigue from the *Partita in B♭* by Bach.

Example 18·3 Bach, Gigue from *Partita in B♭:* mm. 33–40

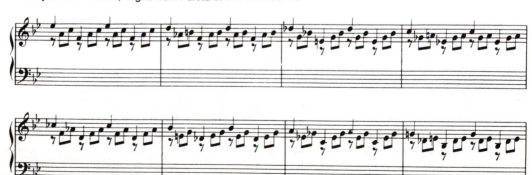

Example 18·4 shows a late nineteenth-century work that begins with a chain of diminished seventh chords. The effect is an obscured tonality and delayed resolution to the tonic.

Example 18·4   Liszt, *Mazeppa:* mm. 1–5

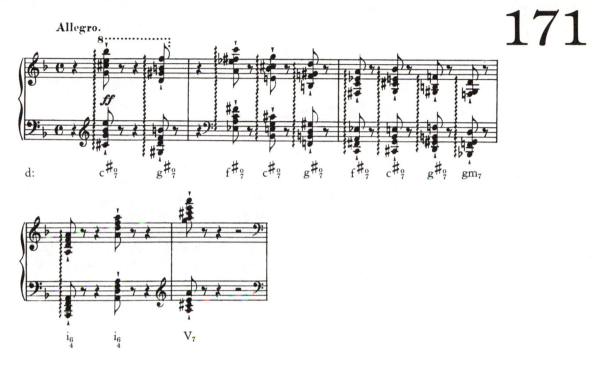

Example 18·5 shows another use of diminished seventh chords in sequence. This technique was common in music for silent movies and later for cartoons, because it can maintain tension and delay resolution almost indefinitely.

Example 18·5

Augmented Sixth Chords

All of the sonorities we have discussed thus far contain various combinations of major and minor thirds. **Augmented sixth chords** contain the interval of the diminished third, or when inverted, the interval of the augmented sixth. These chords are most often found inverted (hence, the name *augmented sixth*) and are classified as Italian, German, or French (the origin of these names is unknown).

Example 18·6

Example 18·6 illustrates the conventional spelling of augmented sixth chords. Observe that the three types have in common three pitches, in this case, Ab, C, and F♯. Here, the German augmented sixth chord has an added Eb, and the French augmented sixth adds a D.

When augmented sixth chords are reduced to root position, they can be seen to function as altered subdominant or supertonic chords (Example 18·7).

Example 18·7

Used in a linear progression, the interval of the augmented sixth resolves to the octave, most often the dominant or tonic six-four chord. The French and Italian augmented sixth chords typically resolve to the dominant, while the German augmented sixth often resolves to the tonic six-four, thus avoiding parallel fifths (Example 18·8).

Example 18·8

Augmented sixth chords may also be spelled enharmonically and used for modulation. In Example 18·9, the German sixth chord is re-spelled as a dominant seventh in the key of Db major.

Example 18·9

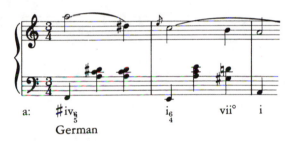

c: German = V₇ in D♭ I₆₄

Examples 18·10 through 18·13 present various uses of augmented sixth chords.

Example 18·10   Beethoven, *Sonata,* Op. 13: mm. 41–47

E♭:   I₆₄   V₇   I   V₄₂   I₆   IV₆ II₆₄   V

Fr. 3

Example 18·11   Schumann, *Waltz,* Op. 124, No. 4: mm. 1–3

a: ♯iv₆₅   i₆₄   vii°   i

German

Example 18·12   Scriabin, *Prelude No. 5,* Op. 11: mm. 10–11

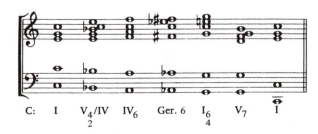

D: V₇/IV   vii°₇/vi   IV₆   Fr. 6   I₆₄

Example 18·13

C: I   V₄₂/IV   IV₆   Ger. 6   I₆₄   V₇   I

In examples 18·14 and 18·15, the augmented sixth chords are spelled enharmonically.

Example 18·14   Chopin, *Prelude No. 4:* mm. 20–25

German

Example 18·15   Donizetti, "Ciascun Lo Dice" from *La Figlia Del Reggimento:* mm. 9–11

From *The Prima Donna's Album,* copyright 1956 by G. Schirmer, Inc. Reprinted by permission.

Neapolitan Sixth Chords

The **Neapolitan sixth chord** is a major triad built on the lowered second degree of the scale (see Example 18·16). It too is typically found in first inversion, although it may appear in root position as well. In the Baroque and Classical periods, it appeared most often in minor keys.

Example 18·16

Example 18•17 shows how the Neapolitan sixth chord normally resolves to the dominant or tonic six-four.

Example 18•17 Schumann, *Waltz,* Op. 124, No. 4: mm. 11–13

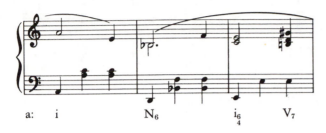

a: i   N₆   i⁶₄   V₇

Examples 18•18 through 18•21 show other uses of the chord. Notice in Example 18•18 that the Neapolitan chord is in root position.

Example 18•18 Chopin, *Prelude No. 20:* mm. 12–13

c: i VI N V₇   i   i

Example 18•19 Mozart, *Fantasia in C minor:* mm. 169–72

c: V   ii°₇ III   ii°₄ III₆   N₆
                         ³

vii°₇/V   i⁶₄   VI   ii°₆   V   i
                            ⁴   ⁵

Example 18·20 Beethoven, *Piano Sonata*, Op. 53: mm. 235–39

C: I V₇/iv iv V₇/iv iv N₆ i⁶₄ V₇ I

Example 18·21 Beethoven, *Sonata in C♯ minor*, Op. 27, No. 2: mm. 1–4

Adagio sostenuto.

c♯: i i⁴₂ VI N₆ V₇
            (V of N)

Ninth, Eleventh, and Thirteenth Chords

Layers of thirds added to a triad or seventh chord produce ninth, eleventh, and thirteenth chords. Notice in Example 18·22 that adding a diatonic fifteenth produces a repetition of the root.

Example 18·22

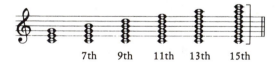

7th 9th 11th 13th 15th

Spacing or voicing is an important consideration in the use of these chords. For instance, in the thirteenth chord, where all the diatonic triads are present, the effect of the sonority can be dissonant or consonant, depending on the spacing of the chord members.

The dominant ninth is the most frequently used of these sonorities. It is built with a major triad, minor seventh, and major or minor ninth. The seventh and ninth (both are usually present in a dominant ninth) resolve down by step. Since a complete dominant ninth chord would contain five notes, the fifth is often omitted.

Example 18·23

Chapter 18
Expanded
Chordal
Vocabulary

177

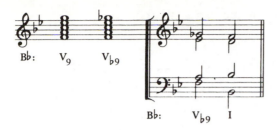

The opening measures of Ravel's *Jeux d'Eau* (Example 18·24) are constructed around a tonic ninth chord. Observe that the triad, the seventh, and the ninth are all major in quality. Example 18·25 uses the ninth chord as a secondary dominant ninth. Notice that the triad is major but both the seventh and ninth above the tonic are minor. This dominant function of the ninth chord is typical of late Classical and early Romantic music.

Example 18·24   Ravel, *Jeux d'Eau:* m. 1

Copyright 1907 by G. Schirmer, Inc. Renewed 1935 by Marie Joseffy. Renewal assigned 1939 to G. Schirmer, Inc. Reprinted by permission.

Example 18·25   Beethoven, *Piano Sonata*, Op. 53: mm. 112–16

Suggested Activities

1. Complete the following augmented sixth chords:

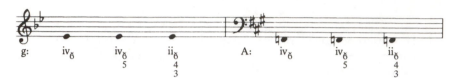

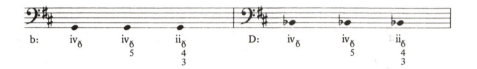

2. Spell the Neapolitan chord in each of the following keys:

C minor	F♯ minor
E major	A major
B minor	F♯ major
F major	D major

3. From each given bass note, write a fully diminished seventh chord and resolve it. Use appropriate accidentals.

4. Analyze the following examples for Neapolitan and augmented sixth chords.

Schubert, "Die Krähe" from *Die Winterreise,* Op. 89, No. 15: mm 1–4

179

Beethoven, *Sonata,* Op. 2, No. 1: mm. 139–52

180

geht, da wel - ken die Li - lien auf je – dem Beet; da muss in die

Wol - ken der Voll – mond gehn, da - mit sei - ne Trä - nen die Men - schen nicht

sehn; _____ da hal - ten die Eng - lein die Au – gen sich zu

Chopin, *Mazurka*, Op. 7, No. 2

181

19

The techniques of diatonic modulation discussed in chapter 15 make available to composers a number of key centers to explore in a composition. However, direct diatonic modulation between certain keys is not possible with this technique. If you wish to modulate, for instance, from the key of C major to the key of G major, you have at your disposal the four chords common to both keys (I-IV, ii-vi, V-I, vi-ii). If you wish to modulate from C major to D major, two common chords are available (iii-ii, V-IV). But direct diatonic modulation from C major to E♭ major is impossible, because no chord is common to both keys.

Composers of tonal music have long been interested in exploring distantly related key centers to which diatonic modulation is not possible. For this purpose, there are two other types of modulation: *chromatic modulation,* involving the use of altered chord tones, and *enharmonic modulation,* requiring the actual or theoretical enharmonic transformation, or re-spelling of a chord to suggest a relationship to another key.

Chromatic Modulation

Chromatic modulation generally involves altering a chord in the old key to make it diatonic in the new key, although the opposite may occur. In some ways this is merely an extension of the concept of secondary dominant function. In the key of C major, for instance, a D major chord (V/V) followed by a G major chord (V) momentarily suggests a change of key, even while it is strengthening the dominant function of the G chord. Ordinarily the use of secondary dominants produces only an indefinite allusion to a new key, since the old key is quickly reestablished. It is possible, however, to turn this suggested change of key into a permanent modulation by simply remaining in the new key and establishing it. The effective strength of a V–I or V$_7$–I progression in a new key can momentarily dislocate the old tonal center, and if reiterated, can erase it completely. A similar effect may also be achieved by using a secondary leading-tone triad (vii°– I or vii$_7^{\circ}$–I).

Chromatic modulation makes it possible to modulate from any key to almost any other key. Through appropriate alterations, a dominant to tonic or leading tone to tonic relationship can be established for any diatonic chord in the old key. If, however, both chords have chromatic alterations, the relationship may be extended to any tonal center the composer chooses. Example 19•1 demonstrates this principle by illustrating a few of the chromatic modulations possible from the key of C major. Remember that the effectiveness of each modulation depends on the type of harmonic progression and cadential resolution that follows it. Examples 19•2 and 19•3 show the use of this technique by Beethoven and Schumann.

Example 19•1

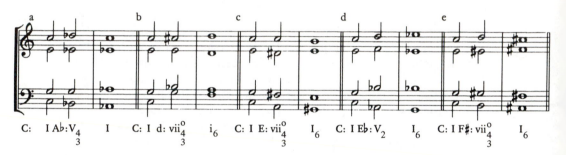

Example 19•2 Beethoven, *Sonata*, Op. 13: mm. 16–25

Example 19·3 Schumann, "Die Lotosblume" from *Myrthen*, Op. 25, No. 7: mm. 10–15

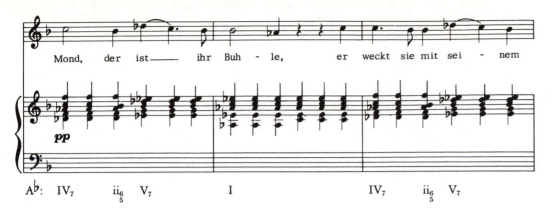

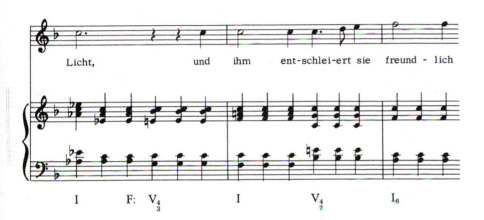

Enharmonic Modulation

In equal temperament, any pitch may be notated enharmonically. For instance, C♯ on the staff will sound the same as D♭, E♭♭♭, or B♯♯. Applied in a tonal sense to a chord, an enharmonic spelling can change the function of the chord. Notice in Example 19·4a that the I₇ chord can be altered and still retain a function in the key of C major. In Example 19·4b, this same chord may be spelled enharmonically and function as the dominant of A♭ major.

Example 19·4

In Example 19•5, the altered mediant chord can be spelled enharmonically as a D♭ major seventh chord. This D♭ chord then becomes a subdominant chord in A♭ major.

Example 19•5 Hugo Wolf, "Das Verlassene Mägdlein" from *Gedichte von Möricke:* mm. 15–21

Certain types of chords lend themselves more easily than others to enharmonic transformation. These include diminished seventh chords and augmented sixth chords. The ambiguity of diminished seventh chords allows any of the four tones to sound and function as the root of the chord. This, plus the potential for enharmonic spellings, makes it possible for a diminished seventh chord to function in many different keys. Example 19•6 gives sixteen resolutions from the same diminished seventh chord. Listen to each and decide if all sixteen are equally appropriate.

Example 19·6

Chapter 19
Expanded
Tonal
Centers

187

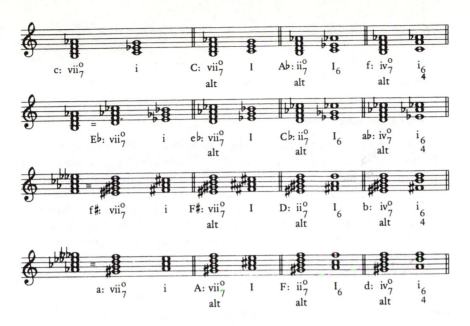

Augmented triads may also be re-spelled and used in enharmonic modulations. The augmented triad occurs naturally as the mediant triad in harmonic minor. Through enharmonic transformation, an augmented triad can be spelled three ways. For example, the mediant triad in D harmonic minor (F-A-C♯), may be re-spelled as A-C♯-E♯ or D♭-F-A. By considering these enharmonic spellings as mediant chords in different minor keys, a modulation to these keys can be effected.

Example 19·7

Finally, the German augmented sixth chord can be transformed enharmonically into a major-minor seventh chord and used as the dominant or secondary dominant of a new key. Similarly, a dominant seventh chord can be converted into a German augmented sixth chord for the purposes of enharmonic modulation.

Example 19•8

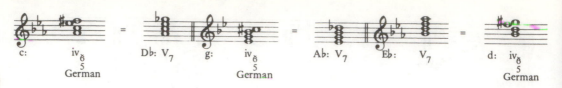

Transient Key Cells

We believe a true modulation occurs only when a composer establishes and remains in a new tonality. Consequently, we suggested in chapter 15 the term *transient key cell* as more appropriate to identify brief explorations of new tonal levels. At times composers have used sequences of these transient key cells. Used in this way, these sequences produce a feeling of continual change of key, which in turn temporarily blurs or completely obliterates any central tonic. Examples 19•9 and 19•10 give two such uses of this technique by Mozart and Schumann.

Example 19•9 Mozart, *Fantasia in C minor*, K. 475: mm. 78–88

Example 19·10 Schumann, *Symphonic Etudes* (XII), Op. 13: mm 41–50

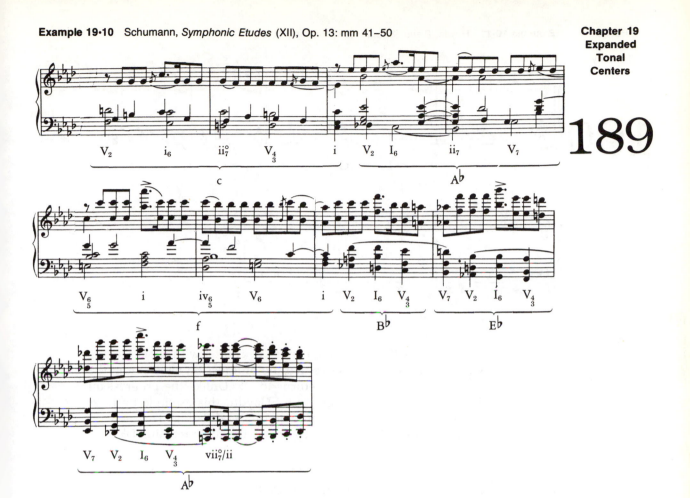

Another way to expand tonal centers is to use chord progressions with root movement in thirds. Chord progressions with root movement by fourths and fifths (I–IV–I–V–I) strongly reinforce the feeling of tonic. Chord progressions with root movement by thirds (I–vi–IV–ii–V–I) can also strongly reinforce the tonic. However, when the third relationship moves through a series of altered chords, the tonality can become more obscured. The technique can be used for modulation as well as for extending the harmonic framework within a tonality.

In Example 19·11, Haydn uses a series of chords with root movement by thirds to move from the development section to the recapitulation (b–G–e⁷–C–a–f♯°–B). The sequence is broken with the use of the final B major chord, which functions as dominant to the tonic key of E minor. Both the harmonic rhythm of one chord per measure and the repetition of the arpeggiated chord in the right hand give a stability to the eight-measure passage.

Example 19·11 Haydn, *Piano Sonata in E minor:* mm. 71–80

In Example 19·12, Liszt uses a series of chords with roots moving down by minor thirds. Observe that the progression moves from the tonic in D♭, to B♭, G, E, and returns to D♭. Unlike the progression in thirds in the previous example by Haydn, this example by Liszt expands the harmonic framework without modulating. The increase in chromaticism adds harmonic color, yet the tonic remains D♭.

Example 19·12 Liszt, *Concert Etude in D♭,* No. 3: mm. 65–72

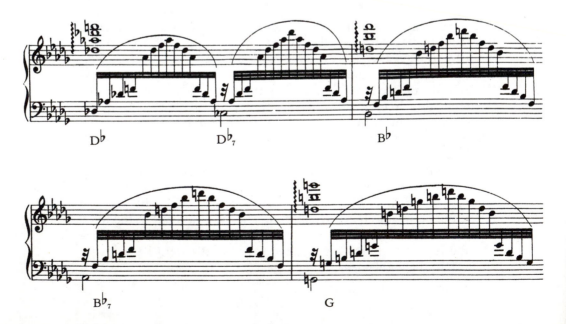

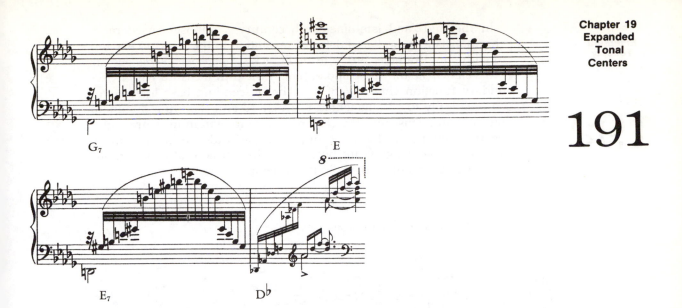

G₇   E

E₇   D♭

Example 19·13 shows the relationship of root movement by thirds and added seventh (from the Liszt *Concert Etude* in D♭). Compare Example 19·13 with Example 19·12.

Example 19·13

Third relationship

Added seventh

In Example 19·14, by Debussy, the chromaticism and progression by thirds totally obscures the feeling of B♭ as the tonal center.

Example 19·14   Debussy, "Danseuses de Delphes" from *Preludes*, Book I: mm. 23–24

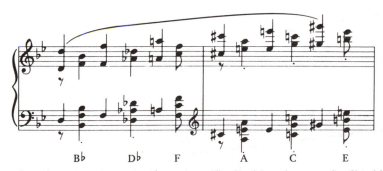

B♭   D♭   F   A   C   E

Copyright 1910 Durand et Cie. Used by permission. Elkan-Vogel, Inc. sole representative, United States.

In the mid- and late-nineteenth century, composers used more chromaticism, as well as a delay of resolution to the tonic, to expand tonality. In Example 19•15, from Franck's *Symphonic Variations for Piano and Orchestra*, the piano enters in the fifth measure with a secondary function chord (V of V). The descending bass line moves chromatically to an augmented sixth chord and then to a dominant ninth chord. This, plus the chromatic progression in measure eight, delays reference to the tonic until the V_7–I cadence in measure 9. This example is significant because of the harmonically ambiguous opening statement by the solo instrument.

Example 19•15 Franck, *Symphonic Variations:* mm. 5–9

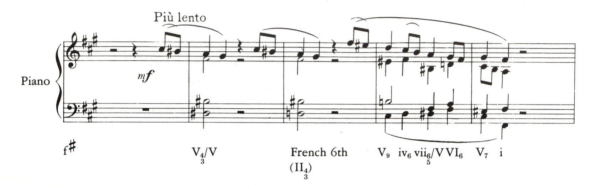

It was noted for Example 18•4 (Liszt, *Mazeppa*) that a series of diminished seventh chords obscured the feeling of tonic. Compare that example with Example 19•16. Notice that Liszt establishes a fourth relationship between these opening diminished seventh chords. This fourth relationship has an ambiguous duality about it. On the one hand it creates a feeling of intervallic stability; on the other hand, it obscures tonal stability and motion toward the tonic.

Example 19•16 Liszt, *Mazeppa:* mm. 1–4

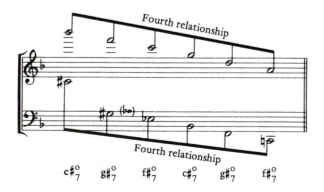

In Example 19•17 by Brahms, the G minor tonic is not heard until the final measure. The opening chord of D is probably a dominant **anacrusis**, or pickup, resolving to a G minor tonic. However, it moves to an E♭ major. The four-measure phrase cadences on a G major chord. The next phrase is a sequence of the first phrase, stated a third higher, and cadencing on a B major chord. A strong D major chord is heard in measure 9, but is followed by a G major chord rather than G minor. Finally, in measure 11, the C minor, D major, G minor progression gives the feeling of G minor (iv–V–i).

Example 19•17   Brahms, *Rhapsody*, Op. 79, No. 2: mm. 1–11

Example 19•18 Brahms, *Rhapsody*, Op. 79, No. 2

iv   V   i

194

Suggested Activities

1. Beginning on a F♯ minor triad, write and play at the keyboard a chromatic modulation to each of the following keys:

V_7 (or inversion) to I in E major, A major, and B major
V_7 (or inversion) to i in C♯ minor, B♭ minor, and A minor
vii_7^{o} (or inversion) to I in D major, A♭ major, and E major
vii_7^{o} (or inversion) to i in B♭ minor, D minor, and C♯ minor

2. Example 19•1 gives sixteen resolutions of a diminished seventh chord. Write a smooth and convincing progression around each of these resolutions.

3. Beginning in C major each time, write and play at the keyboard the following sequences of transient key cells. Discuss how each might be used by a composer of tonal music.

C major: $V_{4/3}$–I   D: $V_{4/3}$–I   E: $V_{4/3}$–I   F: $V_{4/3}$–I

C major: vii_7^{o}–I   e♭: vii_7^{o}–i   b♭: vii_7^{o}–i

C major: V_7 F: V_4 B♭: V_7 E♭: V_4 A♭: V_7

4. Analyze the following examples for chromatic and enharmonic modulations.

Haydn, *Piano Sonata in E♭:* mm. 42–46

Chopin, *Mazurka,* Op. 56, No. 1: mm. 16–27

Poco più mosso.

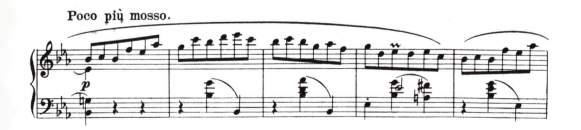

Schumann, "Helft mir, ihr Schwestern" from *Frauenliebe und Leben*, Op. 42: mm. 37–46

Beethoven: *Sonata,* Op. 2, No. 1: mm. 49–59

Schumann, "Reconnaissance" from *Carnaval*, Op. 9: mm. 13–22

Schumann, "Ich kann's nicht fassen" from *Frauenliebe und Leben,* Op. 42

Mit Leidenschaft

Ich kann's nicht fas_sen, nicht glau_ben, es hat ein Traum mich be_ rückt;

_ wie hätt' er doch un _ ter al_len mich Ar_me er_höht und be_glückt?

Mir war's, er ha_be ge_spro_chen: „ich bin auf e _wig dein;" ___ mir

war's_ich träume noch im_mer, es kann ja nimmer so sein,_ es kann ja

nimmer so sein. O laß im Traume mich ster _ ben, ge_wie_get an sei_ner

20

The chord-by-chord analysis emphasized in Part B provides valuable information about the basic harmonic motion of a composition, as well as insight into the relationship of harmonic movement to tonal center. When viewed in a different way, this same analytical information also can provide insight into the more subtle principles controlling the pacing and direction of a particular work.

Harmonic Rhythm and Pacing

The importance of harmonic rhythm and pacing to the structure of a composition can be seen in Example 20•1, the "March" from the *Notebook for Anna Magdalena Bach*. First, notice that the anacrusis, or upbeat of the first two measures, quite apparent melodically, is strengthened by a chord change on the fourth beat of each measure. Then, observe how the harmonic rhythm doubles in measure 7 to establish the modulation to the dominant. This increase in harmonic rhythm, plus the cadential formula I_6–IV_6–ii_6–V–I provides strong harmonic support for the new key level. There is similar doubling of the harmonic rhythm in the B section of the march, both at the point of return to the tonic level (measure 12), and in the final cadential sequence (measure 20).

This piece is essentially contrapuntal and moves in an even rhythm. Analyzing the changes in harmonic rhythm adds insight into the harmonic pacing and into the basic direction and arrival points, thus supporting the view that the fundamental harmonic motion of the composition is I-V: ‖ :V-I: ‖ .

Example 20·1 Bach, "March in D major" from *Notebook for Anna Magdalena Bach*

A different structural use of harmonic rhythm and pacing is apparent in Example 20·2, the Bach chorale *Mach's mit mir, Gott, nach deiner Güt*.

Example 20·2 Bach, "Mach's mit mir, Gott, nach deiner Güt": mm. 1–4

D: I   IV₆ V₆ I vii°₆ I₆ V ⌈vi
                               A:⌊ii I V₆₅ I ii₆₅ V I

Here, a progression, including a modulation to the dominant, that covered nine measures of Example 20·1, takes only four measures (in two phrases). The totally different color and tension are due, in large part, to the faster harmonic rhythm and the even pacing of events. Example 20·3 compares the harmonic rhythms of the two compositions.

Example 20·3

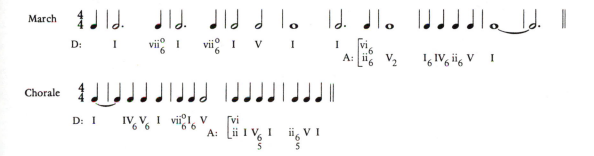

March

D: I   vii°₆ I   vii°₆ I V   I   I ⌈vi₆
                                              A:⌊ii₆ V₂   I₆ IV₆ ii₆ V I

Chorale

D: I   IV₆ V₆ I vii°₆ I₆ V ⌈vi
                          A:⌊ii I V₆ I ii₆ V I
                                  5   5

Similar harmonic rhythm and pacing can, however, produce stylistically different results. Consider Examples 20·4 and 20·5.

Example 20·4 Bach, "Prelude II," *WTC* I: mm. 1–5

Example 20·5 Chopin, *Etude,* Op. 25, No. 12: mm. 1–5

Molto allegro, con fuoco

Both have a similar harmonic rhythm and chord progressions with basically the same harmonic function, including an implied pedal point. Their strikingly different sound can be explained, in large part, by the contrasting keyboard figurations. An important point related to these examples is that pianos of Chopin's time had a damper pedal, thus allowing Chopin to explore a wider pitch range than was possible with the undamped keyboard instruments of the time of Bach.

Structural Harmonic Principles

Harmonic principles influence musical structure, particularly structural development, on more than one level. This was recognized in the early twentieth century by the German theorist Heinrich Schenker (1868–1935).* Schenker believed that certain fundamental principles, understood consciously or unconsciously by great composers, governed all music. These governing principles have as their basis the "sound, or chord, of nature," that is, the overtone series through the fifth partial. Schenker saw this as the tonal center of a work, controlling vertical relationships (chord structure) as well as horizontal movement (melodic and harmonic pitch succession). This natural triad, or **Klang** as Schenker refers to it, appears both vertically and horizontally in a composition, and defines the manner in which a tonality governs an entire work. His analytical system reduces the harmonic and melodic pitches of a composition (the foreground) to a background, or **Ursatz**, identifying the elemental structure of the composition based on the *Klang*. For Schenker, only those pitches and chords which support the *Klang*, or extend it in time, are harmonically important. This is known as *prolongation*. Harmonies appearing around these structural chords act as embellishment, in much the same way that a melody has passing tones or neighboring tones. Thus, a distinction may be drawn between chord-by-chord analysis, or *chord grammar*, and Schenker's system of *chord significance*.† Among other uses, this interpretation can be valuable in identifying harmonic pacing operating on an architectonic level; that is, chords of structural importance that occur within the chord-by-chord progressions.

Important to Schenker's theory is the notion of structural levels, that is, levels of musical understanding. He attempts to show that the foreground of a piece of music—the surface events that the listener hears—has a deeper level of organization. The analysis is one of reduction, of eliminating non-essential, secondary characteristics until a middleground level of understanding is achieved. This middleground brings out important structural events that may be obscured when observing only the foreground. Eliminating more details yields an understanding of the background level, the basic structure controlling the entire composition. Schenker believes that understanding the principle of structural levels and the fundamental organization of a work will lead to a deeper, more broadly based understanding of the music itself. This, in turn, will lead to a more accurate under-

*We do not present a detailed description of Schenker's analytical system. For this we refer you to the books at the end of the chapter. Schenker's system is limited primarily to tonal music, but within these boundaries it is useful for understanding the structural function of harmony, and all musicians should become familiar with it.

†The distinction between chord grammar and chord significance was made in Felix Salzer's *Structural Hearing* (New York: Charles Boni, 1952), Vol. 1.

standing of a composer's intentions and, ultimately, to a more musically correct performance of the work.

Example 20•6, the first eight measures of the Sonata, Op. 2, No. 1 for piano by Beethoven, illustrates the basic concepts and relationships of the foreground, middleground, and background levels of musical understanding.

Example 20•6 Beethoven, *Sonata in F minor*, Op. 2, No. 1: mm. 1–8

Notice that the three levels are arranged on separate systems aligned one above the other, with the foreground at the bottom (Example 20•6c), and the background at the top (Example 20•6a). Let us first examine the middleground (Example 20•6b). The dominant harmony arrived at in measure 8 sounds more important structurally than the dominant harmony of measures 3 and 4. This is because the melodic bb'' of measure 4 acts merely as a neighboring pitch to the ab'' of measures 2 and 5, rather than as a structurally important arrival point. Similarly, the dominant harmony of measures 3 and 4 can be considered a neighboring harmony of the tonic chord which is reiterated in measure 5, and measure 6 can be assigned a passing-tone function. The first seven and a half measures, then, prolong the tonic chord; structurally significant harmonic motion occurs only in measures 7 and 8 with the movement to the dominant half-cadence.

Moving from the middleground to the background (Example 20•6a), we see the controlling structural movement of this short example emerge. No longer is each chord or each measure of equal structural importance. Rather, the underlying structural movement is from the tonic, prolonged for seven measures, to the dominant. This prolongation of the *Klang* in time is important. Notice in Example 20•6 how the content of each level is prolonged at the next deeper level. In large works, Schenker identifies non-harmonic chords, dissonant events, and embellishing events that contribute to this prolongation.

Example 20•7 Bach, "Prelude I," *WTC* I: mm. 1–19

Applied to a larger section of a composition, this kind of background analysis can indicate structural harmonies even more obscure. Example 20•7, the first nineteen measures of the Bach "Prelude No. 1 in C major" from Book 1 of *The Well-Tempered Clavier*, appears, on first impression, to consist entirely of a one-measure, arpeggiated motive, moving harmonically in the key of C major.

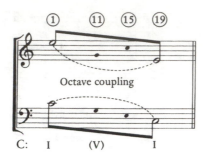

A closer examination reveals that the top voice descends from e'' to e' during these measures while the bass voice descends from c' to c. Although it is possible to see in measure 11 a lesser arrival point on the dominant harmony, these nineteen measures exhibit octave coupling for prolonging the tonic triad and should be considered a structural unit rather than eighteen repetitions of a one-measure motive at a variety of pitch levels. The implications for performance should be obvious.

Examples 20•8 and 20•9 present the Bach chorale "Ich bin's, ich sollte büssen" from the *St. Matthew Passion,* and Schenker's analytical graphs of this chorale.

Example 20•8   Bach, "Ich bin's, ich sollte büssen"

Example 20·9 Bach, "Ich bin's, ich sollte büssen"

From *Five Graphic Music Analyses* by Heinrich Schenker. Edited by Felix Salzer. Dover Publications, Inc., New York. Copyright 1969. Reprinted through the permission of the publisher.

Example 20•9 consists of a foreground, three levels of middleground, and a background. Notice how the middleground graphs reduce, in succeeding steps, the secondary characteristics. Observe also that the more significant structural material that emerges is always found in the preceding graph. Through this process of reduction, Schenker is able to make clear the deeper, controlling level of organization.

Focus

To be able to comprehend, both theoretically and aurally, the harmonic rhythm and the important structural arrival points of a composition, and to be able to apply this information to the formal parameter are essential for an adequate understanding of parametric interrelationship. They are equally important for performers. It should be increasingly obvious that the parameters of music do not function in isolation from one another; rather, they support and define a complex set of relationships, the effects and significance of which all musicians should be able to identify and determine. Schenker's analytical system is important—particularly to performers—because it enables one to begin hearing, even if at first unconsciously, large-scale connections. This will certainly affect how one hears or performs any piece of music.

Suggested Activities

1. Outline the harmonic rhythm of each of the following works:

Mozart, *Piano Sonata in C major*, K. 545 (exposition only)
Bach, Gavotte from *French Suite No. 3*
Schubert, *An die Musik*, Op. 88, No. 4

2. Identify the chord progression and harmonic rhythm of a currently popular song. Using the same chord progression, write two examples in contrasting style by altering the harmonic rhythm.

3. As a class, prepare one or more middleground graphs for Example 20•7, using Example 20•9 as a model. Compare your ideas with Schenker's graphs of the piece in Suggested Reading 3.

Suggested Readings

We urge you to become familiar with Schenker's analytical system. The following works will be helpful:

1. Katz, Adele T. "Heinrich Schenker's Method of Analysis," *The Musical Quarterly* vol. 21 (1935), pp. 311–329.

2. Forte, Allen. "Schenker's Conception of Musical Structure," *Journal of Music Theory* Vol. 3, No. 1. This is probably the best introductory article. Part of this article is reprinted in the Norton Critical Scores edition of the Schumann *Dichterliebe*, along with graphs and other analytical essays by Schenker, Komar, and Salzer.

3. Schenker, Heinrich. *Five Graphic Music Analyses*. New York: Dover Publications, 1969. These analyses include two works by Bach, one by Haydn, and two by Chopin.

4. Salzer, Felix. *Structural Hearing*. New York: Charles Boni, 1952. Volume 2 contains the musical examples for Volume 1.

5. Beach, David. ''A Schenker Bibliography,'' *Journal of Music Theory* Vol. 13, No. 1.

6. Kessler, Hubert. ''On the Value of Schenker's Ideas for Analysis of Contemporary Music,'' *Periodical of Theory–Composition* (Illinois State Teacher's Association) Vol. 1 (1958).

7. Mitchell, William J., and Salzer, Felix, eds. *The Music Forum*. New York: Columbia University Press. This series covers a number of years. They are all useful.

21

We said in chapter 10 that every musical composition has a discernible organizing principle, or structure, resulting from the relationships of its parts. In this chapter we will explore this premise in greater depth, with the help of the vocabulary and information presented in Part B and Part C.

Vocal Idioms

Composers use repetition and contrast to formally organize a piece. The principle of contrast is found in binary form, and contrast and repetition are found in ternary and rondo forms. Vocal music uses many of the same forms associated with instrumental music, such as rondo and fugue. There are, however, two forms that are almost entirely vocal in nature: *strophic* and *through-composed.*

Strophic form, based on the principle of repetition, describes a vocal composition in which the same music is repeated for every stanza of the text. If the repetition is exact, repeat signs are used; if slight melodic variations occur, each stanza is written out. When significant musical changes occur in successive stanzas, the form is known as *modified strophic.*

Through-composed songs are based on the principle of contrast; different music is written for each stanza of the poem. This allows the melodic line to follow more closely the phrasing and dramatic intensity of the text.

Example 21•1, ''Seit ich ihn gesehen,'' from a cycle of eight songs by Robert Schumann, is a strophic setting of a poem.

The two strophes are written out, without repeat signs, and separated by a short piano interlude. The piano accompaniment is an important structural factor in this work. It states the first measure of the vocal melody as an introduction, repeats the last fragment of the first strophe as an interlude, and repeats the opening fragment as a postlude. At the end of each strophe is a *deceptive cadence,* an important device for creating harmonic tension and momentum. This needs the piano to round off the phrase.

Example 21•2, ''Nun hast du mir den ersten Schmerz getan'' by Schumann, is in binary form. The song itself is through-composed;

however, the addition of the postlude, quoting the first song of the cycle, gives it binary form.

Example 21·2 Schumann, "Nun hast du mir den ersten Schmerz getan" from *Frauenliebe und Leben*

214

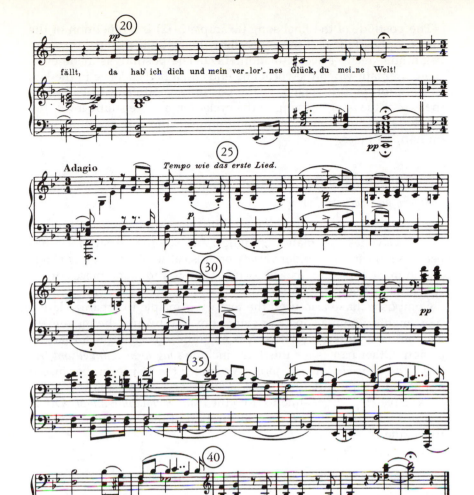

The dramatic, recitative-like intensity of the melody, the key of D minor, and the constantly changing harmonic background all help to project the mood of the song.

In order to understand the relationship between Example 21·1 and Example 21·2, as well as the importance of the piano postlude, we shall discuss the song cycle from which they are taken, *Frauenliebe und Leben.*

The cycle contains eight songs centered around the love and life of a woman. "Seit ich ihn gesehen" (Since I Have Seen Him), the first song in the cycle, describes the woman's feelings as she becomes aware of the person she is to marry. "Nun hast du mir den ersten Schmerz getan" (Now You Have Caused Me the First Pain), the last song in the cycle, describes her feelings at her husband's death. The songs in between describe moods such as her happiness with the approaching marriage, the wedding, the birth of the first child.

The postlude of the final song (Example 21•2) is a repetition of the first strophe of the first song. Recalling the melodic material from the beginning creates a recapitulation effect. The postlude is made even more dramatic when the vocal line ends on a half cadence in the key of D minor, and the piano, in the postlude, modulates to B♭ major, the key of the opening song in the cycle. On a more subtle level, the postlude's echo of the opening song suggests the wife's reminiscence on happier times.

Instrumental Idioms

Binary and Ternary Forms

Binary form is frequently found in the dance movements of Baroque suites (Gavottes, Allemandes, Gigues, and so on). Ternary form has been used in an even wider variety of musical settings—in folk songs and in musical theater, as well as in art songs and piano pieces of the Romantic period.

Composers have also used the ternary principle to organize larger movements within a sonata or symphony. In this use the movement as a whole is in ternary form, A B A, and each section is ternary in design. Other names for this form include *song form, minuet and trio form,* and *compound ternary form.* We prefer the last term, because it applies to a wide variety of musical styles and compositions.

Example 21•3, the Menuetto from the *Piano Sonata in F minor,* Op. 2, No. 1, by Beethoven, is a good illustration of the compound ternary technique.

Example 21•3 Beethoven, Menuetto from *Piano Sonata in F minor,* Op. 2, No. 1

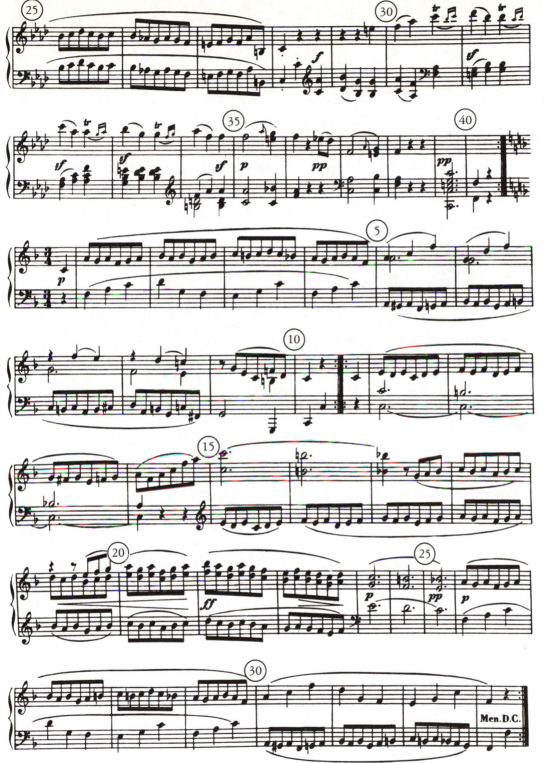

The form of the piece can be diagrammed as follows:

	Minuet			Trio			Minuet	
	A			B			A	
	1–40			1–33			1–40	
a	b	a	c	d	c	a	b	a
1–14	15–28	29–40	1–10	11–25	26–33	1–14	15–28	29–40

In the A sections, the key level is F minor. Tonal contrast is achieved by modulating to A♭ major, B♭ minor, and back to F minor. Having the *a* section return in measure 29 in the left hand rather than the right adds further contrast. The B section (Trio) moves to the parallel key of F major.

Rondo

The rondo principle is based on contrast—for variety—and repetition—for unity. The procedure of statement, departure, and return, gives a strong feeling of stability. In order to distinguish rondo from ternary form, remember that the principal theme in rondo appears at least three times. Contrast is achieved in a variety of ways, the most common being variation in tonal level, with the A section always returning to the tonic key. (See Example 10•9 for a rondo that remains in the tonic key throughout. Contrast there is achieved through other techniques.)

Example 21•4 is a rondo by Beethoven. Notice that it contains three statements of the principal theme, with two contrasting sections. The form can be diagrammed as follows:

A	B	A	C	A
1–16	17–28	29–36	37–74	75–94
F major	C major	F major	D minor	F major

Example 21·4 Beethoven, Rondo from *Sonatina in F major*

220

Sonata Form

Sonata form was illustrated earlier with a Sonatina by Clementi (Example 10•10). In Example 21•5, by Beethoven, the same basic manipulation of parameters is evident, but with an increased harmonic vocabulary, longer transitional passages, and a more sophisticated development section.

222

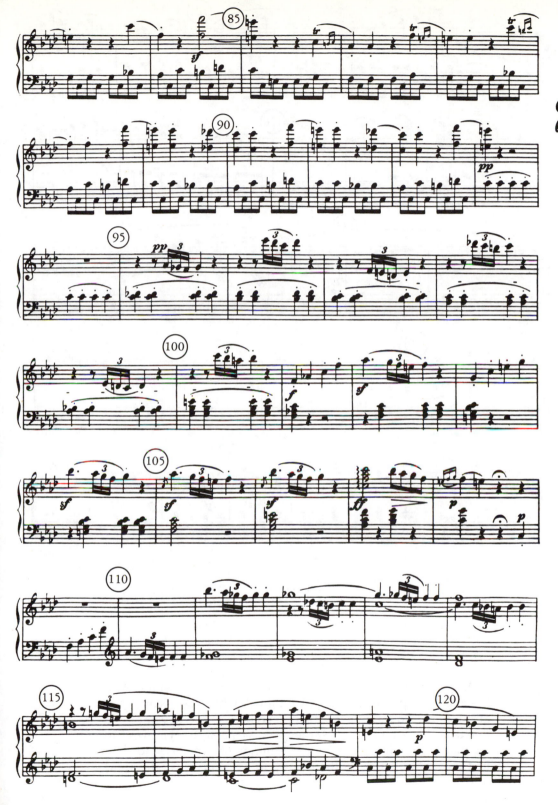

224

Exposition	Development	Recapitulation
1–48	*49–101*	*101–152*
Group I (F minor) 1–20		*Group I (F minor) 101–119*
Group II (A♭) 20–41		*Group II (F minor) 119–140*
Closing Group (A♭) 41–48		*Closing Group (F minor) 140–152*

Observe the contrast in tonal levels. In the exposition, the first thematic group is in the key of F minor, while the second thematic group moves to the relative major (A♭ major). The development section begins by stating the first theme in A♭ major, then moves through A♭ major, B♭ minor, C minor, B♭ minor, A♭ major, and F minor. In the recapitulation, both theme groups remain in the tonic key of F minor.

There are several sections of special interest harmonically. In measure 20, the harmonic shift is clearly to A♭ major, but Beethoven delays the feeling of a strong tonic. Instead, a long dominant pedal is used. Another interesting harmonic usage is the modulation to B♭ minor in measure 55 from the preceding key level of A♭ major. In measures 51 and 52, the chord is a dominant seventh in first inversion. In measure 53, the top note of the chord is altered, and in measure 54, the lower note of the chord is altered, with the resulting sonority an augmented sixth chord (German) in the new key of B♭ minor.

The use of a dominant preparation for the return to an important key level is typical of classical sonata form. We see it in this example in measures 81–100. The harmonic background functions basically as a dominant for approximately twenty measures, setting up a strong expectation for the recapitulation in F minor in measure 101.

Variation Technique

In theme and variation form, the theme is usually a short, separate piece, often in binary or ternary form, followed by a series of variations. This kind of procedure, which dates from the earliest stages of instrumental music, has been used by composers of every period in music history. Of course, the stylistic treatment varies considerably from period to period. Some composers borrow a familiar tune; others compose an original melody. Representative works in theme and variation form include the *Goldberg Variations* by Bach, the first movement of the *Piano Sonata,* Op. 26, by Beethoven, the *Symphonic Etudes* by Schumann, and the second movement of the *Piano Concerto No. 3,* Op. 26, by Prokofiev.

Another variation technique has continuous variations surrounding a repeated melodic figure, or a repeated harmonic pattern. The terms *ground bass, chaconne,* or *passacaglia* are used for this procedure. In the Baroque period, compositions built on a recurring harmonic pattern would probably have been called a *chaconne,* while works built on a repeated melodic figure would have been called a *passacaglia.* However, composers were not consistent in making this distinction. Therefore, to avoid confusion we suggest that both be considered a variation form with either melodic material or harmonic progression constant. Surrounding the constant element are elements of contrast, such as changing rhythmic activity, change of mode, or change in texture. Representative works include *Ciacona* (Chaconne) by Buxtehude, *Passacaglia in C minor* by Bach, "Passacaille ou Chaconne" from *Suite No. 1 for Viols* by Couperin, *Passacaglia* by Walter Piston, and *Passacaglia* by Aaron Copland.

We have chosen the *Passacaglia* by Copland to illustrate this variation technique. The melodic and harmonic materials represent the twentieth century, yet the techniques used in developing elements of contrast are classic.

Example 21·6 Copland, *Passacaglia* Theme

The theme (Example 21·6) consists of an eight-measure melody in 4/4 meter. The earliest passacaglias grew out of improvisatory dance pieces and were most often in a triple meter. Copland has altered this practice. The key signature indicates G♯ minor; chromaticism lessens the distinction of mode.

Following the statement of the theme, there are eight variations and a coda. In the first variation, the theme is clearly stated in the bass, accompanied by an ascending chromatic line in half-notes. In variation two (Example 21·7), the theme is stated again in the bass, while rhythmic activity increases in a countermelody in triplets.

Example 21·7 Copland, *Passacaglia:* Var. 2, mm. 25–26

In variation three (Example 21·8), attention is drawn to the sustained top notes. The theme, though less apparent, is present—observe the final triplet note of the second and fourth beats of each measure.

Example 21·8   Copland, *Passacaglia:* Var. 3, mm. 33–34

Variation four presents the theme in imitation in fugal style. It is
stated first in the bass, then two measures later in the upper voice.

Example 21·9   Copland, *Passacaglia:* Var. 4, mm. 41–45

Variation five is a contrast in tempo (*Doppio movimento*), and in its retrograde-stated theme. Variation six changes the mood with a dotted, dance-like rhythm in the upper part. In this variation the theme appears as the lowest note of an arpeggiated left-hand chord series. Variation seven uses the technique of augmentation (Example 21•10). Sustained whole-notes present the theme, with sixteenth-notes providing an accompaniment above.

Example 21•10 Copland, *Passacaglia:* Var. 7, mm. 88–91

The final variation presents the theme in diminution, and there is a gradual buildup in intensity from this point to the end. At the coda, sixteen measures from the end (Example 21•11), a line of music is added, stating the theme in its middle voice. The added texture, color, and momentum heighten the dramatic ending.

Example 21•11 Copland, *Passacaglia:* Coda, mm. 123–26

Fugue

Melodic imitation has been an important compositional device in the vocal and instrumental music of all periods. It can be found in strict settings (such as canon) and free settings as early as the fifteenth century.

Imitation is an important element of the polyphonic procedure known as *fugue*. Bach developed the fugue to a point considered the standard today. If we tried to define this standard, however, we would have a textbook model that does not exist in music. Although it is impossible to find two Bach fugues exactly alike, it is possible to establish analytical terminology based on common usage with which to understand the structural organization of any fugue.

The *subject* is the melodic or thematic basis of a fugue. The *answer* is the subject transposed, usually to the level of the dominant. A **real answer** is an exact intervallic transposition. A **tonal answer** is an answer with certain intervals adjusted to accommodate the tonality. **Countersubject** refers to the musical ideas that accompany the subject. *Voice* is the term for an individual contrapuntal line—soprano, alto, tenor, or bass—in both instrumental and vocal works. The majority of fugues consist of three, four, or five voices. **Episode** means any section in which the statement of the subject is incomplete or does not appear. Episodes are often developmental. The *exposition* is the opening section, in which all voices state the subject. A later complete statement of the subject is sometimes also called an exposition. However, we use the term *entry group,* numbered to identify each one. A typical fugue pattern is: exposition, episode I, entry group I, episode II, entry group II, etc.

Example 21•12, the three-voice "Fugue No. 2 in C minor" from the *Well-Tempered Clavier,* Book I, by Bach, offers a good introduction to the fugue design.

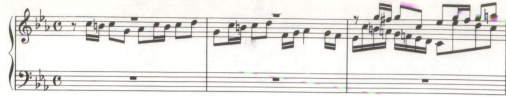

Example 21·12 Bach, "Fugue No. 2 in C minor" from *WTC,* Book I

The subject, stated in the alto, ends with the first note of measure 3. The second voice enters in the soprano, with a tonal answer in G minor. The exposition is completed with the statement in the bass voice in measures 7 and 8. An episode follows in measures 9 and 10.

The next entry of the subject (measure 11) is in the key of E♭ major. Contrasting key levels is important in the organization of a fugue. Observe the key of each entry group after the exposition: E♭ major in measure 11, G minor in measure 15, and C minor in measures 20 and 26.

Focus

The forms discussed in this chapter are applicable to a wide variety of musical styles and situations. We emphasize again, however, that form is only one parameter of musical composition; it can be manipulated, alone and in interaction with other musical parameters, in a variety of ways. Analysis will be more meaningful and less frustrating when each composition is analyzed and evaluated as a total entity, and not solely in terms of textbook-given forms.

Suggested Activities

1. The following works are grouped by type of formal organization. Identify the formal sections; where appropriate, analyze the works harmonically. Discuss elements of unity and contrast for each example. Begin by following a recording of each work with a score.

Strophic
   Schubert, *An die Musik,* Op. 88, No. 4
   Britten, "Lord Jesus, Think on Me" from *Noye's Fludde*
   Schmidt, "Try to Remember" from *The Fantasticks*

Through-composed
   Schubert, "Erlkönig"
   Schumann, "Die Lotosblume" from *Myrthen*
   Riley, *In C*

Compound ternary
   Bach, Menuet and Trio from *French Suite No. 3*
   Schubert, *Impromptu in A♭ major*
   Ravel, Menuet from *Le Tombeau de Couperin*

Rondo
   Schubert, *Ellen's Gesang,* Op. 52, No. 1
   Haydn, Finale from *Sonata No. 12 in D major*
   Bartok, "Evening in the Country" from *10 Easy Pieces*

Sonata form
   Mozart, *Sonata No. 13 in B♭: II*
   Beethoven, *Sonata in E,* Op. 14, No. 1: I
   Kabalevsky, *Sonatina,* Op. 13, No. 1 in C major

Theme and variations
    Beethoven, *Piano Sonata,* Op. 26: I
    Handel, Sarabande from *Suite No. 4*
    Haydn, *Symphony No. 94:* II

Passacaglia-ground bass
    Purcell, "Dido's Lament" from *Dido and Aeneas*
    Bach, *Passacaglia in C minor*

Fugue
    Bach, Fugue No. 21 in B♭, *WTC* vol. 1
    Bach, Fugue No. 16 in G minor, *WTC* vol. 1
    Bach, Fugue No. 17 in A♭, *WTC* vol. 1

2. Analyze harmonically the examples given in this chapter. In cases of frequent chromaticism or modulation, follow the indications of key level in the text.

Part C has provided the additional information and analytical skills needed to explore in depth the parametric interaction in almost any work of tonal music. For this chapter we have selected three works that represent quite diverse compositional control and musical subtlety. As in chapters 11 and 17, we recommend that you attempt your own parametric analyses before reading ours.

Haydn, *String Quartet in F major,*
Op. 3, No. 5: I

Example 22·1

236

238

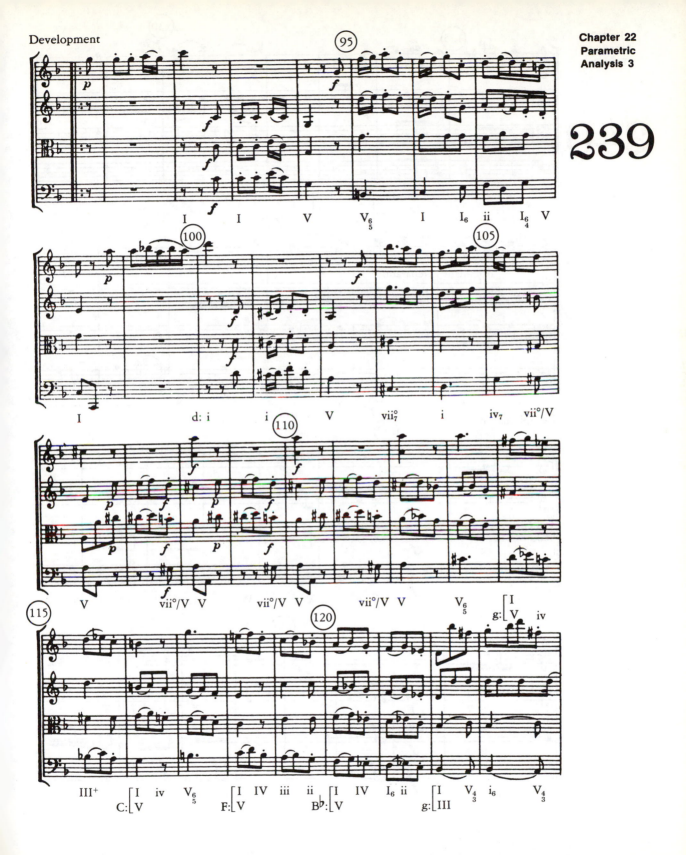

Development

242

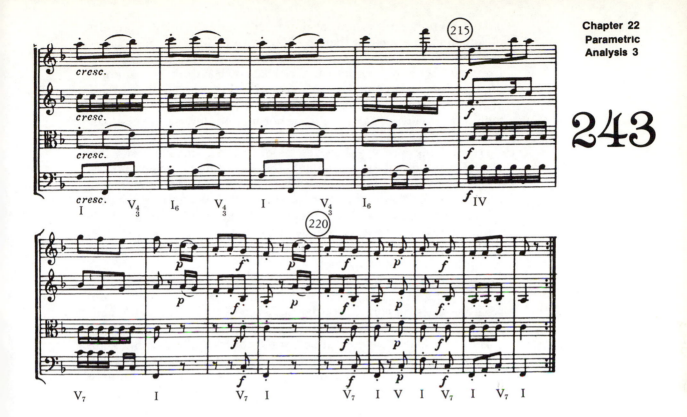

Form

It is typical for the first movement of a classical string quartet to be in sonata form. This early Haydn quartet is no exception. Beginning in F major, it modulates to C major for the B thematic group of the exposition. The development section, measures 91–137, begins in the key of the dominant, C major, but moves through a variety of keys before returning to F major for the recapitulation.

For the most part, the formal structure of the movement is clear and easy to follow, with almost nothing unexpected occurring. We can see the classical principle of symmetry and balance in the lengths of the movement's sections. The overall length of 224 measures divides into an exposition section of 90 measures, a development section of 47 measures, and a recapitulation section of 87 measures.

Symmetry is less evident within the exposition section itself. The A theme, or group of themes, lasts 27 measures, including the four measures of transition. The B thematic group, on the other hand, extends for 63 measures. The following discussion of melody gives one reason for this imbalance.

Melody

Most textbook examples of sonata form give the impression that the juxtaposition and conflict of opposing themes is the major component of sonata form. In many works, however, the harmonic component is equally important. There also are early monothematic examples of sonata form—some of them by Haydn—in which the interplay of key levels is obviously the major component of the formal structure. Example 22•1 is not monothematic. Instead, Haydn uses a number of short themes and motives in free succession. The absence of any systematic development of this thematic material supports our contention that Haydn was equally, if not more, interested in the harmonic potential of sonata form.

The opening A theme shows a melodic balance and symmetry that extends throughout the movement. The ascending motive of the first violin (measures 1–2) is answered by a similar descending motive in the other three instruments (measures 3–4). When the second half of the A theme (measures 5–8) is repeated (measures 13–16), both the dynamics and the range of the melody are altered. Notice, also, that the closing motive of the A section (measures 17–20) is a rhythmic retrograde of the opening motive.

A four-measure transitional section (measures 24–27) leads to the B thematic group. Observe that the transitional section consists of scale passages, in contrast to the melodies of the A and B thematic groups.

The B section of the exposition consists of three themes: B_1 beginning at measure 28, B_2 at measure 42, and B_3 beginning at measure 73. Although the three melodies of the B group contrast with each other as well as with A, they have in common the interval of a rising fourth. Also, the closing motive of the A section is repeated as the closing motive of the exposition.

The development section begins with a statement of the A theme, but fragments of B_1 can be found starting at measure 123, and fragments of B_3 beginning at measure 127. Nevertheless, the major interest of the development section seems to be harmonic rather than melodic.

Harmony

The most significant aspect of the harmonic parameter is the contrast between the stability of the exposition and recapitulation, and the ambiguity of the development section. The exposition moves from the key of F major to the key of C major by common chord modulation in measure 24. C major is firmly established in four measures by an authentic cadence. Aside from the two secondary dominant chords in measures 36 and 37, the harmony of the exposition is diatonic, with a majority of the chords being the primary triads (I, IV, V).

In contrast to the exposition, the development section exhibits a surprising degree of harmonic experimentation. It begins in C major and moves by a direct shift of key to D minor in measure 99. This is followed by a series of secondary leading-tone chords between measures

105 and 112. Measure 114 begins a sequence of two-measure transitory key cells, going through G minor, C major, F major, and B♭ major, and ending in G minor at measure 122. The harmony appears to move to the key of C major in measure 126, but in fact, only passes through C major to reach F minor in the next measure. At this point (measure 127) a dominant pedal prepares for the return of the A theme in the recapitulation and the key of F major.

It is significant that the only augmented sixth chord in the entire movement appears in measure 135. Augmented sixth chords are frequently used to establish the dominant harmony, usually in places where it would otherwise be unclear; this is its function here. The interval of the augmented sixth expands to the octave in measure 136, establishing the dominant harmony in F major for two measures and preparing harmonically for the recapitulation in measure 138.

Donizetti, "Ciascun Lo Dice"
from *La Figlia Del Reggimento*

Example 22·2

246

ha;___ il sol cui cre-di-to con a-mi-stà fac-cian le

pare!___ land-lords our cred-it-ors glad-ly be-come, kind-ly they

I   V₇   I   IV   I   V₇

bet-to-le del-la cit-tà; il reg-gi-men-to che o-vun-que an-

wel-come us in___ ev-'ry home; we who are read-y ev-'ry where to

I   I₆₄ V   I   iv₆₅   i₆₄   V₇

German

iii

dò, ma-ri-ti e a-man-ti___ di-sa-ni-mò, del-la bel-

fight, hus-bands and lov-ers___ wish out of sight, in___ us they

i   iv₆₄   I₆₄   V₇   I   iv₆₄

German

V

Vivace.

tà, oh!___ ben su-pre-mo. E-gli è là, e-gli è là, e-gli è là, dav-

know their dames de-light, yes. From a-far, from a-far, from a-far, yes,

I   iv₆₄   I   V₇   I

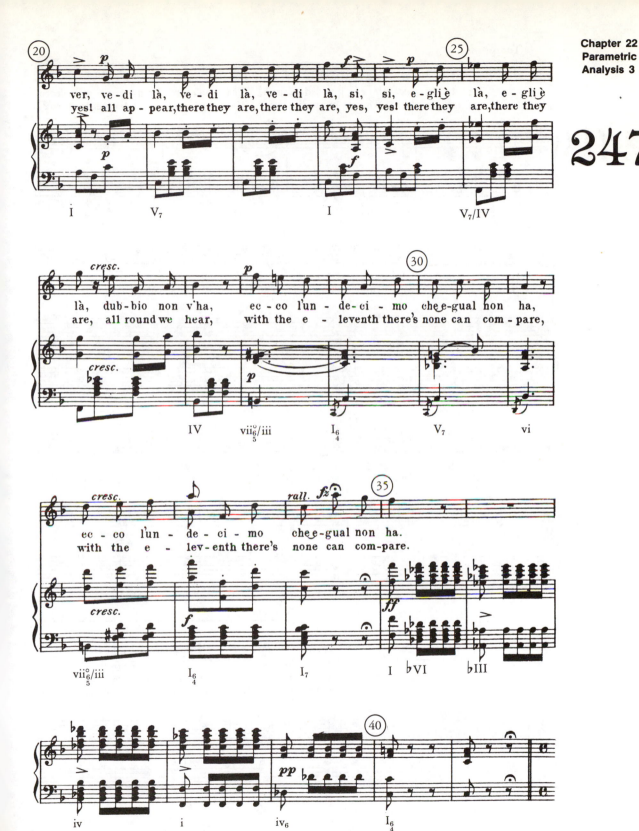

247

248

250

From *The Prima Donna's Album*, copyright 1956 by G. Schirmer, Inc. Reprinted by permission.

Form

The aria of Example 22•2 is in modified strophic form, with a short vocal cadenza as introduction. The first strophe (measures 2–35) is divided into two parts of contrasting character. The second strophe—separated from the first by a short interlude that introduces a new harmonic color—contains slight modifications in melody in order to fit the words, as well as slight changes in orchestration. The second strophe is followed by a short instrumental postlude that concludes the aria.

Melody

The melody is obviously meant to be dramatic in nature. As a result it lies in a range—c' to a''—that best supports the soprano's upper register. Anyone familiar with performances or recordings of this work will realize, however, that performers take liberties with the melody, sometimes improvising a cadenza, other times changing the shape of the melodic line to suit their vocal abilities. Such improvisation is stylistically correct for works from this period.

The melody has a balance of conjunct and disjunct motion, with ascending octave leaps followed by descending scale passages. Important to the work is the repetition of an idea with a change of direction. Measure '28 begins a four-measure phrase with descending motion to a deceptive cadence. The same words are repeated in the following four measures, but the melodic thrust is upward, characteristically a sixth. A fermata emphasizes this leap up to the a'' in measure 34, thus creating a dramatic as well as harmonic cadence. The melody is unified by two underlying rhythmic motives.

Rhythm

Rhythmic contrast in the aria is achieved through a change of meter and tempo. The A section of each strophe is in 4/4 meter and marked *Marziale*. The B sections are written in 3/8 meter and marked *Vivace*.

Each section has its own underlying rhythmic motive. In the opening section the figure ♩ ♪. ♪| ♩ , stated eight times, gives a rather martial effect. In the B section, the figure ♪ ♪| ♩ becomes important in giving momentum and thrust to the line. In the A section, the eighth-note articulation in the accompaniment heightens the dramatic and lyrical quality of the soprano line.

Harmony

The harmonic background includes secondary dominants, augmented sixth chords, and bimodality. These chords, however, are used only at important structural points for color and intensity. Most of the harmony is built around the primary triads. For example, the first eight measures contain only tonic, subdominant, and dominant chords, with each downbeat a tonic chord. The tonal stability created by this progression prepares for the striking contrast of the German sixth chord in measure 10. The augmented sixth chord, spelled in the key of A minor, moves the harmonic level to a transient key cell on iii (A minor). After a cadence in this key in measure 12, another German augmented sixth appears, moving the tonal level by sequence to a cell on V (C major). Following a cadence in this key, there are three measures of dominant preparation for the B section, and the return of F major in measure 17.

A deceptive cadence is often used as a means of extending musical material. This is true of the chord in measure 31. If you perform measures 28–31, changing the D minor chord to F major, you should notice a feeling of finality. If you then perform it again, as written, you should feel the momentum increase in preparation for the progression that follows—vii°/V–I_6^4–V_7–I.

The interlude in measure 35 provides an important touch of harmonic color. The passage may be analyzed as a shift to the parallel minor, or as remaining in F major and using bimodal chords, but either way, what is significant is that it provides the color and feeling of transition needed to conclude the first half of the aria and set the mood for the second half.

The instrumental postlude (measures 75–81)—built entirely on the tonic chord—is necessary to increase the dramatic intensity of the soprano's final cadence, as well as to bring the motion to a conclusion. The effect of the postlude is more important rhythmically than harmonically.

Example 22·3

252

Rhythm

The rhythmic parameter functions as a stabilizing force in the prelude in Example 22·3. Every measure but the final one consists of the rhythmic motive 𝄴 ♩ ♩ ♩. ♪ ♩ . The bass line provides even more stability by moving continually in quarter-notes. Obviously, variety is not Chopin's intent in this parameter.

Melody

The melodic parameter does not add much more variety to the composition. The first four measures consist of a one-measure melodic motive, repeated three times. Even though there are variations with each repetition, it is clear that every measure is melodically related to the first. This relationship continues in measures 5–8. Although the dominant rhythmic motive shifts to an inner voice in measure 5, it returns to the top voice for the remaining three measures. Again, each of these measures relates melodically to the first measure, even though the interval structure of the motive continues to change. Measures 9 through 12 are an exact repetition of measures 5 through 8.

Form

The structure of this prelude is straightforward; its one-part form consists of three four-measure phrases plus a one-measure cadence on the tonic chord. This may be diagrammed as A B B. The dynamic markings in measures 1, 5, and 9 help delineate the formal structure.

Texture

An unchanging homophonic texture is maintained throughout the thirteen measures of the prelude. All vertical sonorities are either triads or seventh chords, but doublings produce five-note, six-note and seven-note chord structures—a rich, thick texture.

Harmony

The parameters discussed so far serve to unify the prelude. So little variety could create a predictable and dull piece of music. In this particular work, however, the elements of unity seem necessary to balance the enormous variety and complexity of the harmonic parameter.

In the A section of the prelude, Chopin has a rather peculiar way of establishing the key center. Measure 1 contains a strong cadence in the key of C minor (i–iv₇–V₇–i). This is followed by similar cadential figures in key cells on A♭, F and G (measures 2–4). Within each key cell the chords are diatonic. These strong cadential figures in different keys work collectively to establish the key of C minor. Notice that the key cells are explored in an order suggesting the classical progression i–VI–iv–V–i (C, A♭, F, G, C)..

Having established the key of C minor in the A section, Chopin remains there for the B section. In one sense, the B section is harmonically more stable than the A, since it remains in one key. At the same time, however, the B section is more chromatic, for the A section functions diatonically within each key cell.

There are several events of harmonic significance in this prelude. First, the second beat of measure 6 is a French augmented sixth chord. This is important because measure 6 is the first measure that remains in the key of the previous measure and does not explore a new key cell. The augmented sixth at this point clearly defines the dominant (G major chord on beats 3 and 4), in a chromatic progression that could otherwise be harmonically unclear. Second, measure 5 contains a diminished triad on the leading tone in root position (beat 3), followed by a dominant triad (beat 4). This is unusual but can be explained, in part, by the chromatic voice-leading in the bass line. Third, measures 2, 8, and 12 contain identical D♭ major chords on the second beat. The function of this chord is different in measures 8 and 12 from its function in measure 2. In measure 2 it is a diatonic, subdominant chord within the transient key cell of A♭. In measures 8 and 12 it is the Neapolitan chord, related to the key of C minor. In both cases the chord is exactly the same. The function of the chord is defined, not by the chord itself, but by the chords that surround it.

**Part D
Alternatives
to
Tonality**

23

The music of the twentieth century can be characterized as unsettling, provocative, and diverse. Many of the stylistic changes of modern music stem from the ultra-chromaticism of the late nineteenth-century romantics, who stretched tonality to its limits. To understand these changes more fully, we will briefly review the tonal system.

Tonality is based on the concept of one central tone: the tonic. The tonic and the triad built upon it function as goals, in a melodic and a harmonic sense. Many of the major forms of eighteenth-century music had the following basic pattern: establish the tonic key, digress to closely related keys, and return and re-establish the tonic key. Tonality, however, can vary in stability. As long as the melody and harmony are diatonic, and as long as they emphasize primary scale degrees and triads, the tonality will be firm and stable. To the extent that melodic and harmonic chromaticism is employed, the tonal center will be less firm.

By the late 1800s, the sense of stable tonality had been seriously weakened by such devices as continuous chains of transient key cells, modulation to increasingly foreign keys, increasingly chromatic melodies, and chordal structures that denied the harmonic relationships fundamental to tonality. In much of this music, identifiable tonal centers no longer existed. A primary difference had arisen between highly chromatic music with definable tonal centers, and atonal music that consciously avoided tonality and tonally related mechanisms.

While the acceptance by composers of atonality signaled their rejection of tonal organization, it did not automatically produce alternative methods of organization. The generally accepted melodic, harmonic, rhythmic, textural and formal practices of the past became questionable when the principle of tonality around which they were organized was removed. The early 1900s saw many composers actively searching for artistically acceptable substitutes for the organizing influences of tonality. Even the music of composers who continued to work within the highly chromatic tonal system was influenced. In this chapter we will explore some of the major parametric changes accepted by composers as a result of this search.

Rhythm

Until the twentieth century, pitch manipulation was primary. The horizontal and vertical aspects of pitch—melody and harmony—strongly influenced how composers manipulated the other parameters. The parameters of rhythm, timbre, texture, and form were subservient to pitch. As tonality and its organizing principles came into question, these other parameters moved up in the parametric hierarchy.

By the early twentieth century, composers were exploring new ways to use the organizational and structural potentials of rhythm. For the most part, composers of the eighteenth and early nineteenth centuries had accepted the regularly recurring accent patterns of symmetrical rhythm. Twentieth century composers, on the other hand, were unhappy with the predictability of this approach. They explored new possibilities for syncopation within symmetrical rhythm. They also turned increasingly to non-symmetrical rhythmic organization. Behind most of this exploration was the growing belief that rhythm no longer needed to depend on melody and harmony, but could in fact influence them. Example 23•1 is important, not only because it

Example 23•1 Stravinsky, *Le sacre du printemps:* mm. 114–125

illustrates Stravinsky's use of syncopation, but also because it represents his use of rhythm independent of melody.

Non-symmetrical rhythms and their metrical ambiguities also helped to establish rhythm as an independent parameter. Examples 23•2 and 23•3 show two well-known applications of non-symmetrical rhythm by Stravinsky.

Example 23•2 Stravinsky, *Le sacre du printemps:* rehearsal No. 142

Example 23·3 Stravinsky, *L'histoire du soldat:* mm. 64–69

Even greater rhythmic complexity is available through the techniques of polyrhythm and polymeter. Example 23·4 gives us Hindemith's use of polymeter in *Kammermusik, No. 2* for piano and twelve solo instruments, written in 1924.

Example 23·4 Hindemith, *Kammermusik, No. 2,* Op. 36, No. 1: mm. 8–10

By the middle of the twentieth century, composers were exploring the rhythmic parameter from opposite directions: increased rhythmic organization and free rhythm. The first approach involves greater compositional control, the other offers performers new freedoms and responsibilities. The advantages and disadvantages of these opposite approaches will be considered in the chapters on 12-tone music and indeterminate music.

Melody

For some musicians, contemporary melodic practices are a continual source of irritation and misunderstanding. The accepted melodies of classical music generally were triadic or diatonic in character, symmetrical in design, and delineated by cadential patterns that asserted and reasserted the tonal center. Even though romantic melodies tended to be more chromatic and less symmetrical, they still had as their goal the melodic cadence and the eventual reaffirmation of the tonal center. With the introduction of atonality, and the consequent reduction of tonal influences, composers began to explore new pitch resources and alternative techniques of melodic construction.

In their search, composers not only developed new pitch resources but re-examined older ones as well. Medieval modes, the Eastern pentatonic system, and gypsy scales of Eastern Europe were among those found useful. Example 23·5 illustrates the melodic use of both the Phrygian mode on A and the pentatonic scale on B♭ in Ravel's *String Quartet in F,* written in 1903.

Example 23·5 Ravel, *String Quartet in F:* I, mm. 55–65

Vln. I

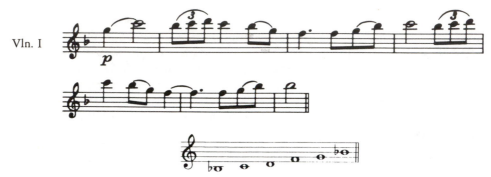

Ravel, *String Quartet in F:* IV, mm. 74–80

Vln. I

Composers also experimented with highly chromatic and **atonal** melodies. The distinction between the two is that a chromatic melody maintains a feeling of pitch center, no matter how vague, and an atonal melody does not. Example 23•6 is an atonal melody by Charles Ives. Notice that it uses all of the pitches of the chromatic scale before repeating any, then repeats the pitch sequence through the eleventh pitch, where the pattern is broken.

Example 23·6 Ives, *Tone Roads No. 3:* mm. 1–12

Andante con moto

Composers have also explored extending pitch resources electronically and with microtones, topics considered in detail in chapters 26 and 27.

Contemporary melodies have sometimes been called unsingable. This is seldom true, but they are indeed more chromatic, more disjunct, and more rhythmically unstable than most melodies written between 1600 and 1900. Composers, in search of new methods of organization, have often carefully avoided all tonal practices, including the basic contours and directions of tonal melodies. Without question, to listeners whose experience has centered almost exclusively around tonal music, many contemporary melodies may not be immediately understandable or pleasing. Wider experience in listening to contemporary music can, however, reveal the unique subtlety and expressiveness of contemporary melodic practices.

Harmony

The acceptance of atonality brought the question of harmonic consonance and dissonance into prominence. The focusing, goal-directed qualities of tonality gave definition to consonant and dissonant harmonies—a tone or chord was increasingly dissonant in relation to its distance from the key center. Without this tonal reference point, consonance and dissonance became increasingly relative. Harmonic practices of the early twentieth century went in many directions in the search for a re-definition of consonance and dissonance.

One such direction extended the harmonic practices of tonal music. Triads, seventh chords, and ninth chords, the predominant harmonic structures of tonal music, were superseded by chords of the eleventh, thirteenth, fifteenth, and seventeenth. Furthermore, extra pitches were often added to triads and seventh chords. These extra pitches were generally dissonant to the chord to which they were added (for instance, F♯ added to a C major chord), and in most cases, served to blur the harmonic implications, but not destroy them. Chords built on intervals other than thirds were also explored, the two most common being those built on fourths (**quartal chords**) and on seconds (**secundal chords**).

One of the more interesting developments in early twentieth-century harmonic practice was the introduction of **bitonality**. *Bitonality* is the simultaneous use of two different key centers,* and is similar to a modal technique accepted by medieval composers but largely unused from the fifteenth century to the twentieth century. Examples 23•7 and 23•8 illustrate this technique as used for voices by Charles Ives and for piano by Darius Milhaud. Also note that the rhythmic pattern cited earlier in Example 23•1 consists harmonically of an F♭ major chord below an E♭ chord.

*The word **polytonality** is often used incorrectly. It means more than two key centers.

Example 23·7 Ives, *The Sixty-Seventh Psalm:* mm. 1–3

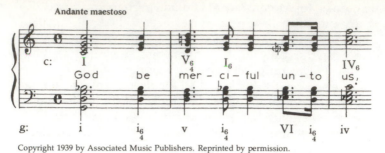

Example 23·8 Milhaud, "Copacabana" from *Saudades do Brazil:* mm. 13–17

The twentieth-century experiments in harmony identified so far are extensions of tonal concepts rather than their replacements. One atonally related substitute is **chord clusters**. Chord clusters may be distinguished from tonal chords with added chromatic pitches by their lack of harmonic function. Instead, chord clusters are used for color. Example 23·9 shows a 10-note chord cluster used by Ives.

Example 23·9 Ives, *Majority:* opening

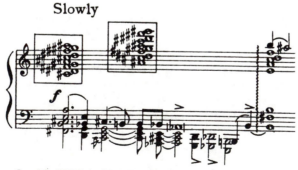

A widely used technique, particularly in impressionistic music, is to move chords or voices in parallel planes of sound. In many instances, parallelism, or **planing** as it is sometimes called, produces unusual sequences of tonal chords which do not function tonally. Examples 23•10 and 23•11 illustrate two uses of this technique by Debussy. In the first instance, all of the chords are major in quality, while in the second, they are first-inversion ninth chords. In both cases the resulting harmonic motion is unrelated to harmonically functional tonal progressions.

Example 23•10 Debussy, *Preludes*, Vol. 1, No. 1 ("Danseuses de Delphes"): mm. 21–24

Copyright 1910 Durand et Cie. Used by permission. Elkan-Vogel, Inc. sole representative, United States.

Example 23•11 Debussy, *Images*, Series 1 ("Reflets dans l'eau"): mm. 20–21

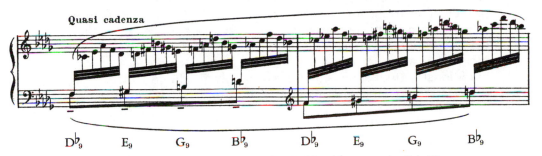

Copyright 1918 Durand et Cie. Used by permission. Elkan-Vogel, Inc., sole representative, United States.

The extension of pitch resources into the atonally based 12-tone system and into microtones, along with the resultant harmonic developments, will be examined in later chapters.

Texture

Devices such as polyrhythm, polymeter, chord clusters, and bitonality brought about changes in the textural parameter in both tonal and atonal music. These and other techniques encouraged a linear approach to music and renewed interest in polyphony. Unlike seventeenth-century contrapuntal practices, which melodically and harmonically related each voice to a common tonal center, twentieth-century counterpoint allowed far more freedom. Unhampered by tonally functional harmonic necessities, composers could allow horizontal considerations to dictate vertical sonorities. At times, this resulted in highly dissonant harmony produced by essentially consonant lines. Freed from the domination of tonal concepts, the equal-voice principle of polyphony was extended to compositions structured in layers of sound. Whether moving independently or combined into thick blocks of color, textural layers of sound are now often used as alternatives to harmonic motion and melodic development.

Timbre

The twentieth century witnessed an unparalleled search for new sources of sound. In the early 1900s, composers extended the pitch range of traditional instruments, explored new ways of combining instrumental timbres, and experimented with untraditional methods of producing sound on traditional instruments (strumming the strings of a piano or placing objects between the piano strings). The opening passage from *Le Sacre du Printemps* (1912), by Stravinsky, which uses a bassoon in its extreme high register, is often cited as the beginning of this interest in new sounds.

In addition to extending the possibilities of traditional instruments, composers explored sounds from sources previously considered nonmusical. Before World War I, the Italian Futurists movement had staged noise concerts in which machines, motors, and other noise-producing instruments played a music based on timbre and texture rather than melody and harmony. The percussion ensemble, particularly with its use of instruments such as brake drums and kitchen utensils, is a similar development. The musical acceptance of unintentional natural sounds and electronically produced sounds (explored in later chapters) is a logical extension.

Form

The majority of classical forms had developed to explore melodic and harmonic tonal relationships. These same forms, however, can be used to structure musical meaning in other ways. Composers of the early 1900s experimented with the parameter of form less than with other parameters, perhaps relying on the clarity of classical forms to support their experiments with melody and harmony. The use of classical formal principles without the underlying tonal structures on which they were based is known as **neoclassicism**.

By the early 1920s, however, the music of more experimental composers seemed to require new types of formal organization. In our later considerations of 12-tone music, electronic music, microtonal music, and indeterminate music, we will discuss alternative principles of organization.

Focus

The twentieth-century acceptance of alternatives to tonality created a vast array of new possibilities for musical expression. A gradual realignment of the relative importance of the parameters of music took place, resulting in a de-emphasis on melody and harmony. The parameters of rhythm, texture, and timbre, on the other hand, became increasingly important. Today, pieces are written in which the melodic and harmonic parameters play no active role or are present only by coincidence. In trying to understand works not structured according to tonal principles, our recommendations at the beginning of chapter 11 seem pertinent: (1) determine the parameters the composer is most interested in controlling, (2) decide the nature and the extent of these controls, and (3) determine how these controls contribute to a successful composition.

To a great extent, twentieth-century music has focused on new methods of organization, new sources of sound, and a re-definition of the roles of composer and performer. In the remaining chapters we will look at 12-tone and microtonal organization, the new sounds of electronic music, and the changing relationship between composer and performer in indeterminate music. To lay a solid foundation for these discussions, the next chapter will cover the changes that have taken place in musical notation, and the relationship of these changes to contemporary musical thought.

Suggested Activities

1. For those students who have had little experience listening to music of the twentieth century, we recommend the following recordings as a place to begin. If possible, follow them with score and look for the techniques described in this chapter.

Debussy, *La Mer* (1903–1905) (Columbia Recording MS-7361);
    Jeux (1912) (Columbia Recording MS-7361)
Schoenberg, *Three Piano Pieces,* Op. 11 (1909) (Dover Records 7285);
    Pierrot Lunaire (1912) (Nonesuch Records 71251)
Stravinsky, *Le Sacre du Printemps* (1912) (Nonesuch Records 71093);
    L'Histoire du soldat (1918) (Vanguard Records 2-Van.
    71166)

2. Write a short composition for three handclappers in which you explore non-symmetrical rhythmic organization. Perform the piece in class.

3. Using polymeter, write a short composition for two wind instruments. Perform the work in class.

4. Write a short bitonal composition for piano. Try to select two keys that, when played together, will produce both consonant and dissonant harmonic combinations. Perform these works in class.

24

Contemporary notation is, for the most part, in a state of misunderstanding and confusion. Many musicians question its necessity, purpose, and value. They point out that the works of such early twentieth-century composers as Debussy, Stravinsky, Schoenberg, Webern, and Copland are all in the same notational framework, even though of significantly different styles. If these composers found traditional notational practices adequate for their ideas, why, question some, must today's composers reject traditional notation? With such a profusion of seemingly individual notational systems existing today, we are forced to admit that the majority of composers must no longer be able to adequately express their ideas in standard notation. Is this plethora of private musical symbols necessary or are composers taking new freedoms too far?

The answer appears to center on the main function of notation. As we said in chapter 2, a notational system is, among other things, primarily an information storage and retrieval system, a graphic means of conveying to performers information essential to an adequate realization of a composer's intentions. When a particular system of notation can no longer efficiently express these intentions, it is inevitable that it will be abandoned in favor of a more appropriate system. That so many of today's composers feel their musical ideas require a new kind of notation should be taken as a clue that their basic musical intentions may have changed. This chapter considers the changes that are taking place in notation. Chapter 28, on indeterminate music, considers possible changes in basic musical intentions.

Categories of Notational Control

Almost every composer today seems to be working with his own private system of notation. To be able to read and comprehend the graphic symbols of one composer no longer automatically ensures that works by other composers will be understood. In this situation it is easy to believe that all of the current notational systems have little relationship to one another. This is not, however, the case. In fact, we group this wide variety into five broad categories, according to the type and nature of the information the composer seeks to convey. We have labelled these five categories of notational control as *operational, nominal, ordinal, interval,* and *ratio notation.**

Operational notation is a system of notation that indicates what the performer is to do rather than what sound is to be obtained. **Nominal notation** is a system that merely names certain events that are to occur. The order of these events is decided arbitrarily. **Ordinal notation** is a type of contour notation in which the order or position of a symbol within a parameter is important. In this system, a parameter is represented as a bipolar continuum and the position of a symbol along that continuum indicates the value of the parameter. Ordinal notation usually involves a two-dimensional graph; the x-axis usually represents time and the y-axis pitch, although other parameters can be so used.

Interval notation is a system of notation that prescribes the division of a parameter into supposedly equal steps. Standard notation is a form of interval notation, with the octave divided into twelve equal half-steps and with durations normally divisible by two (one whole-note divides into two half-notes, and so forth). **Ratio notation** allows even greater control than interval notation. In this system, the relationship between any two items within a parameter is analogous to other relationships within the parameter. A vertical example: two rhythmic patterns occurring against each other, such as seven against six (usually expressed 7:6). A linear example is rhythmic modulation.

Before continuing with a fuller discussion of this typology, let us make a couple of general remarks. First, the interval notation with which we are familiar is a complex system capable of transmitting with precision certain kinds of information. It has existed for over three hundred years because of this precision. Nominal and ordinal notational systems, even though confusing and complex to anyone

*The last four of these categories are derived from types of psychophysical scalar order first delineated by S. S. Stevens ["On the Theory of Scales of Measurement," *Science* Vol. 103 No. 2684 (June 7, 1946), 677–680.], and later applied to music by Ben Johnston ["Scalar Order as a Compositional Resource," *Perspectives of New Music* Vol. 2 No. 2 (Spring–Summer 1964), 56–76].

unfamiliar with them, are used today just because they are not as precise as interval notation and, consequently, allow performers certain freedoms not possible with interval notation. Ratio notation, on the other hand, is usually employed by composers for even greater control than interval notation can offer. Second, these categories of notation are not mutually exclusive. Composers use more than one type in a composition, if doing so best conveys their intentions.

Operational Notation

Operational notation, also referred to as *action notation,* indicates what actions the performer must make rather than what sounds he can expect to hear. This type of notation can vary from tablature to typewritten instructions. In most uses, operational notation is the clearest way of indicating the composer's intentions; in some instances it represents the only way.

Compositions for non-pitched percussion instruments exemplify the situation where operational notation is the only adequate notation available. How can a composer indicate the pitch of a gong, a suspended cymbal, or a triangle? In some instances it is possible to do so, but it is usually much clearer and simpler to use operational notation and ignore exact pitch. Edgard Varese was one of the first composers to explore extensively the new sounds available from percussion instruments. Example 24•1 is the opening measures of his *Ionisation* for percussion ensemble of thirteen players. Notice that, except for the piano, each instrument is notated on a separate line.

Example 24·1 Varèse, from *Ionisation*

Percussion sounds represent only one instance where operational notation is the clearest, most easily understood notation available. Whenever a composer uses non-traditional sounds, notating pitch can be a problem. Example 24•2 gives us a section from Paul Zonn's *Revolutions* for solo clarinet.

Example 24·2 Paul Zonn, from *Revolutions*

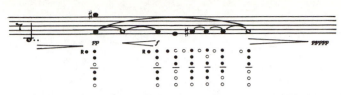

In this example, Zonn utilizes the multiphonic capabilities of the clarinet. **Multiphonics** are sound composites of two or more simultaneous pitches obtainable on woodwind instruments through, in most cases, cross fingerings. They are highly complex sounds. Since no standard way of notating multiphonics has been developed, Zonn indicates fingerings below each sound to make his intentions clear to the performers.

Nominal Notation

Nominal notation allows performers more freedoms than any other type of notation. As a rule, it is also less complex. In nominal notation, the musical events are merely identified as possibilities. There is no attempt to structure or rank them into any kind of contour or scale of sound events.

In *Nonet,* Barney Childs provides nine performers with a set of sound events to draw from. The part for voice is reproduced in Example 24·3. Notice that he has not indicated a rank order for these sound events, such as high to low or loud to soft. Neither has he assumed that all of the events will be used. The performers are given specific instructions on how to structure a performance, but these instructions relate more to chance than to musical considerations.

Example 24·3 Barney Childs, voice part from *Nonet*

VOICE

Durations: = 5-8 seconds, = 3-5 seconds, = 1-3 seconds,

Dynamics: Variable, but generally *mf - pp*

Alternatives furnished (in parenthesis) are for notes which might be out of your range

If you do not have "perfect pitch," use the same text but improvise the pitches

All texts, words, and reading passages in this piece are citations and assemblages from the seventeenth-century English writers Traherne, Walton, Browne, Donne and others

For the following *P* events, select (consecutive, if more than one is needed) syllables from the following text: "Kinds upon the way is in waters cannot be seen first made of wings and black wool feathers likewise about either"

P

any very low note, big blues-y sound, one syllable, ca. 3 seconds, *f*

as high a pitch as you can get, one syllable, ca. 5 seconds, *pp* possible

slow steady gliss, from the top down through your whole range, one syllable, ca. 6-8 seconds, *pp*

any moderately high pitch, tiny vibrato-less child-like tone, one syllable, ca. 4 seconds

any mid-register pitch, sing through at least two feet of large-bore cardboard mailing tube, one syllable, ca. 3 seconds, *f*

any pitch, muted with hands over mouth, one syllable, ca. 4 seconds

ghostly improvised indistinct "sprechstimme," moderate tempo, seven syllables, *pp*

N

Single fingersnap, *ff*

Single clap of the hands, *ff*

Slap leg once, *f*

Rattle fingernails (quasi trill) on the mailing tube, *mf*

Play a short, loud note on a blow-into-it plastic toy instrument
        (not any sort of a whistle)

Snap side of mailing tube once with fingernail, *ff*

For each page's group(s) of events select any correct number of consecutive pitches and set to them the same number of consecutive syllables from the text; the text, as the pitch line, is "circular"— that is, if you begin "hedges being" the next words are "easily April..." use each part of the text only once

The text: easily April himself near and keep the running winter this day shade and that above all echo without standing is under hedges being

Whisper your birthdate (month, day, year)

Whistle any steady pitch, ca. 3 seconds, *ppp*

Hum any steady pitch, ca. 5 seconds, *mf*

Hiss, 5-8 seconds

 Hold 20 seconds, or as long as you can up to that time; any vowel sound, *ppp*

(8)

 This bar repeated once

(8) *fall-ing fall-ing &c.*

(at choice) Three of these *P* events are to be devised yourself; each must use the voice in some way; if a pitch is involved, it must in some way be altered from normal timbre.

Play a sustained note, fluttertongue, on the toy instrument, ca. 3 seconds

Shake a good number of pennies in a china cup, ca. 4 seconds

Rap lightly on edge of cup with a penny

Speak (normal voice, do not declaim!) the word "at"

Read quietly, as if to yourself: "and what proportion this poor globe of earth might bear with it"

Otto Henry's *Omnibus (1)* for an indeterminate number of players (see Example 28•4) is another example of nominal notation. The group procedures listed below the pitch line provide a field of possibilities from which the performers choose the sequence of events for a particular performance. Nominal notation is of value to composers of indeterminate music precisely because its ambiguity not only allows but demands that the performer become involved in the creative process. This type of notation presents performers with a field of possibilities from which to choose; they thereby contribute directly to the direction and shape of the work.

Ordinal Notation

Ordinal notation is a form of contour notation which most often indicates pitch and time—in a general rather than a specific way—by means of a two-dimensional graph. In this system, *where* a symbol occurs on the *x*-axis indicates *when* it occurs in the time scheme of the piece, and *where* it occurs on the *y*-axis indicates its *general pitch level*. The terms *graphic, temporal,* and *spatial notation* refer to particular types of ordinal notation.

Graphic Mobile for three or more performers by William Karlins is a clear example of the two-dimensional, bipolar characteristics of ordinal notation. In Example 24•4 we have one of nine pages of that score.

Example 24•4   William Karlins, from *Graphic Mobile*

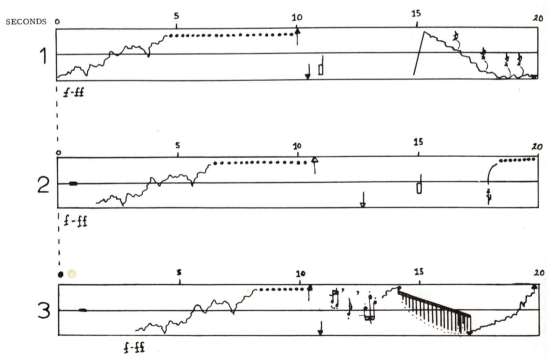

There are three separate parts. The center line of each part indicates the midpoint of the range of the particular instrument selected to perform that part. Above the line is the upper half of the range, and below the line, the lower half of the range. With this system of pitch notation, Karlins is able to indicate **tessitura** (performing range) and graph pitch contours, but is unable to specify pitches.

Time is marked in *Graphic Mobile* in five-second intervals, the entire page of score lasting twenty seconds. Thus, where a symbol appears vertically is a general indication of pitch level, and where it appears horizontally indicates its placement within the twenty-second span of time.

Example 24•5 is a page of score from Earle Brown's *Hodograph I* for flute, piano, celeste, orchestra bells, vibraphone, and marimba. The "explicit" notational section at the top is to be performed in fifteen seconds; where a pitch appears horizontally gives its general placement within this fifteen seconds. Notice that Brown uses lengthened noteheads to indicate sustained pitches.

Example 24•5   Earle Brown, from *Hodograph I*

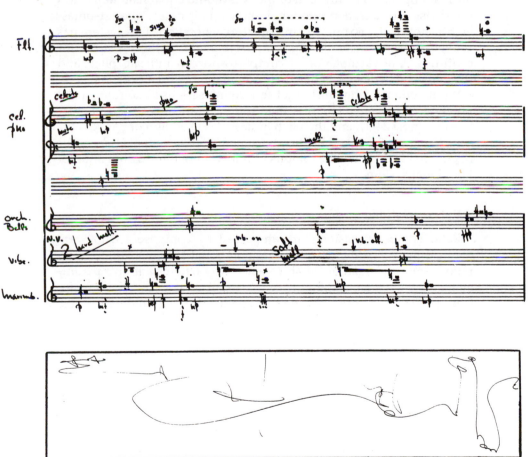

Copyright 1961 by Associated Music Publishers. Reprinted by permission.

The "implicit" notation at the bottom is also an example of ordinal notation, one that allows a great deal more freedom in interpretation. The box represents the entire pitch range of the instrument performing it. Since the time for the entire event is limited to fifteen seconds, the line drawing gives pitch contour within a specified amount of time.

Ordinal notational systems like those used in *Graphic Mobile* and *Hodograph I* allow certain kinds of musical events to occur easily. Other kinds of events would be almost impossible to obtain—diatonic melodies and harmonies, for obvious example. Ordinal notation also has no provision for symmetrical or non-symmetrical rhythmic schemes. On the other hand, this system of notation not only allows, but encourages pitch groupings and complex rhythmic events that would be at best difficult, and in most cases, impossible to notate in traditional notation.

Interval Notation

Interval notation identifies equal divisions within a parameter. In some instances, this system can be thought of as an extension of ordinal notation. The division of the octave into equal half-steps, and the division of duration into whole-notes, half-notes, quarter-notes, eighth-notes, and so on, is a kind of interval notation. This system has proved so valuable for storing composers' ideas that it has lasted for centuries. Interval notation is complex and can indicate pitch and rhythmic subtleties far better than nominal or ordinal notation.

We mentioned previously that few composers use one category of notation exclusively. The rhythmic system used by Varese in *Ionisation* (Example 24•1), and the pitch indications used by Zonn in *Revolutions* (Example 24•2) and by Brown in the upper system of *Hodograph I* (Example 24•5) are all illustrations of interval notation within another notational system.

Ratio Notation

Ratio notational systems are employed by composers who want controls more specific than interval notational systems can offer. In ratio systems the relationship between any two items within a parameter is not only an equidistant but also an analogous relationship. Example 24•6 represents this type of relationship within the rhythmic parameter.

This example, a section from the *String Quartet No. 2* of Elliott Carter, shows his concept of rhythmic modulation. Changing tempi are precisely controlled by relating the basic metrical unit of the new section to a known unit from the previous section. Thus, at measure 183 Carter is able to change the tempo from a quarter-note at mm. 140 to a half-note at mm. 105 by relating the value of the half-note at the new tempo to the value of a quarter-note plus a third of a triplet in the previous tempo.

Example 24·6   Elliott Carter, *String Quartet No. 2*

In the parameter of pitch, Harry Partch experimented with actual ratios for notating the microtones he was employing. Example 24•7 gives us Partch's notation for voice and adapted viola (an instrument he constructed around 1930). The ratios in this example refer to pitch intervals in just intonation.

Example 24•7   Ratio notation of Harry Partch

Focus

Standard notation, a form of interval notation in use from approximately 1600 to the present, is a set of such clearly understood symbols that any system of notation that deviates from it may be immediately suspect. Only if you assume—falsely—that the basic musical intentions of composers will never change, is it difficult to justify current notational practices.

In this chapter we have tried to show that the notational systems adopted by composers will indicate clearly the parametric controls they feel are important, and the degree of control they consider necessary. In most instances composers employ operational notational systems because they store information most clearly and unambiguously. On the other hand, nominal and ordinal systems are useful precisely because their varying degrees of ambiguity not only allow performer involvement, but insist on a contribution to the creative process. The value of performer involvement in the creative process is open to dispute, but given a composer's intentions in this direction, nominal and ordinal systems of notation offer the best available solutions.

Interval systems of notation are still the most widely employed means of communicating musical performance information. Their usefulness has been established over centuries. For composers who feel their musical ideas require even greater degrees of control, ratio systems are available.

Most contemporary composers are looking for a type of notation that will express most adequately their musical thoughts, with a minimum of confusion and false complexity. If a particular notational system appears eccentric or needlessly vague, it may well be that the philosophical basis of the music is not understood. Once a composer's philosophical orientation is appreciated, the seemingly vague notation may turn out to be not only the most adequate and easily understood method of expressing the musical intentions, but, perhaps, the only manner of doing so.

Suggested Activities

1. Using a recording or class performance of a contemporary composition, discuss the parameters the composer is most interested in controlling, and the methods of notation available. If possible, compare your decisions with the composer's score.

2. Perform Greg Bright's *The Balkan Sobranie Smoking Mixture* (Example 11•3). Discuss the parametric controls exerted by this particular notation.

3. Divide the class into four groups and clap the rhythmic modulations in Example 24•6 (*String Quartet No. 2* by Elliott Carter).

4. Using ordinal notation, compose a short work for three instruments. Have the work performed in class without verbal instruction from the composer. Have the composer discuss his or her intentions and the results.

Suggested Readings

1. Karkoschka, Erhard. *Das Schriftbild der Neuen Music* (Celle, Germany: Hermann Moeck, 1966) illustrates and catalogues many examples of contemporary notation.

2. Risatti, Howard. *New Music Vocabulary* (Urbana: University of Illinois Press, 1975) catalogues the various signs and symbols of contemporary notation.

3. Bartolozzi, Bruno. *New Sounds for Woodwind*, trans. and ed. Reginald Smith Brindle (London: Oxford University Press, 1967) explores multiphonics for woodwind instruments. It includes a recording of the sounds and a system for their notation.

4. Pooler, Frank, and Pierce, Brent. *A New Choral Notation*. New York: Walton Music Corp., 1971.

5. Boretz, Benjamin, and Cone, Edward T., eds., *Perspectives on Notation and Performance* (New York: W. W. Norton & Co., 1976) contains essays by such authors as Gunther Schuller, Kurt Stone, Lukas Foss, and Donald Martino. Many of the essays first appeared in *Perspectives of New Music*.

6. Barney Childs has written an excellent discussion on "Indeterminacy" for the *Dictionary of Contemporary Music*.

7. The score for "Nonet" by Barney Childs is printed in *Source* Vol. 3 No. 1 (January 1969), complete with Childs' "event machine," a device for producing chance procedures.

25

The **12-tone system** was developed in the early 1920s by Arnold Schoenberg for the systematic writing of non-tonal, chromatic music. In the late 1800s and early 1900s, tonal music became so chromatic that determining the tonality of a piece was at times difficult or impossible. In the music of Haydn and Mozart and the early works of Beethoven, chromaticism was employed as a means of modulating to a new tonal center, was concentrated in development sections, or was introduced for color within a firmly established tonality. By the time of Chopin, however, so many chromatically altered chords and melodies were being used that in some music functional tonality was actually in question. It is true that tonality is not as firmly established or as evident in the music of Chopin as it is in Classical compositions. With late Wagner, movement through levels of dissonance replaces tonal progression and cadence to such an extent that it is often impossible to determine a fixed tonal center.

This increase in the use of chromaticism as a structural element, and the consequent blurring of tonality, led Schoenberg to conclude that the major and minor scales had all been replaced by one scale: the chromatic scale. He also saw the twelve notes of the chromatic scale as equally important, unlike the notes of major and minor scales, which depend on tonic-dominant function. If the twelve pitches of the chromatic scale are, indeed, of equal importance, then they can function as the source material for a composition. By the early 1920s, Schoenberg had developed a basic system for composing with twelve equal tones.

Rejecting major and minor scales for a chromatic scale organized into a non-repetitive pattern of pitches implies a rejection of other basic principles of organization associated with tonality. The principles of melodic construction, harmonic movement, and formal development essential for tonal music are not normally applicable to music organized in a 12-tone system. More dissonant in style, essentially contrapuntal in texture, 12-tone technique represents a new understanding by composers of how to best express their musical ideas.

The 12-Tone Row

The basic generative material for 12-tone music is the **12-tone row**. The row (referred to as the *prime* or *original* and abbreviated *P* or *O*) is an ordering of the twelve pitches of the chromatic scale. Generally, one row is used as the source material for an entire composition. This means that composers must take care to construct the row so that the order of pitches is appropriate for their ideas, and so that the intervals created by adjacent pitches are acceptable. Since composers who write 12-tone music have generally rejected tonality, they normally avoid interval patterns that suggest tonal relationships (that is, outlined triads) when constructing a row. They also try to avoid too many intervals of the same size, since this limits the melodic possibilities of the row.

Example 25•1 shows the basic row used by Alban Berg for his *Violin Concerto*. The tonal implications are indicated below the row; above the row are marked the kinds of triads available.

Example 25•1   Berg, tone row for *Violin Concerto*

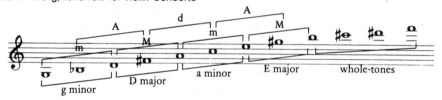

Copyright 1936 Universal Edition. Reprinted by permission.

Although this row has many intervals of similar size, the tonal and triadic possibilities as used by Berg in the composition itself offer advantages which offset this disadvantage.

Far more common for 12-tone writing are the kinds of rows shown in Example 25•2. Both rows explore a variety of intervals while at the same time avoiding tonal implications.

Example 25·2   Schoenberg, tone row for *Fourth String Quartet*
              Dallapiccola, tone row for "Die Sonne Kommt!"

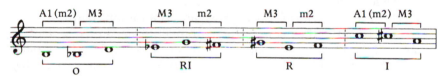

Some composers have developed rows built around segments of two, three, four, or six notes from which the remainder of the 12-tone row is constructed.* In Example 25·3, notice that the row employed by Webern for the *Concerto for Nine Instruments* can be divided into four **trichords**, all of which contain intervals of a minor second and a major third, and the last three of which are the retrograde inversion, retrograde, and inversion of the first. Since 12-tone technique assumes equal temperament, enharmonic equivalents (for example, F#–G♭) are interchangeable.

Example 25·3   Webern, tone row for *Concerto for Nine Instruments*

Forms of the Row

The pitch row from which a composer wishes to construct a composition can exist in one of four forms and still maintain the integrity of the basic row. These four forms are: *original*†*(O), retrograde (R), inver-*

---

*Stravinsky's *In Memoriam Dylan Thomas* uses a 5-note row that is not referable to any complete 12-tone row. Because of pieces such as this, the term *serial music* is now preferred by some theorists. They reason that all 12-tone music is serial, but not all serial music is 12-tone. We see serialism as extending 12-tone pitch manipulation to other parameters, such as rhythm and dynamics.

†Some theorists recommend the use of *prime (P)* instead of *original (O)*.

sion (I), and *retrograde inversion (RI).* Example 25•4 shows the four basic forms of a row used by Dallapiccola in "Die Sonne Kommt!" from his *Goethe-Lieder.*

Example 25•4   Dallapiccola, tone row for "Die Sonne Kommt!"

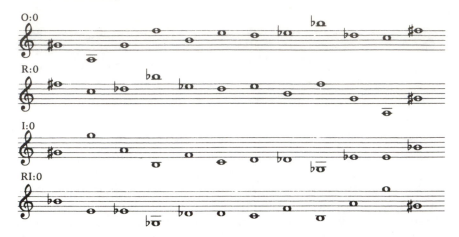

Notice that the retrograde has the pitches of the original in reverse order. The inversion begins on the same pitch as the original and maintains the exact interval size while reversing the direction of each interval. In the retrograde inversion, the pitches of the inversion are in reverse order.

Each of the four forms of the row can, in addition, be transposed to begin on any other note of the chromatic scale. In Example 25•4 above, Dallapiccola's original row begins G♯, A, G, F. At this pitch level, the row is identified as *O:0;* transposed up a half-step (A, B♭, G♯, F♯), the indication *O:1* would be used; transposed up five half-steps (C♯, D, C, B♭), the identification would be *O:5.* Similarly, the inversion beginning on G♯ would be identified as *I:0;* the inversion beginning on B would be labeled *I:3.* The identifications of transposed retrograde and retrograde inversion forms of the row are taken from the original and the retrograde forms, respectively. Thus, in Example 25•4, R:0 begins on F♯, the twelfth note of O:0, and RI:0 begins on B♭, the twelfth pitch of I:0. Since all four forms of the row can begin on any of the twelve pitches of the chromatic scale, a total of forty-eight possible forms of the basic row are available.

Tone-Row Matrix

Since few composers can remember the forty-eight possible forms of a row, many find it convenient to utilize a tone-row matrix for seeing all the possibilities simultaneously. The matrix has the letter names of the pitches of the original row (O:0) written across the top, and the letter names of the inversion pitches (I:0) written down one side. The matrix is filled in with the transpositions of the original row. Reading the completed matrix from left to right gives the twelve possible forms of the original; reading from right to left yields the twelve forms of the retrograde. The columns read from top to bottom give the inversions, and from bottom to top, the retrograde inversions. Example 25•5 is a matrix for the Dallapiccola row of Example 25•4.

Example 25•5

I:0

O:0	G♯	A	G	F	B	E	D	E♭	B♭	D♭	C	F♯	R:0
	G	G♯	F♯	E	B♭	E♭	D♭	D	A	C	B	F	
	A	B♭	G♯	F♯	C	F	E♭	E	B	D	D♭	G	
	B	C	B♭	G♯	D	G	F	F♯	D♭	E	E♭	A	
	F	G♭	E	D	G♯	D♭	B	C	G	B♭	A	E♭	
	C	D♭	B	A	E♭	G♯	F♯	G	D	F	E	B♭	
	D	E♭	D♭	B	F	B♭	G♯	A	E	G	F♯	C	
	D♭	D	C	B♭	E	A	G	G♯	E♭	G♭	F	B	
	G♭	G	F	E♭	A	D	C	D♭	G♯	B	B♭	E	
	E♭	E	D	C	F♯	B	A	B♭	F	G♯	G	D♭	
	E	F	E♭	D♭	G	C	B♭	B	F♯	A	G♯	D	
	B♭	B	A	G	D♭	F♯	E	F	C	E♭	D	G♯	

RI:0

12-Tone Compositional Techniques

There are some general principles of 12-tone writing normally observed by composers of 12-tone music. First, a 12-tone composition uses successive statements of the 12-tone row in its various forms. Then, any pitch from any form of the row may appear in any octave without destroying the inherent quality of that row. Finally, the order of pitches (1 through 12) of a particular series should be maintained, with the following exceptions:

1. A pitch may be repeated once or more—usually in the same octave—before the next pitch is played.

2. A pitch may be repeated out of sequence in such figures as trills and tremolos.

3. Short groups of notes may be repeated occasionally. (Sometimes this has the effect of establishing a pitch motive in the ear of the listener.)

With these general principles in mind, the composer then structures the materials into a musical composition. The row forms selected, and the development of the rhythmic framework for the setting of the pitch material reflect the personal preferences and musical creativity of the composer.

Example 25•6 is Dallapiccola's "Die Sonne Kommt!" for mezzo-soprano and E♭ clarinet. The E♭ clarinet is notated in C in this example. Refer to the tone-row matrix in Example 25•5 as you read our analysis of the piece.

Example 25•6   Dallapiccola, "Die Sonne Kommt!"

Notice first that the soprano begins by stating the original row (O:0). Observe how Dallapiccola has set the first three words of the text, "Die Sonne Kommt!" (The sun comes up!), in an ascending pattern spanning almost two octaves. In measure 6, the soprano begins an inversion of the row (I:1) beginning on a'. Notice that this statement of the inversion begins with a repeated group of notes and culminates in measure 9 with a b'', the highest pitch of the composition.

Shortly before the soprano completes the statement of the inversion, the clarinet enters in canon with the soprano, performing O:0 (measures 8–12) and I:1 (measures 13–16) at the same pitch level and in the same rhythm as the soprano.

While the clarinet states O:0 and I:1, the voice states RI:1 and R:0. Notice that this creates a retrograde in the voice in which measures 9 through 17 mirror measures 1 through 8½. Observe, too, that Dallapiccola has chosen to retrograde not only the pitches but the rhythm of the vocal line as well.

It is significant that only four of the forty-eight possible row forms are used (O:0, I:1, RI:1, R:0). We would expect few pieces to use all forty-eight possible forms, but Dallapiccola could have used more than four. By limiting himself as he did, however, he has developed a symmetrical structure for the vocal line which unifies it musically and formally. At the same time, the clarinet in canon further unifies the work structurally by calling to mind previously heard material.

Vertical Sonorities in 12-Tone Music

The techniques of 12-tone writing lend themselves to linear motion. It does not automatically follow, however, that vertical sonorities are nothing but a byproduct of contrapuntal lines. Composers can, in fact, develop strong tonal progressions within a 12-tone work. Example 25•7 clearly implies a G minor cell and an A minor cell. The row of Example 25•1 was constructed in a manner that allows for such possibilities.

Example 25•7 Berg, *Violin Concerto:* mm. 11–15

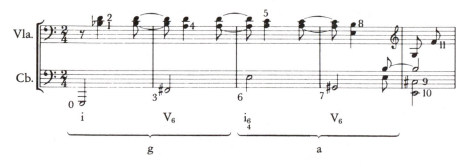

Composers can also consider vertical sonorities in terms of consonance and dissonance, free from tonal implications. Example 25·8 illustrates such a consideration. Notice that all twelve pitches of the row are used in almost every measure.

Example 25·8 Schoenberg, *Fourth String Quartet*, Op. 37: I, mm. 1–3

Composers of 12-tone music are not free to disregard vertical sonorities in their music. Whether they wish to produce implied tonal centers or consonant–dissonant atonality, they must be sensitive to the harmonic aspects—the piece must make some kind of tonal or atonal sense. Twelve-tone technique, like all other systems of writing, must be tempered by musical reason.

Extended Serialism

Beginning in the 1940s, certain composers applied the techniques of 12-tone pitch manipulation to other parameters of music. The term **serialism** refers to this approach. These composers reasoned that the ordering and structuring of rhythm, tempo, articulation, and dynamics could be pre-compositionally determined. Although each composer tended to develop a unique system, the strict ordering of parameters other than pitch followed processes similar to 12-tone pitch manipulation or, in some cases, other numerical schemes devised by the composer.

If a process similar to 12-tone pitch manipulation is used, the pitches of the original row (O:0) are numbered 1 through 12 and a number matrix is developed from the pitch matrix by substituting the appropriate number wherever a particular pitch occurs in the matrix. By assigning twelve levels to whatever the composer wishes to control serially—dynamics, rhythmic values, articulations, or the like—the number matrix orders these musical elements within the composition. It is also possible to develop a numerical scheme apart from the pitch matrix. As long as the composer can relate rhythmic values, dynamic levels, and the like, to the numerical scheme, the scheme can be used to predetermine the order of these musical elements.

Many students feel that serial music is composed within guidelines so technically strict that it is mathematical and void of any personal expression or creativity. Granted, the chromatic, often disjunct melodies of much of 12-tone writing are less personal in character than diatonic melodies with which we are more accustomed. This, however, is more a result of composers' turning to atonality to find resources for their musical ideas. The 12-tone system, as such, is only a means of ordering and structuring atonal material, much as tonality structures ideas around tonic-dominant function and shifting tonal centers. We need only consider the writing of fugues in the 1700s or the techniques of rhythmic modes and isorhythm prevalent in the 1300s and 1400s, to realize that both tonal and modal music could also be highly organized. There is certainly room for creative individuality within the rules and conventions of 12-tone music. Overcoming the limitations and restrictions of 12-tone technique is similar to the problem faced by eighteenth-century composers in trying to transcend the limitations and restrictions of classical harmony and form.

Suggested Activities

1. Write a 12-tone row utilizing as many different intervals as possible between a minor second and a major seventh, while at the same time avoiding three successive pitches that might outline major or minor triads.

2. Write a 12-tone row in which the last six pitches are an inversion of the first six. (The inversion must, of course, begin at a different pitch level.)

3. Prepare a matrix for one of the above rows.

4. Using various forms of the row from the matrix of activity 3, write a short contrapuntal exercise for two or three instruments. If possible, perform the work in class.

5. Write a short exercise for solo instrument and three "accompanying" instruments, using only one form of the row at a time, and distributing the pitches between the four parts. Perform the work in class.

6. Prepare a matrix for the Schoenberg *String Quartet No. 4* in Example 25•8. Obtain a score and a recording of this work and analyze the 12-tone manipulation Schoenberg employs. (This may be best accomplished as a class project rather than as an individual one.)

Suggested Readings

This chapter has introduced the basics of 12-tone technique. For anyone interested in more detail, we recommend the following:

1. Josef Rufer was a student of Arnold Schoenberg in the 1920s. His *Composition With 12 Notes*, trans. Humphrey Searle (London: Barrie & Rockcliff, 1954) provides insight into Schoenberg's approach to serial music.

2. Reginal Smith Brindle's *Serial Music* (London: Oxford University Press, 1966) is written for composers interested in exploring serial compositional techniques.

3. Ernst Krenek, *Studies in Counterpoint* (New York: G. Schirmer, 1940) explores a 12-tone approach to counterpoint.

4. George Perle's *Serial Composition and Atonality*, 2nd Ed. (Berkeley: University of California Press, 1967) is an excellent study of serialism and the chromatic atonal style of writing which preceded it.

5. Folkways has produced a recording demonstrating 12-tone compositional techniques (Folkways FT-3612).

26

Microtones are pitches that create intervals smaller than a half-step. The use of microtones is more than a recent occurrence; ancient Greek theorists wrote about them and experimented with them. Composers today are probably more aware of microtonal possibilities than at any time in the past three hundred years. However, making performers aware of the potential, and convincing them to extend their abilities in the direction of microtonal music, will remain a major problem.

Microtones appear in twentieth-century music for a variety of reasons. They can arise by chance or as noise, either in pieces for traditional instruments or in electronic music. They have also been used as embellishments in otherwise tonal pieces. Composers such as Charles Ives, Ernest Block, and Béla Bartok have experimented with ornamental microtones to simulate the sounds of out-of-tune bands or East European folk music. When occurring by chance or as embellishment, microtones seldom serve a structural function. They do add timbres not otherwise available, but this in itself may not be sufficient reason to expect performers to develop microtonal performing abilities.

Twentieth-century composers have also approached microtones more systematically. Some prefer to subdivide the half-steps of the equally tempered scale into quarter-tones, eighth-tones, or some other mathematical division of the octave. This makes available 12, 24, 36, or 48 equally tempered tones per octave. Other composers use some system of tempered just tuning or extended just intonation. A 31-tone temperament was advocated by the Dutch composer Adriaan Fokker, and there is a rather large group of Americans who advocate this and the less widely recommended 19-tone temperament. The best known of these advocates in the Netherlands is Henk

Badings. In the United States, Joel Mandelbaum at Queens College, Abram Plum at Illinois Wesleyan University, Robert Chamberlain at Webster College, and Easley Blackwood at the University of Chicago, plus other, less active composers use 31-tone or 19-tone temperment. Other composers who use microtones based on extended just intonation include Harry Partch, Ben Johnston, Lou Harrison, and La Monte Young. We feel this second approach is a strong reason for twentieth-century performers and listeners to concern themselves with microtonal music.

Extended Just Intonation

Equal temperament has been the accepted practice in Western European music for almost two centuries. It is easy for us to forget that equal temperament developed as an eighteenth-century compromise that allowed keyboard and other fixed pitch instruments to play music in all major and minor scales. Although equal temperament allows a keyboard instrument to play in all keys, it does so by making all intervals except the octave acoustically out of tune. In equal temperament, perfect fifths are not pure fifths vibrating at a ratio of 3:2, only close approximations. Likewise, perfect fourths are not exactly 4:3, major seconds only approximate 9:8, and so on for all intervals except the octave, whose vibrating ratio is exactly 2:1.

It is this discrepancy between the possibility of acoustically pure intervals and the reality of only close approximations that leads some composers to call equal temperament irrational. They insist that consonance and dissonance can be physically described in terms of vibrating ratios. (For instance, the acoustically correct major seventh (15:8) is heard by the ear as more dissonant than the acoustically correct perfect fifth (3:2) because the major seventh has a more complex vibrating ratio.) Maintaining the integrity of the concept that dissonance is proportional to the complexity of the vibrating ratio should be, they believe, a primary concern of all musicians. Equal temperament, of course, does not maintain this integrity. Only the octave vibrates at a simple ratio. All intervals but the octave vibrate at a level of complexity which produces chords that microtonal composers describe as equally gray in quality. To them, the clear brightness of simple ratio intervals, the harsh dissonances of complex ratio intervals, and the consonant-dissonant interplay between the two are noticeably missing from music written and performed in equal temperament. In an attempt to regain these lost qualities, these composers use microtones in a system of extended just intonation.

In order to create a just intonation pitch system, a few intervals—easily and precisely tuned by ear—are chosen. These intervals are used to generate the pitches of a microtonal scale. Harry Partch, the

best-known microtonal composer of the twentieth century, chose the
unison, octave, perfect fifth, major third, natural seventh, and natural
eleventh as generative intervals. The natural seventh and natural
eleventh, although derived from the harmonic series, are unfamiliar
to most musicians, and microtonal scales generated from these intervals force Partch at times to rely on fixed-pitch instruments rather
than the hearing and tuning abilities of his performers. Still, by combinations of these generative intervals, Partch has created a variety of
scales in extended just intonation. Although he is most often associated with the 43-note scale, this is only one of many scales he has
developed.

Ben Johnston, a University of Illinois composer, has used the unison, octave, perfect fifth, and major third as generative intervals.
The advantage of using only these intervals is that they are familiar
to musicians and can be precisely tuned.* Johnston's system produces
a scale of fifty-three tones per octave. Example 26·1 gives the microtonal pitches within the whole-step c' to d'. Notice the system of accidentals employed by Johnston to notate these pitches. Notice too the
vibrating ratios below each of the pitches. While c to d is a relatively
simple ratio of 9:8, c to c double-sharp plus is an astounding 1125:1024.

Example 26·1

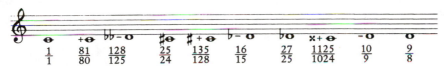

*Since 1972 Johnston has extended his systematic use of microtones to include
the natural seventh and, more recently, the natural eleventh as generative
tones.

Example 26•2 represents one way Johnston makes use of these expanded pitch resources at the beginning of the second movement of his *String Quartet No. 2* (Nonesuch Records H-71224), written in 1964.

Example 26•2 Ben Johnston, *String Quartet No. 2:* II, mm. 1–6

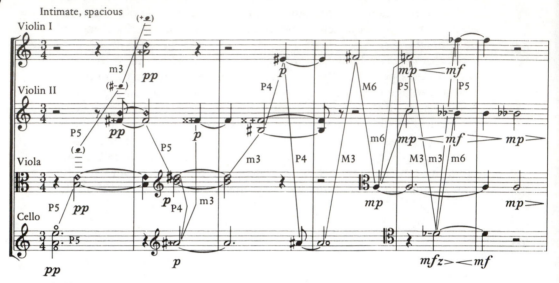

The lines connecting pitches between the four parts indicate how to tune the microtonal pitch inflections. (The lines, but not the interval identifications, appear in the original score. We have identified the intervals to make them clearer.) Performers can reasonably be expected to hear a few basic intervals in just intonation, such as the octave, perfect fifth, and major third. By indicating these interval relationships with connecting lines, Johnston has provided the performers clues sufficient to adjust the tuning by ear as they play.

Notice also that the second violin begins on an F-sharp plus harmonic. This is done to obtain an accoustically pure perfect fifth, with the B sounded by the viola. Likewise, the entrance of the first violin must be an A-plus harmonic to produce an acoustically pure minor third.

Example 26•3 is the opening bars of the first movement of this same quartet. It is both microtonal and serial. Each measure utilizes a 12-tone row composed of four trichords:

C Eb E	B G♯ G	Bb Bbb Gb	Db D F +
O	I	R	RI

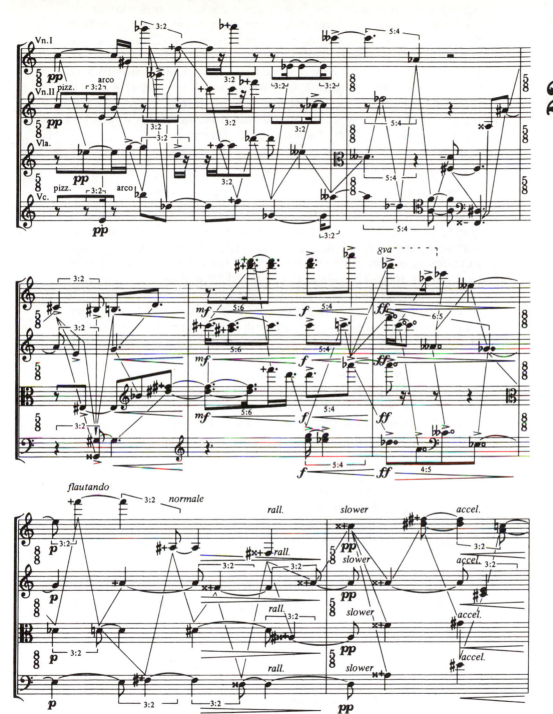

Notice that the last three trichords are the inversion, retrograde, and retrograde inversion of the first. Each measure of this movement, moreover, uses a row form that is one microtonal step higher than the previous measure; that is, measure 1 begins on C, measure 2 on C plus, measure 3 on D double-flat minus, and so forth. These first three measures show the three basic microtonal row forms employed in this movement. Measure 4, beginning on C♯, is a transposition of the first measure. The result of this type of 12-tone microtonal manipulation is a highly chromatic texture that stands in opposition to the diatonic texture of the second movement.

Notating
Microtonal Music

Notating microtones is difficult. Composers can try, as in the Johnston Quartet (Examples 26•1 to 26•3), to use standard pitch notation supplemented with a few microtonal pitch inflections. Even though Johnston uses fifty-three pitches per octave rather than the twelve of standard notation, he uses only two additional signs: +, meaning raise by one comma, and −, meaning lower by one comma. The comma in this instance, is 21.5 cents, or about one fifth of a semitone. These two signs, combined with familiar sharp, flat, doublesharp, and double-flat signs, are sufficient to notate the entire 53-note scale.

Other composers recommend altering the traditional sharp and flat signs to accommodate microtones. Russian composer Ivan Wyschnegradsky, who works chiefly in quarter-tones, recommends the addition of four new signs. These are shown in Example 26•4.

Example 26•4

+	pitch raised by a quarter-tone
♯	pitch raised by 3 quarter-tones
h	pitch lowered by a quarter-tone
♭ʰ	pitch lowered by 3 quarter-tones

Moravian composer Alois Hába also recommends altering the existing sharp and flat signs to accommodate quarter-tones, but suggests different alterations.

Example 26•5

L or ♭	pitch raised by a quarter-tone
♯	pitch raised by 3 quarter-tones
♩ or ♯	pitch lowered by a quarter-tone
♭	pitch lowered by 3 quarter-tones

Mexican composer Julián Carrillo developed an entirely new system of notation capable of expressing up to ninety-six tones per octave. Working on the principle that even semitone music is too difficult to read, Carrillo took the many clefs and accidentals, the numerous ledger lines, and even the traditional staff itself and reduced them to a system of three lines and twelve numbers. The main reference point is a long horizontal line representing c′, with a line above or below for octave identification, as required. Example 26•6 gives the notation of a chromatic scale in whole-notes, and Example 26•7 represents, respectively, a whole-note, a half-note, a quarter-note, an eighth-note, and a sixteenth-note, on the pitch D♯′.

Example 26•6

Example 26•7

For microtonal music, Carrillo's notational system remains basically the same, except that relative numbers are used. For example, in half-tone music whole numbers *0* through *12* represent the span of an octave; in eighth-tone music an octave requires the whole numbers *0* through *48*; and in third-tone music, *0* through *18* represent an octave. To work from this notation, a performer must become familiar with the relationship of the numbers in the particular microtonal system being employed. Example 26•8 shows how a Carrillo score appears in this notational system.

Example 26·8 Carrillo, from *Preludio a Cristobal Colón*

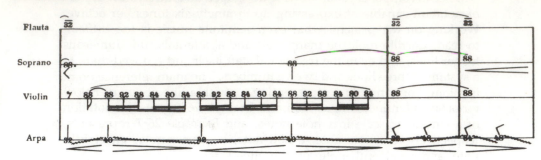

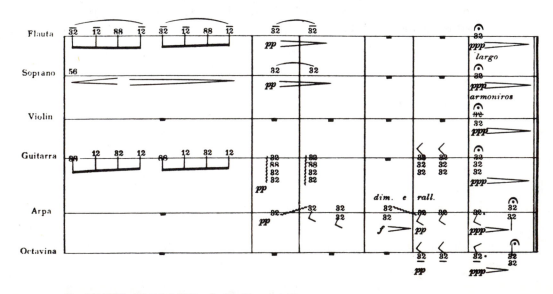

Harry Partch has experimented with a variety of notational systems, including indicating vibrating ratios directly, indicating certain ratios with code numbers, and using tablature to show how to make the sounds on the instruments he has designed for his music.

Focus

Microtones appear in twentieth-century music by chance or as noise, as ornamental embellishments in otherwise tonal music, as subdivisions of equal temperament, or as extended just intonation. The system of extended just intonation offers, we feel, the most compelling rationale for microtonal music. To subdivide equal tempered scales into quarter-tones, eighth-tones, and so on, merely extends the acoustical irrationality of equal temperament. Composers who wish to write microtonal music must either turn to electronic realization, write for fixed-pitch instruments such as re-tuned pianos, or convince performers of the validity of re-educating their hearing. Only the last offers the possibility of general understanding and acceptance of microtonal music. Furthermore, if performers are to learn new ways of hearing, they can do so far more easily with a system based on familiar intervals.

Regardless of the ways in which microtones are produced, notating them will continue to be a major problem for composers. The general acceptance of a totally new notational system, such as the one suggested by Carrillo, seems impossible, at least in the foreseeable future. Equally unlikely is the widespread use of ratios or ratio codes, since they are virtually meaningless to anyone unfamiliar with microtonal scale construction. Alterations to standard notation, however, can be equally confusing. In Johnston's notational system, for instance, D double-flat minus appears on the staff as higher in pitch than C♯, when in fact the opposite is true. Nevertheless, the use of altered standard notation does appear more advantageous than any other system proposed so far.

In an article written for *Perspectives of New Music* (suggested reading 2), Ben Johnston makes a convincing case for microtonal music:

> If we are not to be faced eventually with the splitting apart of the art of music into an art of pitched sounds and a separate art of non-pitched sounds, we must greatly refine our understanding of pitch relationships. Such understanding must be not only theoretical (intellectual) but also practical (audible by ear in actual musical compositions). The relations between component pitches of very complex sounds include a great many with which our traditional pitch system is powerless to deal. We are, therefore, accustomed to hear, more and more, relationships which demand a more comprehensive vocabulary of pitch intervals than we now have.

Suggested Activities

There is, unfortunately, only a limited selection of microtonal works on recordings. From among those currently available, we recommend:

Carrillo, *Mass for Pope John XXIII* (CRI S-246)
Ives, *Three Quartertone Piano Pieces* (Odyssey 32160162)
Johnston, *String Quartet No. 2* (Nonesuch 71224)
Partch, *Delusion of the Fury* (Columbia M2-30576)
       Music of Harry Partch (CRI 193)
       The World of Harry Partch (Columbia MS 7207)
       And On the Seventh Day Petals Fell in Petaluma (CRI S-213)

Suggested Readings

1. *Genesis of a Music* by Harry Partch, 2nd Ed. (New York: Da Capo Press, 1974), offers a comprehensive understanding of Partch's work with microtonal music. A review of this book by Garry Kvistad and Allen Otte is available in *Numus West* (June 1974). It includes a bibliography of literature written by or about Partch, as well as a list of recordings of his music and films about his work.

2. Ben Johnston has written numerous articles that deal with his work with microtonal music:

"Scalar Order As a Compositional Resource," *Perspectives of New Music* vol. 2 no. 2 explains the development of the fifty-three note scale.

"Proportionality and Expanded Musical Pitch Relations," *Perspectives of New Music* vol. 5 no. 1 explores a rationale for microtonal music.

"Three Attacks on a Problem," *Proceedings of The American Society of University Composers* vol. 2 (April 1967) considers microtonal music from philosophical, theoretical, and practical positions. It also includes a discussion of his *String Quartet No. 2.*

"Phase 1-a" (with Edward Kobrin), *Source 7* (1970) presents one-dimensional ratio scales and a Fortran IV program for generating them.

"Tonality Regained," *Proceedings of the American Society of University Composers* vol. 6 (1972) presents basic ratio scale theory, extending "Phase 1-a" to two-dimensional scales.

"Microtones" and "Harry Partch," entries in *Dictionary of 20th-Century Music,* describe historical use of microtones and in particular Harry Partch's use of them.

"The Corporealism of Harry Partch," *Perspectives of New Music* vol. 13 no. 2 stresses Partch's aesthetic and philosophic point of view.

"Harry Partch's *Cloud Chamber Music,*" ed. Ronald Byrnside, (Urbana: University of Illinois Press, in press) is an analysis of a work by Partch for a text of analyses of twentieth-century music.

3. *The Proceedings of the American Society of University Composers* vol. 2 (April 1967) contains a section on "Microtonal Music in America," including articles by Peter Yates, Joel Mandelbaum, and Lejaren Hiller.

4. Gerald R. Benjamin, "Julian Carrillo and 'Sonido Trece.'," *Yearbook of the Inter-American Institute for Musical Research* vol. 3 (1967) is a discussion of Carrillo's microtonal music.

27

A discussion of electronic music suitable to a theory text such as this one presents certain difficulties. Electronic music is sufficiently established as an art form and so widespread (from movie scores to television commercials) that every musician should have an understanding of its basic principles and techniques. It is not our intention in this chapter, however, to discuss highly specialized electronic theory or technology. Rather, we will briefly introduce three technical methods of electronic composition and then search for a musical understanding of electronic music and of the ways composers control musical parameters electronically.

An immediate problem we face is the meaning of the term *electronic music*. Many musicians use the term to identify all music produced electronically. This definition is too broad, however, for it includes music not generally considered electronic, such as that produced by electric guitars and organs, amplified rock singers, and phonograph records. Further confusion exists because the term applies to music of vastly differing styles, much as the term *flute music* applies to diverse styles of music.

We will start with a discussion of three technical processes for producing sound on tape: the tape studio, the synthesizer, and the computer. These three approaches differ in terms of what kinds of electronic manipulation are easy and what kinds are difficult or impossible. These differences create stylistic techniques and characteristics which we identify as synthesizer-produced or studio-produced.

The Tape Studio

Tape studios have existed since the late 1940s. They are usually equipped with sound generating equipment, sound modifying equipment, and sound mixing and recording equipment. Composers using tape studios distinguish between kinds of source material. One group feels that natural sounds—sounds from musical instruments or from the environment—provide more interesting timbres than any that can be electronically produced. The term **musique concrète** (concrete music) is associated with this kind of music.

Other composers believe that pure electronic sounds provide better source material because of their steady-state characteristics and lack of complexity. For these purposes, signal and noise generators are utilized to produce a variety of wave forms, including sine waves (a pure fundamental tone, without overtones), square waves (a tone with only odd-numbered partials), and white noise (a static-like sound resulting from an infinite number of random frequencies). Combining several waves yields even more complex waves.

Having selected the source material for a composition, the next step is to alter and modify this material to make it musically usable. The sounds, either concrete or electronically generated, are stored on magnetic tape. Because tape can be cut, rearranged, and spliced together again without altering the sounds on the tape, it allows the composer to rearrange a familiar sound into an unidentifiable sound-complex. Since tape recorder speeds are known precisely in inches per second ($7\frac{1}{2}$ or 15 ips), exact lengths of time can be calculated and complex rhythmic schemes developed merely by measuring lengths of tape and splicing them together. Taped material can also be played backwards, transposed by varying the speed of the recorder, subjected to reverberation, superimposed by overdubbing, and made to repeat continually by splicing the tape into a loop. These are simple techniques that anyone with a home tape recorder of good quality can experiment with.

Even more complicated sound-modifying equipment is found in the tape studio. This equipment includes filters (high-pass, low-pass, octave, third-octave, and variable band-pass filters) that eliminate various bands of sound within the frequency spectrum; ring modulators that give an output signal the sum and difference of two input signals; frequency shifters that shift a signal up or down by a fixed increment; envelope shapers that control the attack-sustain-decay characteristics of a sound; and mixers that combine a variety of signals into one composite sound.

After a composer has selected and modified a collection of sounds, the next step is to combine them meaningfully into a piece of music. An important characteristic of the tape studio is that the entire process of composing a piece is, from start to finish, a manual operation. Mixing and shaping a musical composition from an assortment of isolated fragments requires hundreds of separate operations and tape splices.

A composer's creativity determines the choice of source materials, and how they are modified and combined. The following two compositions represent distinctly different approaches to the creative possibilities of the classic tape studio. These pieces, like all those mentioned in this chapter, are available on commercial recordings. In listening to these pieces, try to determine the relationship between the sounds of the source materials and the modified sounds in the finished composition, as well as how the sounds are grouped and arranged in the composition to achieve a structural unity.

Vladimir Ussachevsky,
A Piece for Tape Recorder **(1956)**
(Composers Recordings
CRI-112)

Ussachevsky limits the basic source material of his compositions because he believes an overabundance of sounds can weaken the structural unity of an electronic piece. For this particular work he used the following source materials: concrete sounds—a gong, a piano, a cymbal stroke, a kettledrum note, jet plane noises, several chords on an organ—and electronic sounds—four pure tones from an oscillator, a tremolo produced by the stabilized reverberation of a click from a switch on a tape recorder.

Luciana Berio,
Thema—Omaggio a Joyce **(1958)**
(Turnabout TV-34177)

The sound source for this composition is a female voice reading from Joyce's *Ulysses*. Berio breaks the text into sound families, which are then grouped by vocal color or noise content and rearranged and transformed.

The Synthesizer

In some ways, a synthesizer is an extension of a tape studio, while in other ways it is an entirely new approach to electronic music composition. Like the tape studio, a synthesizer is made up of components—called *modules*—that generate, modify, and mix sounds. There are several advantages of a synthesizer over a tape studio. Synthesizers tend to be more compact, and their various modules are more compatible with one another, making sound modifications such as filtering or modulating, easier to accomplish. In addition, the synthesizer has two features—voltage control and sequencing—which make possible many complex manipulations not available with a tape studio.

Modules of a synthesizer can be controlled manually or with a controlling voltage. If the applied voltage is changed, the module to which it is applied responds instantly with a change in output. Thus, the output from a particular module can be used to influence one or more other modules, which in turn can be made to influence the original module. This enormously complex process can produce extremely complicated sound alterations. Through the application of voltage control, oscillators can be made to change frequency, amplifiers to change amplitude and envelope characteristics, and filters to change operating characteristics at any rate of speed. When a touch-sensitive ribbon or keyboard is used to apply the control voltage, each point along the ribbon or each key applies a different voltage predetermined by the composer.

A sequencer is a group of steady-state voltage generators preset to turn on and off in sequence. As they turn on and off, they apply a sequence of different voltages in a prearranged order. When used as voltage control, the sequencer can establish a chain or sequence of manipulative events of great complexity, resulting in a sequence of complicated sound events. The simpler sequences of sound can often be heard as an ostinato pattern, but the capabilities of a sequencer go far beyond this.

A final advantage of the synthesizer is that it allows the composer to hear or sample the various manipulative techniques as they occur. Hearing the work in progress is always an advantage to a composer; in the case of voltage-controlled material, instant monitoring is sometimes essential.

Morton Subotnick,
Silver Apples of the Moon **(1967)**
(Nonesuch H-71174)

This composition was commissioned by Nonesuch Records and was realized using a Buchla synthesizer. The two-sided nature of the phonograph record led Subotnick to divide the work into two major sections. With careful listening you can hear a number of ostinati patterns, produced with a sequencer, which overlap in fascinating ways.

Andrew Rudin, "Kouros" from
Tragoedia **(1967–68)**
(Nonesuch H-71198)

Tragoedia, the second electronic composition commissioned by Nonesuch Records, was realized with a Moog synthesizer. It is written in four movements of 10, 7 1/2, 5, and 15 minutes, respectively. The sound sources are white noise, sine, triangle, pulse, and sawtooth waveforms. The first movement, "Kouros," is in five equal sections. The first four sections are built on a dynamic and textural crescendo design, the fifth section serves as an epilogue. From his sound sources Rudin structures twelve different timbres that present ordered ideas against shifting random figurations.

Computer Applications

Any sound, no matter how complex, can be described as a series of numbers representing changes in pitch, timbre, and amplitude during the life of the sound. This knowledge led composers in the late 1950s to experiment with computer-generated sounds. Since then, many programs have been developed which allow composers to synthesize sounds with the aid of a computer.

There are three basic steps in synthesizing sound by computer. First, the composer decides the characteristics of the sounds to be used and codes this information for the computer. Second, the computer reads this information and produces a numerical description of each sound. Third, the output from the computer is fed into a digital-to-analog converter that transforms the numerical information into sounds on magnetic tape, for play back.

Computer generation of sounds brings its own problems. For one thing, it is highly expensive. A completed composition has many sounds happening consecutively and simultaneously, all of which must be described to the computer for numerical representation. This is time consuming, even for a computer, and may require hours of expensive computation for a few minutes of music. A second problem is that the composer is unable to hear the work until the entire process is complete. Consequently, a programming mistake will not be detected until the computer computations have been made and the final step of conversion is completed. (A faulty computation has occasionally resulted in several expensive minutes of absolute silence.)

Even with these problems, composers continue to use computers to generate sound. For them, the amount of control possible makes the computer preferable to the tape studio or synthesizer.

Charles Dodge,
Changes **(1967–70)**
(Nonesuch H-71245)

The texture of *Changes* consists of three elements: lines, chords, and percussion. In addition, the pitch content is based on a 12-tone row. The lines consist of 6-note segments of the row, the chords of 3-note to 6-note segments of the row, and the percussion duplicates or linearizes the pitch content of the chords. The timbre change of the percussion sounds result from components of the sound decaying at different rates of speed.

Notating Electronic Music

In music written for traditional instruments, notation serves, in part, as an information storage and retrieval system, allowing performers to realize the composer's intentions. With electronic music, the idea of a middleman interpreter does not exist. The electronic composition exists in its final state on the magnetic tape, ready for performance at any time. A score for storing the composer's intentions is unnecessary.

Still, composers occasionally devise scores for their electronic compositions. The U.S. Copyright Office insists on a score from a composer wishing to register an electronic composition. Ussachevsky has indicated he spent forty hours preparing a score for *A Piece for Tape Recorder* in order to copyright it. Other composers prepare a score for other people to see how the finished composition was arrived at.

There are two kinds of electronic pieces that seem to demand a score for legitimate musical reasons. One is the live electronic piece, which exists only in performance and never on tape, and for which the performer/technician must have specific information in order to carry out the composer's intentions. The second type is a piece combining electronic sounds with live performance, in which situation the performers need to know how to synchronize with the tape. To prepare a score of this type, composers have resorted to clock-time indications, descriptive phrases, or line drawings.

Focus

Electronic music first began to attract the attention of the general public in the 1950s. It was a common fear then that electronic music would replace live performers and result in the dehumanization of music. From our perspective today, we can safely say that electronic music is simply one more style of musical expression to co-exist with the many styles already available.

Whether composers work in a tape studio, with a synthesizer, or with a computer, they are faced with the same problem that confronted Mozart, Beethoven, and Chopin, that is, how to structure materials so that listeners can hear formal associations and coherency within a piece. Although electronic composers need a broad background in electronic theory and technology to handle their equipment, such background does not in any way replace a comprehensive musical background. With a few individuals, technological knowhow and musical understanding have combined to produce electronic compositions of outstanding quality.

Suggested Activities

1. The source material for each of the following electronic compositions is a single sound. Listen to each in terms of how the sound is modified and how these modified sounds are combined into a musically coherent structure.

Hugh LeCaine, *Dripsody* (Folkways FM-3436)—a drop of water.
Jean Eichelberger Ivey, *Pinball* (Folkways FM-3436)—a pinball machine.
Ilhan Mimaroglu, *Prelude XI* (Turnabout 34177)—a rubber band.

2. Although electronic music composition requires a synthesizer or a well-equipped tape studio, a few experiments can be performed in the classroom.

Record some sounds from members of the class (hand claps, whistles, vocal pitches, and the like). Experiment with changing the speed of the recorder. Notice how the sounds differ at different speeds. If a second tape recorder is available, retape the sounds at faster and slower speeds and play them back at different speeds to hear greater differences.

Tape some sounds from a contact microphone placed inside a piano and on the bell of a brass instrument, such as a trombone. Listen to the sounds and discuss their usefulness as source material for electronic music. Experiment with changing the speed of the tape recorder.

Record a variety of sounds from members of the class. Cut the tape into random lengths of two to fifteen inches and splice these random lengths together. Listen to the results. Experiment with changing the speed of the tape recorder.

Record a variety of sounds from members of the class. Splice the tape into a loop. Play this loop on the tape recorder, experimenting with changes in speed and volume.

Suggested Readings

1. The best source for a general, non-technical understanding of electronic music is the November 1968 issue of the *Music Educators Journal,* devoted entirely to electronic music.

2. Schwartz, Elliott. *Electronic Music: A Listener's Guide* (New York: Praeger Publishers, 1973) provides a more detailed approach from the listener's point of view.

3. Appleton, Jon, and Perera, Ronald, eds., *The Development and Practice of Electronic Music* (Englewood Cliffs, N.J.: Prentice-Hall, 1975) is an even more comprehensive study, with a great deal of technical information not available in Schwartz.

4. Ussachevsky, Vladimir. "Notes On A Piece For Tape Recorder" in *Problems of Modern Music* (New York: W. W. Norton & Co., 1960) is a good, non-technical discussion of the compositional process of this piece. The article is also available in the April 1960 issue of *The Musical Quarterly.*

5. Beaver, Paul, and Krause, Bernard. *The Nonesuch Guide To Electronic Music* (Nonesuch Records HC-73018) is a two-record set that demonstrates the basic source materials and some of the manipulative techniques available on a Moog Synthesizer.

28

Until recent years, composers and performers have rejected, almost unanimously, the possibility that the performer could share in the creative process with the composer. The task of the composer was to notate musical ideas as clearly and completely as possible, and the function of the performer was to realize the intentions of the composer as accurately as the notation would allow. Since the 1950s, this clearcut division of labor has been increasingly blurred. Many composers prepare scores that critics claim are more art than music, and performers are routinely expected to improvise—at times, from minimal information. The terms **indeterminate music** and **aleatoric music** are used for this new kind of composition, that is, music composed by chance procedures or that is in some way unpredictable until actually performed.

There are some historical precedents for some contemporary indeterminate music. The idea that a good performance demands an accurate score is a relatively recent one. It has never been accepted in jazz, whose vitality depends in large part on solo and group improvisation. In chapter 16 we drew a parallel between the jazz pianist and the seventeenth-century keyboard continuo player, who was expected to realize an accompaniment from the harmonies implied by a given bass line. Anyone familiar with Baroque trio sonatas understands the amount of ornamentation required in these pieces. We also know that the cadenza of eighteenth-century and nineteenth-century concerti allowed the soloist improvisatory freedom until performers stopped the practice and the fully notated cadenza became necessary.

These and other precedents relate to the work of only some composers writing indeterminate music. Other music in this style can only be explained as the product of a new aesthetic. This changing attitude about artistic function will be examined in the second section of this chapter.

Degrees of Freedom

Some musicians mistakenly believe the element of performer freedom is all or nothing. Either performers are told exactly what to do, or they are given unlimited freedom to do whatever they want. In actual practice this is not true. The degrees of freedom given to performers and the improvisational demands made on them vary from composer to composer.

Example 28•1 is the first movement of Morton Feldman's four-movement piano work *Last Pieces,* written in 1959.

Example 28•1   Morton Feldman, *Last Pieces:* I

At first glance this movement appears to be an endless succession of pitches, punctuated occasionally by a tie or a fermata. Does this mean that the performer can do anything he wants with these pitches? No, for Feldman has actually controlled many of the parameters in *Last Pieces.* For instance, he has indicated the piano as the performance medium, the particular pitches to be played, the order in which the pitches are to sound, the general dynamic level, and the overall tempo of the movement. The major freedom allowed the pianist is the duration of each sound. This gives the performer some control over the formal structure of the movement.

In the mid-1950s Pierre Boulez turned from writing extended serial music to writing music with some indeterminacy. His *Troisième sonate pour piano,* composed in 1957, consists of four movements. In performance, the pianist chooses the movement with which to begin and plays the four movements in one of several orders predetermined by Boulez. In certain movements the pianist is allowed to determine the order of performance of carefully and precisely notated musical units. In works of this type, performers are asked only to choose from among already notated musical units, not to improvise fresh musical materials.

A work in the same category, though freer, is Karlheinz Stockhausen's *Klavierstück XI* for piano (Example 28•2).

Example 28·2 Stockhausen, from *Klavierstück XI* for piano

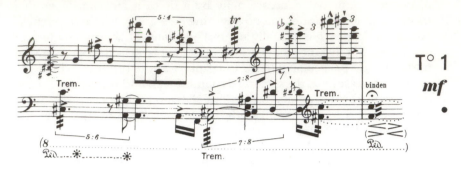

T° 1

mf

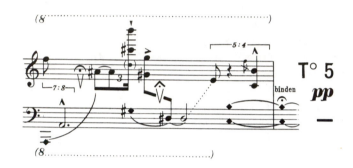

T° 5

pp

T° 5

mf

T° 4

f

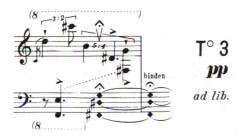

Here the pianist is given a large one-page score with eighteen musical events of varying lengths, and asked to perform them at random. Performing directions are carefully indicated and each event can be played more than once. Events performed a second or third time are altered by adding or omitting notes, or by transposing octaves. Stockhausen suggests that performance end when an event is played a third time.

A similar musical mobile is Earle Brown's *Available Forms I* for chamber orchestra (1961). This piece (Example 28•3) consists of six unbound pages, with four or five events in score form on each page. The conductor, in structuring a performance, is free to start with any event, repeat or omit pages or events, and decide the order and duration of events. Within events, orchestra members are given both specific pitches and line drawings of pitch contours.

Example 28·3 Earle Brown, from *Available Forms I*

The examples given thus far all structure elements of chance within certain clearly defined limits. Other compositions allow many more degrees of freedom. *Omnibus (1)* by Otto Henry (Example 28•4) is a composition of indeterminate length for an ensemble of a indeterminate number of players of pitched instruments.

Example 28•4   Otto Henry, *Omnibus (1)*

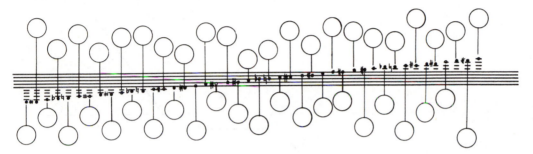

Each pitch sustained (*pp*) until next is located. Accent beginning. Try to connect without breaks. Breathe where necessary.

1st note held until 2nd located (*pp*). Skip 2nd note (rest). Locate 3rd, play, skip 4th, etc. Each note gets louder.

Odd-numbered pitches sustained, swelled, slurred to even-numbered pitches. Cut off sharply.

Each pitch moves immediately to Octave, 5th, 3rd, above or below (vary). This pitch held briefly; decrescendo and stop.

Each pitch is tonic of Major, Minor, or Chromatic scale (vary). Held until next pitch is found, then diatonic or chromatic intervals are filled in...no matter if second pitch is outside scale.

Pitch No. 1 (short, detached) is repeated immediately following all other pitches (longer, *mp*). Hurry.

Each pitch is embellished with staccato repetitions in fanfare style. Hurry.

Begin staccato, *ff*. Each successive note gets longer, softer.

Every other pitch receives different ornament, special effect (trill, mute, vibrato...make your own list). Vary dynamics.

Henry instructs performers to add to their chromatic pitch line a clef appropriate to their instrument, and to randomly number the playable pitches. The numbering system is to be changed from time to time as the performers grow accustomed to it. To structure a performance of *Omnibus (1)*, the performers agree on the order of procedures given below the pitch line and number them. All performers follow the same order of procedures but use their own individual ordering of pitches. The performance consists of at least one cycle through the group procedures.

David Cope's *Towers* (Example 28•5), for any number of players, on any types of sound-producing instruments, is even freer in the types of musical decisions allowed performers.

Example 28·5   David Cope, *Towers*

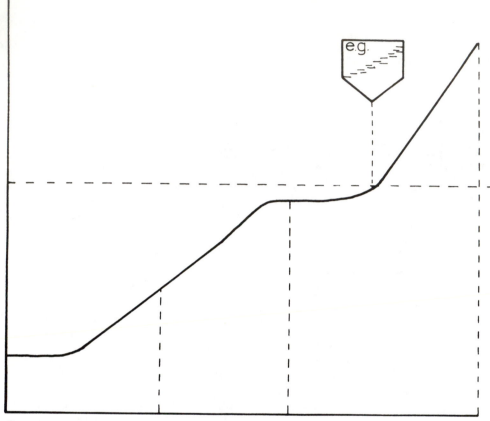

Percussive sound effects
of indefinite pitch. Do
not play 'notes' in a
traditional manner.

Play 'notes' of
distinct pitch but
only with effects—
tremolo, vibrato,
etc.

'Straight' single notes.
Rest before and after each
sound. Each higher than
the last. No effects. As
in e.g. above.

Silence

The horizontal dotted line on the score is a center identification. Below this line, in proportion to distance, sounds are soft, low, slow,
and subtle. Above the line, in proportion to the distance, sounds are
loud, high, fast, and harsh. The score recommends a conductor for
indicating the beginning and end of events and to keep the length of
events proportional to the total length of the piece, as agreed upon
by the performers.

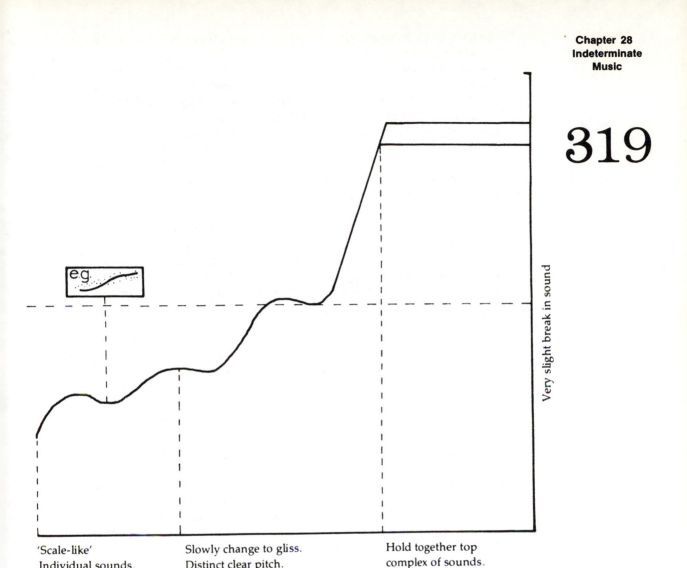

Very slight break in sound

'Scale-like'
Individual sounds.
Short. Staccato.
Add voices slowly.

Slowly change to gliss.
Distinct clear pitch.

Hold together top
complex of sounds.

A New Aesthetic

Even with the degree of indeterminacy Cope allows in *Towers*,
certain basic musical principles still seem to be operating. The page
of score given in Example 28•5 clearly shows a two-part formal structure. The first event moves from low, soft, percussive effects to high,
loud, isolated pitches. The second event moves from short, individual
pitches to a sustained complex of high-pitched sounds. Both events

illustrate growth processes similar to those of much tonal, serial, and electronic music.

Some composers of indeterminate music, however, have rejected all relationship with the past, preferring instead to base their music on totally new criteria. Of these composers, John Cage is perhaps the best known. His music is probably less understood and more controversial than the music of any other major contemporary composer.

After years of exploring new sound sources for music (Cage is credited with developing the percussion ensemble and the prepared piano), he began, around 1950, to radically alter his conception of the role of the composer. From his study of oriental philosophy, particularly Zen, Cage accepted the notion that art could sober and quiet the mind, thereby making it susceptible to divine influences. This state could be reached, however, only if music rejected European cause-and-effect thinking. Cage recommended substituting a purposeful purposelessness or a purposeless play, which, in fact, he saw as an affirmation of life—a way of waking up to reality. For music, sounds must be allowed to be just sounds. Furthermore, sounds not intended must be encouraged.

In order to produce non-intentional music, Cage decided he had to remove his personality from the art of composing. To accomplish this, he turned to chance procedures for making musical decisions. Most notable was the *I Ching,* or *Chinese Book of Changes,* an ancient method of oracle consultation, obtained from one of a possible sixty-four figures or hexagrams determined by throwing yarrow sticks or by tossing coins.

By 1952 Cage had extended his new beliefs to the point of writing *4'33",* a three-movement composition during which no sounds are intentionally produced. The title of the work is derived from the total performance time, in minutes and seconds. Although this work may be performed by any instrument or combination of instruments, the strong charisma of pianist David Tudor, who gave the first three performances, has had the effect of limiting *4'33"* to piano.

In the first performance, which took place at Woodstock, New York, on August 29, 1952, Tudor used a stopwatch to differentiate movements of 33", 2'40", and 1'20". In addition he indicated the beginning of each movement by closing the keyboard lid, and the end of each movement by opening it. Cage has said these particular lengths of time were determined by chance and could have been any others. Nevertheless, Tudor's performances caused musicians to think of *4'33"* in terms of the structure of its initial performance.

As originally written, *4'33"* consisted of five pages on which were drawn one or two heavy vertical black lines, plus one blank page. The piece was written in a time–space notation whereby each seven-inch page equaled fifty-six seconds of time. The black lines, on which minutes and seconds were indicated for each movement, served to divide the time continuum, showing visually the temporal function of the space of each page. When published by Henmar Press in 1960, however, *4'33"* consisted of only a single sheet of paper on which the three movements were indicated by Roman numerals, below each of which the word *Tacet* was written. This, of course, completely destroyed the time–space function of the original notation.

4'33" is not a silent piece, but a piece in which accidental sounds inherent in the performance situation are allowed to be themselves and to be reflected upon by the audience. It is this admission of environmental sound into music that gives *4'33"* its importance. Cage, of course, would consider the importance of *4'33"* to be not so much the admission of environmental sounds into music as the admission of music into life. To him, silence is not silence, but the whole world of sound, presenting, to those who will listen, "nature in her manner of operation."

Variations I, composed in 1958, represents an even more radical example of Cage's rejection of music as a finished product.

Example 28·6 Cage, from *Variations I*

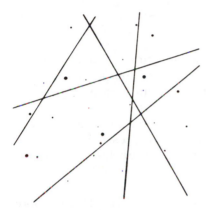

Copyright © 1960 by Henmar Press Inc. Reprinted by permission.

This work, for any number of players playing any kinds of instruments, presents the performer with six square sheets of transparent material from which he is to construct his part. Five of these sheets have five lines each, arranged in various figurations, which represent lowest frequency, simplest overtone structure, greatest amplitude, least duration, and earliest occurrence. The performer is not, however, told which line represents which characteristic. The sixth sheet contains dots or points of four graduated sizes, representing, respectively, one, two, three, and four or more chords.

To prepare a performance of *Variations I,* the performer or performers must place one of the transparencies with lines in any position over the transparency with points. By assigning one of the indicated meanings to any of the lines, and measuring a perpendicular dropped from a point to a line, the performer determines the physical nature of a sound. When one of the larger points is chosen, several measurements are necessary to determine the nature of the interval or the aggregate. The other transparencies with lines are thus employed according to the number of sounds to be determined.

If this all sounds both complicated and vague, that is intentional. The notation for *Variations I* is an excellent example of Cage's concepts of music as process and sounds as "events in a field of possibilities." Furthermore, by requiring that the performer make decisions and take actions within "a field of possibilities," Cage has further removed his own taste from the compositional process.

A new aesthetic of musical function, such as that accepted by John Cage, requires of listeners and performers a new approach to music. If this kind of music seems meaningless or uninteresting, we must ask ourselves if we have preconceptions that automatically block us from experiencing it. According to Cage:

> *The early works have beginnings, middles, and endings. The later ones do not. They begin anywhere, last any length of time, and involve more or fewer instruments and players. They are therefore not preconceived objects, and to approach them as objects is to utterly miss occasions for experience.**

Focus

Throughout this chapter we have tried to demonstrate that indeterminate music represents a broad continuum of composer–performer freedoms and controls. One side of this continuum is anchored in tradition, the other represents the antithesis of Western musical thought. It is important to acknowledge that chance procedures offer valid musical alternatives to composers for expressing their artistic ideas. Indeterminacy is not necessarily in contradiction to traditional musical thought, though some composers have found it convenient to employ it this way.

A major stumbling block to some musicians' acceptance of indeterminate music is a vague feeling of uneasiness that composers and performers of chance music are charlatans. American composer Barney Childs, writing in the first issue of *The Composer* magazine, acknowledged that "Bad indeterminate music is fatally easy to write—and to play." Does the potential of indeterminacy outweigh the possibility of undetected musical charlatanism? Perhaps this question is best answered for each piece individually.

Suggested Activities

1. Ask three pianists to prepare independently a performance of Feldman's *Last Pieces* (Example 28•1). Compare the different interpretations. Are there any areas of continuity among the three performances?

2. Perform in class Otto Henry's *Omnibus (1)* (Example 28•4). Perform it again at the next class meeting and compare similarities and differences.

---

*From *Silence* (Middletown, Conn.: Wesleyan University Press, 1961), p. 31

3. Write a piece, for four or more instruments, that has only one in-determinate element.

4. Compose a piece for the physical space in which class is held, using only those objects ordinarily in the area. Prepare a score for the work. Discuss the results.

Suggested Readings

1. Childs, Barney, "Indeterminacy and Theory: Some Notes," *The Composer* vol. 1 no. 1, and Reynolds, Roger, "Indeterminacy: Some Considerations," *Perspectives of New Music* vol. 4 no. 1 offer good initial readings on the topic of indeterminacy.

2. Arguments against indeterminacy may be found in Billy Jim Layton, "The New Liberalism," *Perspectives of New Music* Vol. 3 No. 2.

3. A book exploring recent developments in indeterminate music is Michael Nyman, *Experimental Music: Cage and Beyond* (New York: Schirmer Books, 1974).

29

Our contention throughout this book has been that major stylistic changes in music occur when composers alter their conceptions of the relative importance of the parameters of music, and their opinions of parametric balance and interaction. We have suggested that musical insight can be gained through analysis of a composer's approach to parametric importance and interaction. We believe this is especially true of the diverse and often contradictory styles of twentieth-century music. To conclude Part D, we have selected three contrasting works. We again recommend that you attempt your own analyses before reading ours.

Debussy, "Danseuses de Delphes" from *Preludes*, Book I

Rhythm

Although written in non-symmetrical rhythm, this prelude moves at a steady pace. It has a main rhythmic motive (♩ ♫. ♫ ♩) but one that is continually extended and transformed. Although much that happens rhythmically in the prelude can be related to this motive, the motive itself occurs without alteration only twice, in measures 1 and 6. We see extensions of the dotted-eighth/sixteenth-note figure in measures 2 and 3, with the even eighth-notes of measures 4 and 5 providing rhythmic contrast. This same rhythmic development occurs in measures 6–10.

Example 29·1

326

Beginning with measure 17 the relationship of rhythmic events to the opening rhythmic motive is less obvious, but still present. In measure 17 it can be seen functioning in diminution (♩. ♫♪♩), and in measures 19 and 20, in augmentation (♩. ♩ ♪|♩.). The continual extension and transformation of the rhythmic motive gives the rhythmic parameter a unifying function.

Form

The prelude exhibits few of the characteristic eighteenth-century and nineteenth-century formal principles. Its form can best be described as a juxtaposition of structure. The material of the first five measures is repeated in measures 6 through 10, with contrast achieved by a thicker texture and octave expansion of the melodic cell. Measures 11–20 represent an even greater contrast of material. The ascending half-step character of the opening measures is replaced in measure 11 by a descending figure based on thirds. Measure 21 is reminiscent of the beginning, more because of the texture than anything else, since the characteristic rhythmic motive is absent. The beginning is more directly hinted at in measures 25 and 26, where the opening material is quoted in rhythmic diminution. This occurs for only two measures, however, and the concluding measures bear little resemblance to the first ten measures.

It is possible to see this prelude as a loosely structured A B A' form (A, measures 1–10; B, measures 11–20; and A', measures 21–31), but this interpretation requires too loose a definition of ternary form to be of much value. It seems more reasonable to say that measures are grouped—because of similar characteristics—into sections that are juxtaposed. Unity of form is achieved by a similarity in texture and the unifying rhythmic structure.

Melody

Traditional melodic shape and development are replaced by planes of sound that sometimes move chromatically and at other times in parallel or contrary motion. The inner voice in measures 1 and 2 can be seen and heard as a chromatic plane of melodic sound. This chromatic motion continues in the lower voices of measures 3 and 4. Contrasting parallel motion can be observed in measures 4–5 and 9–10, as well as in the ascending parallel chords of measures 23–24. Planes of sound move in contrary motion throughout the prelude. The expanding motion between the right-hand chords and the bass line in measures 1 and 2 is reflected in the converging contrary motion in measures 11 and 12.

Harmony

Chord-by-chord analysis gives little insight into the harmonic organization of this piece. Debussy appears to be more interested in the color of a particular chord than in its diatonic function. The relative importance of a chord in relation to the tonic is subservient to color or sonority.

There is still, however, a feeling of tonic to dominant progression between measures 1 and 5, and again between 6 and 10. In both cases, the chords in between are generally non-diatonic and unresolved in the traditional sense. In measure 1, the three chords are quasi I–IV–V. With the alterations formed by the melodic line in the inner voice, the

E♭ and F chords become augmented in quality rather than major, as they would be in a diatonic progression. (Play these measures as major chords and compare them with the tonal instability produced by the augmented chordal structures.) After a repetition of this same pattern, an ascending chromatic pattern begins that prepares for the arrival on the dominant in measures 5 and 10. Important to the pacing and momentum to the dominant is the contrast of the parallel chords in measures 4 and 5, and 9 and 10. Also important in establishing the strength of the dominant sound is the C major chord (measures 5 and 10), felt as a secondary dominant. Nevertheless, the chromatic chords and chords with an added sixth constantly blur any chord-by-chord, tonally functional progression.

At the beginning of the suggested B section (measure 11), there is a modal influence. Over a dominant pedal, the Dorian mode is used for the ascending parallel chords. This, plus the contrary motion in the upper voices, produces a striking contrast in texture and color. A feeling of unity is achieved at this point with the basic rhythmic motive. Another striking harmonic usage are the parallel major chords, moving upward by thirds, in measures 23 and 24.

The harmonic parameter in this prelude is a combination of non-functional, modal–tonal harmonies that often move in blocks of sound in parallel or contrary motion, more important as planes of color than as harmonic progressions. It is important to realize that tonal harmonies can occur in non-functional harmonic settings. Debussy's use of parallelism and chromaticism as color rather than as harmonically structural elements represents a far more significant break with the principles of tonality than is evident from listening to the prelude itself.

Webern, *Variations for Piano,* Op. 27: II

Since Anton Webern is one of the pioneers of 12-tone composition, his choice of a pitch row and the means of manipulating it seem the most logical place to begin an analysis of this piece.

It might have been possible to extract a row from the beginning of this second movement and call it the original row (O:0) were it not for the fact that the entire three-movement work is based on a row not used in the second movement. Example 29•2 is a pitch matrix based on the row extracted from the first movement. The forms of the row in the second movement are indicated.*

*We have constructed this 12-tone pitch matrix based on the basic row for the entire work so that you can analyze the first and third movements if you wish.

Example 29·2

	I:1			I:11			I:4		I:6			
	E	F	C#	D#	C	D	G#	A	Bb	F#	G	B
O:11	D#	E	C	D	B	C#	G	G#	A	F	F#	Bb
	G	G#	E	F#	D#	F	B	C	C#	A	Bb	D
	F	F#	D	E	C#	D#	A	Bb	B	G	G#	C
O:4	G#	A	F	G	E	F#	C	C#	D	Bb	B	D#
	F#	G	D#	F	D	E	Bb	B	C	G#	A	C#
	C	C#	A	B	G#	Bb	E	F	F#	D	D#	G
	B	C	G#	Bb	G	A	D#	E	F	C#	D	F#
O:6	Bb	B	G	A	F#	G#	D	D#	E	C	C#	F
	D	D#	B	C#	Bb	C	F#	G	G#	E	F	A
O:9	C#	D	Bb	C	A	B	F	F#	G	D#	E	G#
	A	Bb	F#	G#	F	G	C#	D	D#	B	C	E

On the score (Example 29·3) we have indicated the order in which the selected rows are used.

Some musicians feel that once all the rows comprising a particular 12-tone work have been detected, analysis is virtually over. We strongly disagree. Determining row usage alone is practically useless. It is similar to an analysis of a Beethoven piano sonata based on observable scale passages only. If we are to discover how Webern structured this movement, we must examine parametric interaction and independence, just as we did in chapters 11, 17, and 22. We do not expect to find functional harmonic motion and diatonic melodic construction in a 12-tone work, but it should be possible to discover alternate means of parametric control which will be useful for greater musical understanding and for performance.

331

Melody

For a 12-tone work, the composer must choose carefully the row forms and transpositions to be used. Notice that Webern has limited his choices to four transpositions of the original row and four transpositions of the inversion. Since he consistently uses a transposition of the original and a transposition of the inversion simultaneously, the following pairs of pitches result:

I6:	Bb	A	C#	B	D	C	F#	F	E	G#	G	D#
O4:	G#	A	F	G	E	F#	C	C#	D	Bb	B	D#

O11:	D#	E	C	D	B	C#	G	G#	A	F	F#	Bb
I11:	D#	D	F#	E	G	F	B	Bb	A	C#	C	G

O6:	Bb	B	G	A	F#	G#	D	D#	E	C	C#	F
I4:	G#	G	B	A	C	Bb	E	D#	D	F#	F	C#

I1:	F	E	G#	F#	A	G	C#	C	B	D#	D	Bb
O9:	C#	D	Bb	C	A	B	F	F#	G	D#	E	G#

Paired in this way, two important facts appear. First, the forms of the row elide, when used in this order; that is, the last notes of the first pair are the first notes of the second pair, and so on. Second, two pitches always coincide: A and D#. (Keep in mind that enharmonic spelling allows D# to appear as Eb.) The score shows that Webern has emphasized A (measures 1, 9, 13, and 19) by using it consecutively and in the same octave, while de-emphasizing D# by using it as a non-consecutive grace note (measures 6 and 21) and as a member of a three-note chord (measure 15).

Melodic motion in this movement seems to function as paired events rather than melodic lines. Except for the four sequential pitches in measures 10–11 and 16–17, these events are of only three types: two notes; two notes, each preceded by a grace note; and two 3-note chords. The interest in these events is mainly intervallic rather than melodic, and a melody, in the classical sense, does not exist.

Form

At first, this movement appears to be in simple binary form. It divides into two distinct sections, and even includes the traditional repeat signs at the conclusion of each section. Within this simple form, however, is a more complex compositional device. Although difficult to see because of the constantly shifting clefs, this movement is a strict canon in contrary motion. The subject is stated first in the right hand, and imitated at the distance of one eighth-note by the left hand. This order reverses in measure 5, is reinstated in measure 8, reverses again in measure 17, and is again reinstated in measure 18.

In a canon in contrary motion, the two voices mirror each other. In this particular canon, the mirror, or point at which the voices coincide, is the pitch a'. Each of the thirty-one pairs of pitches are equidistant from a'. For example, the f#' in measure 7 is three half-steps below a', while the c'' that follows is three half-steps above. Although it does not function as a tonic in the classical sense, a' is the tonal center of this movement, and may be heard as the central pitch, with the other pitch events moving toward or away from it.

Rhythm

Webern has written the movement in duple meter, apparently for the convenience of the performer, for the fast tempo and irregular rhythms create a non-symmetrical rhythmic organization that destroys any feeling of duple meter. Additionally, the movement uses only four separate rhythmic units. These are

1. ♩♪ 𝄾   2. ♩♪ 𝄽   3. ♫♫ 𝄾   4. ♩♪ 𝄽 𝄽

Unit 1 is used thirty-three times and unit 3 is used ten times; units 2 and 4 each appear only twice. In performance, therefore, the impression is of a 3/8 meter, with occasional measures of 5/8.

Thomas Albert,
A Maze (With Grace)

Example 29·4

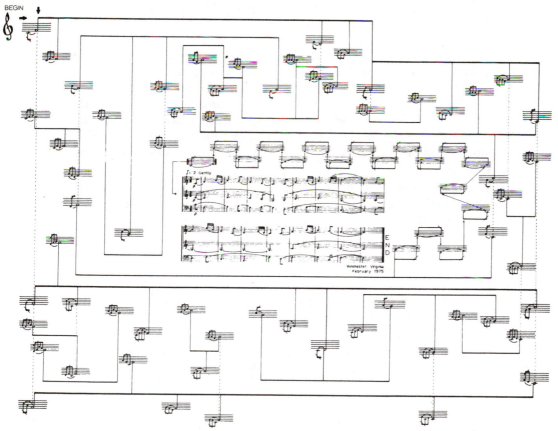

Performance Instructions

1. Any size ensemble is permissible, but one of at least eight performers is preferable. All pitches MUST sound as written, although octave placement is at each individual's discretion.

2. All performers begin simultaneously at "begin." After that, each proceeds at his own speed and in any direction. Any gesture may be followed by any other, as long as the two are connected by a straight line (either a horizontal beam or a vertical broken line). All gestures in the outer section are to be read as graced, sustained pitches.

3. It is anticipated that during the course of playing, performers will discover dead-ends in the maze; when this occurs, the individual performer may choose to back-track and try another route, or pause ten seconds and start again at "begin."

4. Performers may move freely around the maze, but should avoid entering the center section of the maze, which in turn leads to the hymn, and thus the end of the piece. The gate to enter the center is found near the lower right center of the page (by the end of the hymn), and must be passed over until the end of the piece is imminent.

5. Ending the piece: By prearranged signal, performers begin to enter the final gate one at a time. Once a performer enters this section (which is made up of gestures which are exact retrogrades of those found along the outer perimeter of the page), his options are strictly limited to following arrows and playing each gesture in turn. Note that along the top edge of this section, the gestures must be read from right to left. As each performer reaches the last gesture (a sustained F with a grace-note C at the end), he repeats it until all have reached that point. The ensemble stops simultaneously, and the three-part harmonization of "Amazing Grace" is played together, after which the piece is over.

6. Within these guidelines, the performers are free to realize the piece as their discretion dictates. Live performers may be augmented (or replaced) by tape, either purely electronic or concrete; or a drone (open fifth, F-C) may be superimposed over the whole; or voices may be used. It should be noted that although the piece is harmonically static, it is a very strict study of a pentatonic scale on F. For this reason, care must be taken to prevent the accidental sounding of either E or B♭, as these pitches would introduce an element of harmonic tension totally alien to the quiet, restful nature of the piece.

7. The total duration of the piece is indeterminate, and thus left to the performers' discretion. It is suggested that some general time be agreed upon prior to performance, preferably ten minutes or longer.

A Maze (With Grace) is typical of much of the indeterminate music being written today. The work is in two distinct sections. The first section, the maze, is the main body of the piece, and is of indeterminate length and free form. The second part is a pentatonic harmonization of the original hymn tune, *Amazing Grace,* with its conventional meter and phrase structure preserved. Since the two sections are dissimilar in musical intent and internal structure, we will analyze them separately.

The Maze

Melody

Rather than a continuous flow of pitches with characteristic high points and cadences, melody is reduced to seventy-nine gestures, or fragments. Sixty-one of these gestures consist of sustained pitches preceded by one to four grace notes, while eighteen are the reverse—that is, sustained pitches followed by one or two grace notes. The sole pitch resource is the hymn *Amazing Grace* on a pitch center of F. Since it is a pure pentatonic melody, only five different pitches are used throughout: F, G, A, C, and D.

The first sixty-one gestures are extracted from the hymn in three steps. The first step (Example 29·5) uses the first note of the original melody to grace the second, the third and fourth to grace the fifth, and so forth. In this way, nine different gestures are derived, using one or two grace notes per fragment, thus preserving the overall outline of the hymn tune.

Example 29·5

The second level of extraction (Example 29·6) uses the second note of the hymn to grace the third, and so on, resulting in nine more gestures, with one grace note per fragment. The relationship of these gestures to the hymn is less obvious.

Example 29·6

The third level (Example 29·7) is more indirect. It combines one first-level fragment with one of the second level (where both end on the same note), thus producing forty-three different gestures, with three or four grace notes per fragment.

Example 29·7

The last eighteen gestures are the retrograde forms of the first two levels (Example 29·8).

Example 29·8

The order in which these gestures are played is not predetermined, but is left to each performer's discretion, within certain guidelines. Thus, the melody played by one performer differs from that of another, and from one performance to the next.

Harmony

A Maze (With Grace) is harmonically static. Because of the restricted pitch material (the F pentatonic scale), and the freedom allowed in both the melodic movement and the number of performers, it is almost certain that all five pitches will sound at any given moment of a performance. There is, then, no conventional harmonic movement, but rather a buildup of a steady sound state with subtle but constantly shifting pitch colorations and emphases. This absence of harmonic tension-release reflects the ambivalent tonality of the pentatonic scale, which, lacking any half-steps, also lacks the strong resolution tendencies of the major–minor scale system.

Rhythm

The maze section of the composition is in free rhythm—the tempo and duration of each gesture, as well as the placement and duration of rests, are left to the performer's discretion. The underlying concept of graced, sustained pitches is drawn from the basic rhythmic pattern of the hymn tune, which generally alternates short notes (one or one and one-half beats) with longer ones (two or more beats).

Timbre

Since instrumentation is unspecified, timbre is not controlled by the composer. It is wholly a result of the instruments chosen for a particular performance.

Texture

According to the instructions, all performers begin at the same place simultaneously, after which each moves at his own pace and in any direction. In this sense, the texture may be described as polyphonic. On the other hand, it could be said that the texture is of uniform density—a kind of unstable stasis, the net result of the constantly moving lines. Texture is actually the primary parameter of this piece. With melody reduced to short gestures and harmonic progression non-existent, it is the subtle changes in pitch and timbre which draw the listener's attention.

Notation

The first sixty-one gestures are arranged around the page in a maze (including deadends—an inevitable element of mazes) and the performers directed to follow straight lines to determine order. The lines they follow are of two types: (1) broad beams that connect stems, and that also indicate general duration; and (2) vertical broken lines connecting note heads, which join one horizontal plane with another.

The arrangement of the gestures on the page is not haphazard. The twenty-five gestures ending on F are grouped on the left side and extend to the left center; the twelve ending on C are grouped on the right; sixteen gestures ending on A are spread throughout the upper and lower center; the four D gestures are placed two at the top center and two at the bottom center; and the four ending on G are placed in the bottom half of the page. The last eighteen gestures (the retrogrades) are all grouped in the center of the page, beginning at the lower left corner of the hymn harmonization and proceeding up and to the left.

In addition to this organization, the gestures are notated on staves of four sizes, reflecting the four levels of extraction. The largest staves are the nine fragments of the first level, and are found around the perimeter of the page. The next size is used for the nine fragments in the second level, and are generally placed just inside the outer group. The third size encompasses the forty-three gestures of the third level and are scattered throughout the page. The smallest staves represent the last level of derivation (which is farthest removed from the original melody), as well as the coordinated harmonization. Both of these are found in the center of the page. Thus, it is theoretically possible for a performer to structure his melodic movement to coincide with the extraction process, a procedure which would impart some logic to the unfolding of the melody, but which is not a necessary part of the piece.

The Hymn

Melody

The melody is an exact quotation of the original. It is a typical one-part, double-period form, with four-measure antecedent and consequent phrases in each eight-measure period. The first phrase ends on the dominant pitch, but implies the tonic triad. Its consequent ends on a half cadence. The second period antecedent phrase is similar in structure to the first phrase, with an identical cadence, and its consequent draws the hymn to a close on an authentic cadence. The phrase structure may be diagrammed A B A' C.

Harmony

The harmonization of the hymn is unconventional, because it uses only the pitches of the pentatonic scale. Thus, it does not allow the subdominant or leading-tone triads, nor, indeed, for any triads which might use these scale degrees. No tertian chords are used either, but rather two types of quartal chords. The first type includes those which may be described as "open fifth" chords, used as "tonic" and "dominant," respectively.

Example 29·9

The second type includes quartal triads and their inversions, which are used to fill in the supertonic, mediant, and submediant harmonies.

Example 29·10

Focus

The music of the twentieth century, particularly that written since 1950, is strikingly diverse in compositional concepts and techniques. Within the limitations of this chapter, Albert's *A Maze (With Grace)* appears in many ways to be the musical antithesis of Webern's *Variations for Piano*. Such contradictions did not exist within Baroque, Classical, or Romantic styles. In those styles, certain basic assumptions regarding both the individual parameters and parametric interaction can be made. Similar basic assumptions cannot be made about twentieth-century music. The work of each composer must be approached individually.

As you continue to hear and study today's music, remember these two final points. First, the various current compositional styles in which composers work do not have to be in competition with one another. While we all have our own preferences, there is no reason why this diversity of styles cannot musically coexist. Surely the current coexistence of Medieval, Classical, and jazz styles suggests that survival of the fittest is not the system under which music functions. Second, the techniques of parametric analysis recommended throughout this book will yield valuable information about music in any style. As you apply these techniques to new music with which you come in contact, your musical understanding will continue to expand.

acoustics The science that deals with the study of the physical properties of sound.

Alberti bass A broken-chord device employed in keyboard music for adding horizontal motion to the harmonic structure. In most pieces using Alberti bass, the right hand plays the melody and the left hand outlines the harmony in broken-chord fashion. The two most common Alberti bass patterns are do-sol-mi-sol (1-5-3-5) and do-mi-sol, do-mi-sol (1-3-5, 1-3-5).

aleatoric music Music composed by chance procedures or left in some way unpredictable until actually performed. Most theorists use the term interchangeably with *indeterminate music*.

anacrusis An upbeat or pickup.

atonal Without a pitch center; unrelated to a key.

augmentation Lengthening the time value of notes. A rhythmic figure written in augmentation lengthens each note by a fixed value, the most common being double.

augmented sixth chord A triad or seventh chord that contains the interval of a diminished third. This chord is generally used in inversion, in which case the diminished third appears as an augmented sixth. Three types are common: French, German, and Italian. Augmented sixth chords function tonally as altered subdominant or supertonic chords.

bimodal chord The substitution of diatonic chords from a minor key with the parallel major, or vice versa. The device is used in tonal music to vary harmonic color.

binary form A two-part organization based on contrast. The first part, or A section, usually modulates to the dominant, or to the mediant in minor. The second part, or B section, begins in the new key and returns to the tonic. The melodic harmonic and rhythmic material of the B section generally contrast with that of the A section.

bitonality The simultaneous use of two different key centers within a composition. It is based on a modal technique of medieval composers, and was commonly used by composers of the early twentieth century.

cadence A temporary or permanent point of rest within a composition. As such, it generally indicates an important structural point. In tonal music we find a variety of cadences, including authentic (V-I), plagal (IV-I), half (-V), and deceptive (V-vi).

canon A compositional technique in which a second voice, and sometimes a third, strictly imitates a first voice at a fixed interval of time.

cantus firmus A pre-existing melody used as the basis for a new composition. The most frequently used melodies have been Gregorian chants.

chord A vertical structure created when three or more pitches are sounded simultaneously. The basic chord of tonal music is the triad.

chord cluster A vertical sonority, generally of six or more pitches, used as color. Chord clusters may be distinguished from tonal chords with added chromatic pitches by their lack of harmonic function.

chromatic Moving in semitones, or incorporating them, rather than being limited to the pitches of the diatonic scale.

continuo Used in ensemble music of the seventeenth and eighteenth centuries and consisting of two instruments. One, such as viola da gamba or bassoon, played the bass line, while the other, usually harpsichord or organ, played the harmonies suggested by the bass line. The written continuo part consisted of the bass line with numerals beneath it.

contrapuntal texture Two or more equally important melodic lines occurring simultaneously.

countersubject In polyphonic music (such as a fugue), the musical material that accompanies the subject, or thematic material.

diatonic Using the pitches of a major or minor scale. In general, diatonic material is distinguished from chromatic material by the use of more whole steps and fewer semitones.

diminution Decreasing the time value of notes. A rhythmic figure written in diminution shortens each note by a fixed value, the most common being one half.

dissonance Sounds considered discordant or unpleasing to the ear. Historically, there has been no fixed standard of dissonance; sounds considered dissonant during one period have come to be considered consonant during another.

duplum In thirteenth-century organa and clausulae, the second, or middle voice; the part above the tenor.

enharmonic Two pitches with different identifying names but sounding alike. In equal temperament, any pitch may be identified by more than one name: C#–Db, D#–Eb, E#–F, and so forth. This is not true for other types of tuning, where C# and Db, for example, are heard as different pitches.

episode Any section of a fugue in which the statement of the main subject is incomplete or does not appear. Episodes are often developmental.

fauxbourdon A sequence of parallel sixth chords (in first inversion) producing a bass line that is not the root of the chord; hence, a false bass.

figured bass A notational practice for keyboard during the seventeenth and eighteenth centuries in which the bass line had a set of numerals under it implying the harmony. The performer was expected to improvise accompaniment from the suggested harmonies.

form The principle of organization which structures a composition. Every musical composition, without exception, has a discernible shape or structure known as the form. Although organizing procedures can be used freely each stylistic period has evolved a characteristic set of formal procedures.

free rhythm A type of rhythmic organization in which both proportional time values and recurring accent patterns are avoided. Increasingly popular with composers since the 1950s, free rhythm uses such devices as non-proportional rhythmic symbols and rhythmic structure based on time lengths.

harmonic interval The distance between two simultaneous pitches.

harmonic rhythm The frequency or rate of chord change within a tonal composition.

harmonic series The set of tones produced by a string, air column, or vibrating surface by the simultaneous vibration of its entire length and fractional lengths. These secondary vibrations are not as loud as the fundamental frequency; the ear hears one composite sound.

harmony The horizontal progression of chords in a particular work. Harmony is generated directly from the work's basic pitch resources.

hemiola A type of syncopation prevalent in the fifteenth and sixteenth centuries based on the relationship of 3 to 2; that is, three notes in the normal time for two, or vice versa.

homophonic texture One predominant melody plus accompaniment. Often, the accompaniment is chordal or it outlines chords.

Hz (Hertz) The unit of measurement of frequency, or vibrations per second. *Hz* has replaced *c.p.s.* (cycles per second) as the name of the unit, since the initials *c.p.s.* had more than one scientific meaning.

indeterminate music Music composed by chance procedures or left in some way unpredictable until actually perfomed. Most theorists use the term interchangeably with *aleatoric music*.

interval notation A system of notation that prescribes the division of a parameter into supposedly equal steps. Standard notation, in use from the early 1600s to the present, is one form of interval notation, with the octave divided into twelve equal half-steps and with durations normally divisible by two.

inversion The process of turning an interval or a melody upside down. In melodic inversion the interval remains the same and the pitches change, while in harmonic inversion the pitches remain the same and the interval changes.

isorhythm A fourteenth-century rhythmic device in which one rhythmic pattern, usually of three or four measures and most frequently in the lowest voice, is repeated throughout a composition.

Klang Heinrich Schenker's term for the sound, or chord, of nature and consisting of the overtone series through the fifth partial. This natural triad appears vertically in a composition as chord structure and horizontally as melodic and harmonic pitch succession, and defines the manner in which a tonality governs the entire work.

melismatic style In a vocal piece, setting several pitches to each syllable of the text.

melodic interval The distance between two pitches in succession.

microtone An interval smaller than a half-step.

modulation Changing keys within a composition by moving the pitch materials from one key level to another. Almost every long piece of music contains some change of key or shift of tonality; this provides tonal interest and contrast. Unlike a transient key cell, modulation is a more stable change of key, in which the new key is firmly established and remained in for a longer time.

monophonic texture One melodic line without accompaniment.

monothematic Containing one major theme or thematic idea.

motive A short arrangement of pitches identifiable as a melodic unit. The motive usually lends itself well to further transformation or development.

multiphonics Sound composites of two or more simultaneous pitches obtainable on woodwind instruments through, in most cases, cross fingerings. Most are highly complex sounds.

musique concrète (concrete music) The use of natural sounds rather than purely electronic sounds as the source material for electronic music. Composers of *musique concrète* feel that sounds from musical instruments or from the environment provide more interesting timbres than can be electronically produced.

Neapolitan sixth chord A major triad built on the lowered second degree of the scale; normally resolves to the dominant or tonic six-four chord.

neoclassicism The twentieth-century use of classical formal principles without the underlying tonal structures on which they were originally based. The style represents a reaction to the emotionalism of late romantic music.

nominal notation A system of notation that merely names certain events that are to occur. The order of events is decided arbitrarily.

non-symmetrical rhythm A rhythmic organization that retains the proportional time-value scheme of symmetrical rhythm but avoids any recurring pattern of strong and weak accents.

operational notation A system of notation that indicates what the performer is to do rather than what sound is to be obtained. Operational notation varies from tablature to typewritten instructions.

ordinal notation A type of contour notation in which a parameter is represented as a bipolar continuum and the position of a symbol along that continuum indicates the value of the parameter. Ordinal notation usually involves a two-dimensional graph, with the x-axis representing time and the y-axis pitch.

ostinato A melodic or rhythmic pattern or phrase that is repeated over and over for the entire length of a composition or section of a composition. This repetition, in the same voice and at the same pitch level, helps unify the composition.

overtone The pitches of the harmonic series above the fundamental frequency.

parametric analysis A way of musical analysis that looks at each parameter of music (that is, melody, harmony, rhythm and meter, timbre, texture, form, and so on) individually and collectively. By analyzing how a composer emphasizes, manipulates, and integrates the various parameters of music in a particular composition, the principles underlying its style can be made more apparent.

partial All of the pitches of the harmonic series, including the fundamental frequency.

period The combination of two or more musical phrases. If a period consists of two phrases, the first generally ends with a feeling of incompleteness that the second phrase acts to complete.

phrase The basic unit of melodic construction. It gives a feeling of completeness, although the degree of completeness may vary with the setting in which the phrase is used. Historically, phrases have tended to be symmetrical in length, that is two, four, or eight measures each.

planing The moving of chords or voices in parallel planes of sound, producing unusual sequences of tonal chords that do not function tonally.

polymeter The simultaneous use of two or more meters within a composition.

polyphonic texture Two or more equally important melodic lines occurring simultaneously. Polyphony may be imitative or non-imitative. Imitative polyphony uses the same melodic material in more than one voice, as in a round, canon, or fugue. The term is synonomous with contrapuntal texture.

polyrhythm The use of contrasting rhythmic patterns within the same metric organization. These contrasting rhythmic patterns suggest the simultaneous occurrence of more than one metrical scheme.

polytonality The simultaneous use of more than two key centers within a composition. The term is often used incorrectly to indicate the use of *two* key centers, the correct term for which is *bitonality*.

quartal chord A chord built on the interval of a fourth, for example, C-F-B♭.

ratio notation A system of notation in which the relationship between any two items within a parameter is analogous to other relationships within the parameter. A vertical example: two rhythmic patterns occurring against each other, such as 7:6. A linear example is rhythmic modulation.

real answer An exact intervalic transposition of the subject or thematic material of a fugue, usually to the level of the dominant.

retrograde The writing of a melody or rhythmic pattern backwards, that is, beginning with the last note and ending with the first. This device, used as early as the thirteenth century, is a basic technique of 12-tone composition.

retrograde inversion The combination of inversion and retrograde, producing an upside down, backward version of the original.

rhythmic cell A short rhythmic figure or unit used repeatedly in a composition. Some compositions are built almost entirely on three or four rhythmic cells.

rondo A formal principle of repetition and contrast involving a statement and restatement of A material, interspersed with contrasting digressions, or episodes; for example, ABACA or ABACADA.

rounded binary form A two-part structure in which a portion of the A material is repeated at the end of the B material. Sometimes this repeat only hints at the A material, while at other times a considerable amount is repeated. Although similar to ternary form, the rounded binary retains its two-part structure with repeat signs in the middle and at the end.

secundal chord A chord built on the interval of a second, for example, C-D-E.

sequence The repetition of a melodic pattern at a new pitch level, usually a second above or below.

serialism The extension of the techniques of 12-tone pitch manipulation to other musical parameters, such as rhythm, articulation, or dynamics.

seventh chord A four-note chord consisting of a triad plus the seventh above the root of the chord. The additional note adds tension to the chord and to the harmonic progression.

sonata form A formal procedure involving three distinct sections: exposition, development, and recapitulation. While the term *sonata* *form* applies specifically to the structure of a single movement, the term *sonata* usually describes an instrumental work in three or four movements.

standard notation The notational system in widespread use from approximately 1600 to the present, symbolizing pitch by means of notes on a staff (adequate for conventional intervals of a half-step or larger) and durations by means of the shapes of the notes.

strophic form A vocal compositional procedure in which the same musical material is repeated for every stanza of the text.

subject The major melodic material of a contrapuntal composition, such as an invention or a fugue.

syllabic style In a vocal piece, setting each syllable of the text to a separate pitch.

symmetrical rhythm A rhythmic organization characterized by regularly recurring patterns of strong and weak accents, clearly indicated by means of bar lines; and by a proportional system of time values, that is, only multiples or fractions of the basic beat.

syncopation A shifting of the normal accent structure of a composition in symmetrical rhythm; for instance, placing emphasis on normally weak beats, or holding weak beats through strong ones.

tablature A system of notation that indicates not what sounds to play but what actions the performer must make to produce the desired sounds.

temperament A system of tuning fixed-pitch instruments, especially keyboard instruments, in which slight adjustments are made to pure intervals to equalize inherent discrepancies of pitch. The two major systems are meantone temperament and equal temperament.

ternary form A three-part structure (ABA) of statement, departure, and return, based on the principle of contrast and repetition. The most important contrasts generally involve a change of melody, rhythm, and key in the departure section.

tessitura The normal range of an instrument or voice.

theme The basic melodic material of homophonic compositions such as sonatas, symphonies, and theme and variations.

timbre The quality of musical sound by which we discriminate between musical instruments, even those at the same pitch. Timbre, or tone color, is different for each instrument, because each produces its own unique vibrational pattern.

tonal answer A transposition of the subject or thematic material of a fugue in which some intervals are adjusted slightly to accommodate the tonality.

tone row An arbitrary ordering of the pitches of the chromatic scale to produce the basic generative material for 12-tone music. One row is generally used as the source material for an entire composition. Some composers have worked with tone rows of fewer than twelve notes.

transient key cell A tonal shift to a new pitch level for only a few measures, without firmly establishing the new tonality.

triad A three-note chord constructed by the superposition of thirds. Four species are possible: major, minor, augmented, and diminished. The triad is the primary structure of tonal music.

trichord A three-note chord. The term is used in 12-tone music to identify a group of three notes that are in some way related without being tonal. The relationship may be either vertical or horizontal.

triplum In thirteenth century organa and clausulae, the top voice of three voices; two voices above the tenor.

tune An easily recognized, easily remembered melody, such as a folk song or a popular song.

12-tone row *See* tone row.

12-tone system A procedure developed in the early 1920s by Arnold Schoenberg for the writing of non-tonal, chromatic music. In this system, the twelve pitches of the chromatic scale are of equal importance.

Ursatz Heinrich Schenker's term for the background or elemental structure of a composition based on the *Klang*, or chord of nature. The Ursatz is arrived at by a process of reducing the harmonic and melodic pitches of a composition.

350

351

352

INDEX OF COMPOSERS BY PERIOD*

*Page numbers are in parentheses.

354